DEADLINE
POETS SOCIETY

DEADLINE POETS SOCIETY

A WRITER'S LIFE IN NEWSPAPERS

BILL OSINSKI

Library of Congress Control Number: 2020925997
ISBN: Hardcover   978-1-6641-4992-2
                   Softcover   978-1-6641-4991-5
                   eBook   978-1-6641-4990-8

Print information available on the last page.

Rev. date: 01/14/2021

To order additional copies of this book, contact:
Xlibris
844-714-8691
www.Xlibris.com
Orders@Xlibris.com
822724

CONTENTS

Trail of Folly

Life and Death in The Coal Mines

More Misadventure!

FOREWORD

to Deadline Poets Society
By Dave Barry

I GOT TO KNOW Bill Osinski in the 1980s, when we were both sent by our newspapers to cover presidential races and national political conventions.

We ran into each other here and there, and soon became friends; we hoisted post-deadline beers in a variety of dive bars, including one in New Orleans where the specialty cocktail was served in a large Styrofoam toilet.

In those days newspapers sent scores of people to cover the conventions.

Most of these people were Serious Journalists reporting on Serious Political Issues. Bill and I were not. I was writing humor columns, and Bill was writing features about whatever caught his attention — the unusual, the thought-provoking, the quirky, the wild and the weird. In those days many newspapers employed people like Bill — good writers who had an eye for stories that might not qualify as big news, but made for good reading.

There aren't many such writers working in today's Internet-driven newspaper business: The emphasis is on cranking out stories fast to feed the 24/7 news cycle, and to garner as many clicks as possible. Reporters have less time to poke around looking for offbeat stories, or to craft their prose. More and more, journalism is quick hits, superficial coverage, snap judgments, hot takes, snarky tweets.

We're told that this trend is unavoidable, because of economic forces and changing reader habits. And maybe it is unavoidable. But that doesn't mean it's good. Fewer and fewer newspaper journalists today have the time, and freedom, to write the kind of thoughtful stories and columns that Bill Osinski crafted during his long and prolific career. Bill had an excellent ride. Thanks to this book, you can go back and ride along with him. And speaking as his one-time drinking buddy, I promise you won't be bored.

INTRODUCTION

T HE NEWSPAPER BUSINESS can't even get its own obit right.

Sure, the internet didn't help. Newspapers were certainly high on Craig's Hit List. But the actual cause of death was suicide.

Newspapers starved themselves to death, when they stopped producing a daily diet of articles that readers might actually need, or, perish the thought, want, to read. Journalists got tired of journalism, so the people decided they could live without newspapers.

So what? Nothing really terrible has happened since society's watchdogs were put to sleep, right?

Well, define "terrible". Or, do a cost/benefits analysis on disposing of the truth. Credibility has become a quaint concept. Integrity is for fools. Lies are as handy as hundred-bullet magazines.

How many of the 70 million or so people who voted for Trump were daily readers of real newspapers—10 percent, 1 percent?

We need Abraham to start bargaining with God on America's behalf. If he can find 10 honest newspaper readers in Trump Nation, maybe we'll all be spared.

While there seems to be broad agreement that newspapers are in their death throes, not many realize that these bad times came just after the industry's Golden Age. Of course, not many newspaper people were aware of this – until the good times were all gone and they'd all followed each other into the abyss of the internet.

The web was the future, and most papers diverted more and more resources from their print products into their digital endeavors. What kind of businessmen deliberately drive away their most loyal customers? The newspapers became thinner and less interesting, while the goal of making profits from the internet proved highly elusive. Actually, they haven't figured it out yet.

The recessions of the 70s and 80s brought serious attrition in the ranks of daily newspapers. Bad for the papers that died, but very good for the survivors. All but a few metropolitan newspapers gained monopolies in their market. This meant they could, and did, charge whatever they chose for advertising space.

Which, in turn, meant that newspaper profits were literally obscene. Some of the less responsible newspaper chains would cashier any publisher whose paper did not achieve a profit margin better than 20 per cent. Small wonder, then, that a large majority of the papers chose profits over quality.

There were some holdouts, however. At the Louisville Courier Journal, where I worked in the late 70s and early 80s, the publisher, an affable, benevolent, second-generation aristocrat named Barry Bingham, Jr., annually hosted a Christmas party at his home for the state news staff. The CJ was at that time a statewide institution – and took that responsibility seriously. The CJ bore the costs of delivering the paper statewide every day – from Paducah in the west to Pikeville in the east.

I remember this particular Christmas party, because in his annual report, the managing editor apologized for having to raise the profit margin from three per cent to four per cent. Even though it was not meant as a joke, such a statement would get an editor laughed out of the boardroom today.

In those days, a newspaper could be as good as it chose to be. If it wanted to hire great reporters and editors, who would produce first-rate journalism, it could do so. If it wanted to be a cash cow for corporate headquarters, it could do that. More papers chose the latter, but a significant number of papers strove to earn and to keep their readers' trust every day. Imagine that.

When a big story broke, these newspapers sent their best writers into the field with a mandate to take the readers to places the readers couldn't go, to introduce them to extraordinary people they'd never meet otherwise, to do it all on deadline – and to "make it sing."

I was that guy for 11 different newspapers for more than 36 years.

Of course, I wasn't the only reporter doing this stuff. Most good newspapers had writers in residence. In this book, I offer samples of some of my best work, as a tribute to my fellow dinosaurs.

Oh, the places I went, the things I saw, and the people I met! I covered popes and presidential candidates, tornadoes and tsunamis, murder trials and cults. I'll never forget the stoic mountain woman who lost three sons and a grandson in a coal mine explosion; the world's smallest BMOC, a young man who had no legs but a fully-developed ability to flirt; the marine who was seeking permission to die, sir; the suburban housewife who turned the tragedy of her daughter's death into a mission to bring life and hope to those in India's leprosy colonies.

I made the migration from the Rio Grande Valley to the Ohio tomato fields with a family of migrant farm workers. I went to work with outlaw coal miners. I followed a childless Ohio couple who ventured to the Brazilian hinterlands to adopt a child. When no one, including my own newspaper, wanted me to stay on the story, I investigated the man who became the target of the nation's largest child molestation prosecution ever directed at a single individual. While police supporters marched in protest with my name on a casket, I pursued the truth in the slaying of a suspected cop-killer, until it was proven that the police executioner had shot the suspect in the back. I refused to accept the guilty verdict against a man for the savage double murder of his stepdaughter and her boyfriend, helping the man get released from death row; and I returned to the case 25 years later, when the real killer confessed.

I'm not saying today's reporters are not capable of doing similar things. I'm just saying, their newspapers would not give them such opportunities.

I had no credentials for becoming a reporter – except that I was curious about the world, and I loved to write.

Growing up in Mobile, Alabama, the first newspaper I read was the Mobile Press Register. My interest was largely confined to the sports pages, and I remember reading a columnist named Ross Smitherman (how in the world did my memory dredge up that name?) and thinking it was really cool to write something and get your name in the paper nearly every day.

During my high-school years at McGill Institute, a parochial boys' school, I was an insufferable smartass. I thought I could satisfy a sophomore short-story writing assignment by handing in a piece with a plot borrowed from "The Gift of the Magi". My mother Helen told me, "Billy, you'd better start over." But I knew better. I was shocked, shocked I say, when Brother Juan stormed by my desk and threw down my story, bellowing in a voice loud enough for the whole room to hear, "Osinski – F!" I never again thought for a moment about plagiarism.

I majored in Engineering Physics at Florida State University. Coming from a family of seven children, my focus was finding the best starting salary. Nevertheless, I took two elective writing courses from Michael Shaara, winner of the Pulitzer Prize for his novel "The Killer Angels" which many believe to be the finest war novel ever written. Shaara didn't teach me to write. In fact, the first thing he said was that nobody can teach anybody else to write. But he told us to sit down and write, and not to get up until we'd written something. I cranked out the copy, and he told me I was pretty good. I didn't know it yet, but I was set on my path of life.

In 1967, my wife Eileen and I set out as newlyweds for the opposite corner of the country, where I had accepted a job as a materials engineer with Boeing, the aircraft manufacturer. Less than three years later, the bottom dropped out of the aerospace industry. The Boeing workforce in the Seattle, Washington, area was at about 100,000 when we first arrived. When we left, it was approximately 30,000. During this first jobless period of my life, I wrote my first article for pay for *Technology Review*, a science-for-layman's magazine published by Massachusetts Institute of Technology. It was a sardonic piece on the indignities and anxieties of going through a period of mass layoffs. A later letter to the magazine editor complained that I was nothing but a scurrilous humanist – an accusation to which I gladly plead guilty, and still do.

We were getting ready to evacuate Seattle, when I attended a speech by San Francisco Chronicle columnist Art Hoppe. At that time, my favorite newspaper reading was the satire columnists, like Hoppe, Russell Baker, Mike Royko, Art Buchwald, and Erma Bombeck. I had written several columns in that genre, and after the speech, I approached Hoppe and thrust an envelope of my columns into his hands. I told him we were heading back to Florida, and I asked if I could meet with him to discuss my work. He graciously agreed, and we set a date.

I showed up at the Chronicle offices at the appointed time, but Hoppe's secretary gave me the bad news that Hoppe was called out of town. I was devastated. We went back to Florida, and I took a job at a state agency that helped the unemployed find jobs. The irony was lost on me.

About a month into my new career, I received an envelope forwarded from my former address in Seattle. It was from Hoppe. In his letter, he apologized for missing our appointment. He said he had searched the Seattle phone directory and hoped he was writing to the right Bill Osinski. He gave me some high compliments on my writing. He also added a note from his boss echoing that assessment.

I parlayed that letter, and some family connections, into my first job at a newspaper. It was at the now-defunct (funny how that term applies to so many newspapers now) Tampa Times. They actually ran a couple of my satire columns, but they decided I should also learn to become a reporter. My education lasted 36 years.

I never wanted to get "promoted" to the exalted rank of editor. First, I could not imagine myself in a job so dispiriting as being a newspaper editor, where the responsibilities consist mainly of meeting with the same group of pasty-faced people two or three times a day.

Second, boys just want to have fun. It is far and away more fun to be out in the field, getting to the story, finding the people with stories to tell, and getting them to trust you to tell their stories, then writing the story in a manner that will entice people who may not give a damn about the story to read it anyway. I truly believe that nobody in the newspaper business makes enough money to justify not having fun at the job.

There is also in the newspaper craft a mystical element of nobility.

One of my most memorable assignments was to go to Poland in 1979, to cover the first return to his homeland of Pope John Paul II, the first Polish Pope. I worked out a deal with my editors at the Louisville Courier Journal. I would travel at my own expense and on my vacation time. The paper agreed to print my coverage as a long-form story in their Sunday magazine (another lamented casualty of our time of diminished literacy). Also, the paper agreed to get photographer's credentials for my father, Ed, who'd been a photographer in the U.S. Army Signal Corps. Dad didn't want to go at first, but afterwards he relentlessly showed his photographs and re-told the stories of traveling with his son in his homeland.

At the end of the papal trip, the Pope summoned all the media members who'd been following him to a farewell address. It was held in a walled courtyard in Krakow. We crammed the space to overflowing.

The Pope thanked us and warmly encouraged us to practice and to elevate our craft.

"To pursue the truth," he said, "is a noble calling."

I have tried to live according to that principle. It's been a great life.

UNFORGETTABLE FOLKS

Photo of Becky Douglas and Saral, the resident of a leprosy colony in India. Saral had been a beggar, but after she received a microloan from Rising Star Outreach, she purchased a dairy cow and now has a small herd. Photo by Jean Shifrin.

Bill's notes: This story started as a throwaway feature assignment from my boss in the suburban section of the AJC, who had had a brief conversation with someone promoting Rising Star Outreach. As soon as I met Becky Douglas, though, I saw it as much more. I expanded the scope of my story and called the Sunday editor downtown and promoted it for Page One. They took it, making my suburban boss very angry with me for going around him. He'd wanted to hoard the story for just his section. But my small act of defiance yielded big benefits. The story led to major donors enlisting in Becky's crusade. She has realized her dream of buying land in India and building boarding schools that serve hundreds of children from the leprosy colonies. Her non-profit, Rising Star Outreach, also maintains mobile medical services and micro-loan programs aimed at bringing self-sufficiency to the colonies. Becky now has the support of major charitable foundations and even bigger dreams for Rising Star.

HERE COMES THE suburban super-mom, rolling into a leper colony with a smuggled wheelchair. She dances with the afflicted, scrapes their sores with a pocketknife and — hardest of all — convinces them that their lives are worth something.

The smuggler, whom they call "the little white woman," also happens to be a concert violinist who has raised nine children.

What's wrong with this picture?

Absolutely nothing, says Becky Douglas of Norcross. To her, it makes all the sense in the world that she frequently forsakes a life blessed with abundance to go halfway around the globe to places that define misery, to touch the lives of people even India's "untouchables" won't touch.

Her associates call her a Mother Teresa figure, pointing to her efforts to raise more than $250,000 in less than four years for poverty relief in India and to her plans to create a home and school for more than 300 children of lepers.

At first, though, the quality of her mercy was somewhat strained.

"It was scary," Douglas, 52, says of her early encounters with the lepers. She says she was worried that she might contract the disease herself. "I've got nine children to raise," she recalls thinking.

Later she learned that, although leprosy can be contracted via airborne bacteria, it is easily treatable in its early stages. "The hardest thing was to make myself look at them," she said. But once she did, she saw what was truly ugly: the fact that she was holding back. How could she help these people if she would not touch them?

"I told myself, 'You can't let this suffering go on if there's anything you can do about it.'

She did what she could, and that has turned out to be more than she ever imagined herself capable of doing, Douglas says. "If I've learned one thing, it's that one person can make a difference," she said. "If every person in America lifted just one other person up, what a different world it would be."

Before this, her life was full and comfortable. Her husband, John, is an attorney specializing in international finance. She typically performed a dozen or so violin recitals a year. Their home is in a subdivision of mini-estates in Peachtree Corners.

They first expanded their family horizons in 1996, when a friend called and asked Douglas if she would take in two Lithuanian orphans. The children were a brother and sister; the girl had a life-threatening medical condition. Douglas agreed on the spot. When her husband got home, she told him, "John, you're not going to believe what I did today." The Douglases adopted the two, adding them to their seven biological children.

LEGACY OF A TRAGEDY

It took a family tragedy, however, to launch Douglas' mission to India. In April 2000, the Douglases' daughter Amber, in her early 20s, took her own life. She had long battled bipolar disorder. In going through her daughter's things, Douglas learned that Amber had been making regular donations to an orphanage in India.

As a tribute to Amber's memory, she decided to learn more about the orphanage, and in 2001 she went to India to see it for herself. She learned that Amber's orphanage was doing relatively well financially, but she was stunned by the overall dimensions of the poverty she saw. "So many people needed help," she says.

She learned that there is a whole subclass of outcast children: the sons and daughters of lepers. Though they may not have the disease, they suffer the same social stigma as those who do, she explains, so they frequently have no one to care for them.

Douglas was introduced to a man who took in children from the streets. "He had these 25 beautiful little untouchable children. I asked him, 'How do you feed them?' " The man answered, "We eat every other day."

It was through this Good Samaritan that Douglas first experienced the plight of the lepers. Estimates of the number of people in India who have the disease vary widely; some government agencies place it in the tens of thousands, while some private relief agencies place it in the millions.

Douglas brought her cause home to Peachtree Corners. In 2002, she sponsored an orphaned Indian girl, Esther Muthuswamy, to come to Norcross on a student visa to receive the education she had never gotten in India. Now, Esther plans to return to India as a teacher.

"We teach the girls in India that they can be anything they want to be," Douglas says. In 2003, Douglas and four friends formed Rising Star Outreach, a nonprofit company devoted to raising money for Indian orphans, children with disabilities and children of lepers. It's a strictly volunteer organization. "We're the world's cheapest people," she says. "We don't get paid, and we don't pay anybody for anything." When Douglas travels to make presentations to church or community groups or to groups in private homes, she pays her costs, just as she and others in Rising Star do when they travel to India.

FRUITFUL SERENDIPITY

Her efforts have gained the attention of important people in India. About three months ago, she received a phone call from a woman she did not know. The woman, Padma Venkataraman, is the daughter of a former president of India and a well-known activist against poverty and for women's rights. The two women have formed a partnership, plugging Douglas' fund-raising skills into Venkataraman's network of Indian social service programs.

"Becky has a lot of compassion, and she's really committed to the cause," Venkataraman said from India in a recent telephone interview. Also, they share a common philosophy about the best way to assist the lepers. "Many people work with the leprosy people, but often they just want to feed them, give them trinkets," Venkataraman said.

In her programs, self-sufficiency is the goal; small loans are made to enable people in the leper colonies to do things such as buy an iron or raise livestock, she said. "What is most rewarding is when these people prove to themselves and prove to the world that they can be productive," Venkataraman said.

Serendipitous things like her linking with Venkataraman have happened regularly since she started Rising Star, Douglas says. "We're all convinced that God is opening doors." The people who have joined her crusade believe that Douglas is a marvelous instrument of a godly enterprise.

"The people in the villages love her," says Tom McKinney, an Atlanta financial consultant and a board member of Rising Star. "When she comes to their town, it's as if a queen has arrived. But she is able to do what she does in such a humble way. The only one I can compare her to is Mother Teresa," McKinney said, adding that Douglas has modeled some of her poverty-relief efforts after those of the revered Roman Catholic nun and Nobel Peace Prize winner.

Adrienne Cohen, another Rising Star board member, calls Douglas "the most remarkable woman I've ever met." Cohen says Douglas' obvious sincerity touches the audiences at her fund-raising presentations, just as it does the people in the leper colonies. And she's having a greater impact than even she realizes, Cohen says. "Even if she saved just a few children, that would be incredible. But she's done so much more than that. She's given herself completely to her cause."

FAMILY REWARDS

Working with the poorest and most wretched of the poor has yielded great rewards for Douglas and her family. She recalls the time she enlisted her daughter Dianna in a wheelchair-smuggling conspiracy.

Dianna, then 24, was accompanying her on a trip to India. Douglas wanted to take two wheelchairs to a leper colony. Airline officials wanted to charge a tariff that amounted to more than the wheelchairs were worth.

Douglas came up with an idea. All the way to India, she pretended to be disabled, and her daughter used one of the wheelchairs to push her around the airports. (As far as is known, the other wheelchair is still in the custody of the airline.) She even limped to the airplane restroom so her "disability" would seem more real. Dianna was embarrassed by the charade, and she complained to her mother for most of the journey. But when they arrived at the leper colony, the daughter understood why her mother had broken the rules.

The leader of the colony, a man whose leprosy had left him with stubs for limbs, came crawling to Douglas to express his joy that she had brought a wheelchair. Having a wheelchair meant that the lepers no longer would have to perform amputations of diseased limbs on one another. With the wheelchair, they could push an afflicted person the 18 miles to the nearest village, where the amputation could be performed at a medical clinic.

The reluctant Dianna soon became a favorite of the villagers, and they inquire about her every time Douglas returns. There have been similar benefits for the rest of the family, Douglas says. "My children have never known want, or known anyone in want," she says. Now, five of them have done service as Rising Star volunteers. One son asked that the money for his Christmas gift be given instead to Rising Star. "This experience has brought out a tenderness we didn't know existed in them," Douglas says of her children. "It's helped make my kids into real people."

As for herself, she says she is aware of what she has given up for Rising Star. There's less time for her family, and she has scaled back her recitals to three or four a year. She misses her music, especially the feeling of having a concert hall full of people applauding. But what she receives from the poor has more than made up for the loss, she says. "It's much more meaningful to hug a leper child."

Bill's notes: The campus newspaper at Western Kentucky University in Bowling Green published a short feature on Sam Early, a freshman who often preferred to get around on his hands rather than his legs — because he had no legs. I quickly set up a meeting with Sam, and he turned out to be earthy, funny, and in most ways a typical freshman. He refused to give in to his disabilities, and he hated nothing worse than someone else's pity. He became a bit of a national celebrity after this story. Less than a year later, Sam and his girlfriend Newtie were married.

LOUISVILLE COURIER JOURNAL, OCTOBER 23, 1978

BOWLING GREEN, KY. - There are only 2 feet, 9 inches left of Sam Early, but that just makes him the world's smallest Big Man On Campus.

Sam Early stands on his hands as proof that life with half a body can be full. His body ends just below his belt buckle.

"I don't feel like I've missed anything," Early said. "You're just as handicapped as you think you are."

Except for a pair of legs, this freshman agriculture major at Western Kentucky University is missing very few of life's necessities for any Joe College. He has a special girlfriend, drinking buddies, and a car. He shoots pool, lifts weights and swims.

If he needs any help, there's a small coed cadre of "Sam's Angels" he can call on.

For the most part, though. Early prefers to do things for himself.

He abandoned his wheelchair about five years ago, shortly after an operation that rid him of useless legs that had been crossed since his birth.

"When I got to high school, I just said, 'To hell with it,'" Early said of his decision to rely on self-propulsion.

Now he walks from his car to his classes on hands strengthened by years of doing farm work.

The sight of a full-sized head bobbing along less than three feet above the sidewalk causes a set of reactions that Early takes in stride. Older people tend to cluck their tongues in pity, which only bothers him when he's already in a bad mood.

Early said he likes the way children usually respond to him. One time a little fellow asked him if he were one of Santa Claus's elves.

Most of his mobility comes from the Chevy he drives with the aid of hand controls and a special car seat When he applied for his driver's license, he told the clerk his correct height. The clerk said she'd leave that spot on his license blank.

When he and his girlfriend, Newtie Fane, take a stroll around campus, legs are strictly optional for them both. Ms. Fane, a 19-year-old, first-year social-work student, uses metal crutches to aid legs weakened by a life-long battle against cerebral palsy.

Early has two artificial limbs, but they are almost always left in his closet "To be treated like anyone else, you can't feel sorry for yourself," Early said.

Ms. Fane reinforced that sentiment "Some handicapped people just vegetate," she said. "They get all this money coming in from the government, and they just sit back and be handicapped."

The anxieties that Early and Ms. Fane have are not related to their impairments but are the ones shared universally by college freshmen: Will she pass her sociology course? Can they spend the time they want together and study, too? How do you cook for yourself, when the most you ever did at home was boil water? Can I make it my first time away from home on my own? What will winter bring?

When they found each other in August as newly enrolled students, they rekindled a friendship that began about five years ago at a summer camp. Their first meeting occurred when Early was using himself to play a practical joke, Ms. Fane recalled.

The joke was one of his standards, one in which he pretends to be stuck in a hole and asks for help. "All these cheerleaders were there, and he was just looking for girls to pull him out of the hole so he could scare them to death," she said.

Ms. Fane admitted to being a little unnerved herself at seeing Early for the first time. One night after lights out at the camp, she said, Early raided her cabin and nearly scared her to death when he climbed up the posts of her bed and latched on to her neck.

Her revenge was sweet, literally. "We poured some of that chocolate glitter all over him," she said. "He looked like one of those chocolate-covered cherries!"

Except for their meetings at summer camp, their friendship was kept up only by exchanging letters. For the rest of the year they went home, Early to the Pulaski County community of Mount Victory, near Somerset, and Ms. Fane to Louisville to fight separate battles against the way other people viewed their disabilities.

Ms. Fane said her parents had to challenge the Jefferson County school board to keep her enrolled in the regular public schools. "I'm left-handed," she said, "but they kept trying to teach me to write with my right hand. I was reading and writing everything backwards."

Early said he didn't have much problem getting into the Pulaski County schools, but moving around once he got in was a different story. The school superintendent approved his attendance at the public grade school only on the condition that Early stay in his wheelchair.

Once he entered high school and lost his legs, Early shunned the chair for good. When graduation time came, Early said, his parents tried to persuade him to use his artificial legs to receive his diploma at the ceremony.

But Early had always moved among his classmates on his hands, and that's the way they wanted to see him off. A group of the school's seniors got together, he said, and persuaded Early's parents to let him march down the aisle on all twos.

Since Early is one of seven children of a farm family, there were financial, as well as physical, questions about whether he'd be able to go on to college. The car that solved many of those problems was a gift from his family and friends in the community.

Not surprisingly, Ms. Fane's absence from Early in those years made her heart grow fonder for other boys. "I was going with this guy; he was almost beautiful," Ms. Fane said. "But he wasn't my type."

She turned to Sam as soon as they arrived at the Western campus. She arrived before her roommate, and during her first night in the dorm she imagined all sorts of frightful things were outside her room.

"She kept me up on the phone all night long," Early said. Since then, the couple has become a regular item on campus.

When classes and some studying are done in the evenings, Early goes over to Ms. Fane's dorm, balances on one hand and pitches pebbles at her window to signal her that their date should begin. They are together often, but Early manages to get in a little free-lance partying.

He has developed a fondness for socializing with the "good ole farm boys" at the residence house operated by the agricultural fraternity on campus.

While they share mutual problems and affections, Sam Early and Newtie Fane come from different backgrounds. "We grow taters and beans, and they grow petunias and roses," said Early, assessing the difference between his family and Ms. Fane's.

Ms. Fane has had to work to polish some of Early's country-boy manners and to refine his tastes, which run to squirrel and groundhog at present. "She's changed me quite a bit," Early said. "I don't burp as much, and now I spit when she isn't looking."

For his part in the cross-culture effort, Early said, "I'm going to get me a hillbilly dictionary."

Their adjustments to life away from home weren't automatic, they said. "I'm really scared about making it here," Ms. Fane said.

Because she has overcome her handicap enough to enter college, she said, some instructors have assumed that she is a genius. "I'm not, I'm just average," she said.

Early said that he worried about physical obstacles before he came to Western. "I sort of dreaded it," he said. "I was afraid I was going to have to walk up that hill all the time."

Each of them is convinced they can make it and use their college degrees to enter professional careers. Ms. Fane said she intends to become a social worker. She has seen relationships between caseworkers and clients turn sour, she said, and when she has clients of her own, "Mine won't be bitter."

BILL OSINSKI

Early is also fairly certain of his life plan. He wants to run his own farm and perhaps teach agriculture at the high-school level. He doesn't believe the hard work connected with farming is beyond his capabilities.

He's already an accomplished tractor driver, and by carrying a feed bucket in his mouth, he can slop hogs with anybody. Tending dairy cows is no problem, he said, but he sometimes makes steers skittish.

"Beef cattle run me all over the field like I'm a dog," he said.

When Sam and Newtie talk, Sam's disability is not only glossed over, it is seemingly obliterated from their thinking. Ms. Fane told of how Early makes rules: "He really put his foot down."

He teased Newtie when she stole his cap: "I'm gonna kick your butt!"

Speaking of how exercise makes him feel, Early said: "When you get done lifting weights, you feel like you could jump to the sky."

Although Sam and Newtie have been categorized as "special education" students all their lives, they both refuse to accept the label. "I don't feel like it's any different than anybody else going to college," Early said.

Bill's notes: Saving Baby Kathleen was much more than a medical achievement. It was, as I wrote in the lead of this story, a miracle. Not only did the U.S medical personnel save a wounded and orphaned infant, they affirmed their own humanity. I was able to get this story only because I defied my boss, who did not want me to do another piece on the documentary film project on Vietnam helicopter rescues. I relied on my judgment about what makes a good story. The story I produced became the catalyst for the reunion of Kathleen with the people who had saved her. It is certainly one of my favorite newspaper stories, because it affirms the triumph of good over evil.

DOWNIEVILLE, CALIF. — Out of the massacre came a miracle.

In a Viet Cong attack on a village in May 1969, everyone was killed — except a baby girl found wounded in her dead mother's arms.

U.S. soldiers, helicopter crewmen, medics, nurses and doctors saved her life. They gave her a name, Kathleen.

Eventually, the Americans came back home, not knowing what became of Kathleen. But they never forgot her.

About 12 years ago, she began a search for answers about her past. On Monday, they will finally meet again.

Baby Kathleen is now Kathleen Epps, a Northern California wife and mother with three daughters of her own.

The prospect of Monday's reunion at a Texas army base thrills her yet makes her anxious.

"What would be an appropriate gift for saving my life?" said Epps, who was adopted by a U.S. Navy officer. "I can't show up with nothing. What should I bring after 34 years?"

Two of her rescuers — a Lithia Springs paramedic and a Marietta real estate broker — say Kathleen has already given them a priceless gift.

"She was a bright spot in a very bad time. She made all the rest of it bearable," said Richard Hock, a former medic who lives in Lithia Springs and is one of Epps' godparents. "Of all the things that stuck with me from Vietnam, I've always wondered what happened to that child."

Still, Hock said he, too, is worried about gifts for the reunion. "I wish I had something to bring her from back then," he said. "But all I can bring is my memories and myself."

BENDING THE RULES

Flight records show that Huey helicopter commander David Alderson was called to perform a "dustoff" rescue on May 15, 1969, after American soldiers reported finding wounded Vietnamese civilians in a village. "Dustoff" is the term used for a no-landing, in- and-out helicopter rescue mission.

It was a day when Alderson would log more than 12 hours in the air and make at least three trips to Third Field Hospital. He recalled a medic telling him that they had a wounded child, who had been locked in the tight embrace of her dead mother for more than two days. The soldiers pried the two apart to rescue the baby.

"We thought the baby was going to die," Alderson said. Had he radioed his base for instructions, he probably would have been told to go to a Vietnamese hospital.

Instead, Alderson headed for Third Field Hospital, a U.S. facility set up in a converted school in the heart of Saigon. "Every now and then, we just didn't call in," he said. "In this case, a lot of people bent the rules."

For most of that day, the staff at Third Field Hospital had struggled to keep up with a heavy flow of casualties, recalls Donna Rowe, the head triage nurse, who now lives in Marietta.

But when the radio call came in — "Will you receive civilian casualties?" — there had been a brief slowdown.

Had she followed the rules, Rowe would have redirected the Huey. Third Field Hospital was primarily for wounded American soldiers. Wounded Vietnamese civilians were the lowest priority guests.

"Tell 'em to come on," Rowe said.

Hock, the former medic, remembers that moment well.

"We [he and Rowe] just looked at each other and knew it was the right thing to do," he said.

Hock took the baby from the ambulance drivers who'd shuttled her in from the helicopter landing pad across the street from the hospital.

The baby was near death, said Darrell Warren, another medic on duty. She was dehydrated, malnourished and had fragmentation wounds in her abdomen and lower chest. "She was blowing up on her own blood," Rowe said. Rowe said the baby was rushed to the X-ray room so pieces of shrapnel from the attack could be located.

On the way from X-ray to the operating room, Rowe saw a chaplain, the Rev. Luke Sullivan, and pulled him into the crowd that was half-running down the hospital corridor.

"Father, come with us, you have to baptize this baby," Rowe said.

She knew that if the baby were baptized by a Catholic priest, and if she survived surgery, she could find a bed at a nearby Catholic orphanage.

Sullivan said he didn't have the holy water for a baptism. Rowe suggested that tap water would suffice.

So, there was a Catholic baptism, with Rowe, a Methodist, serving as godmother, and Hock, then a Methodist, and Warren, a Mormon, as co-godfathers.

But no one knew the baby's name. Rowe said she should be christened Kathleen Fields — the first name from the Irish ballad "I'll Take You Home Again, Kathleen."

Rowe and the others then took Kathleen to the operating room, where a surgeon removed the shrapnel and stabilized Kathleen. "She was so tiny, she only went from here to there," Rowe said, indicating the distance from her elbow to the palm of her hand. "They had to use the smallest tools we had."

After the surgery, they made a crib for Kathleen: an orange crate lined with warm towels. They fashioned diapers from washcloths reinforced by sanitary napkins.

Then, a medical staffer wondered about stretching the rules to treat a Vietnamese baby.

"Captain, there's going to be some heat over this," Rowe recalls hearing.

"What are they going to do, send me to Vietnam?" she answered.

The next day the hospital commander approached Rowe. "Captain, I understand we have a civilian patient," he said.

"Yes, sir, we do," she said.

"Well done," the commander said.

From then on, the baby became the darling of the hospital staff. "Every spare moment, we spent with her," said co-godfather Warren.

He and the other hospital staffers were touched by the baby who smiled more than she wept, he said. "Kathleen was one of those special little people who grabs you and pulls the good things out of you," Warren said.

They cadged money from other staffers, telling them to cut back on beer, to buy baby clothes and supplies. They painted the classroom ward where the baby was kept. "We were like two idiots," Warren said of his and Hock's attempts to care for the child. "If it wasn't for Donna showing us how to be parents, that baby would've been in a lot of trouble."

A few days after Kathleen arrived, three soldiers in combat gear came into the hospital. They asked if the hospital had treated a wounded baby, and if it had survived.

Rowe directed them to Kathleen's room, where they visited briefly, then headed out. As they passed Rowe, one of the men said, "Thank you."

"Those combat troops did something exceptional and wonderful. They could have kept right on walking," Rowe said. "But they were compassionate and caring. They were Americans."

But there were still challenges ahead: The baby couldn't eat. Rowe said Kathleen could not tolerate cow's milk or goat's milk. It wasn't until Red Cross workers brought in soy-based formula that the baby started to thrive.

After about two weeks, Kathleen was healthy enough to be transferred to St. Elizabeth's orphanage. Rowe told the men to scrounge extra food from the hospital mess to take with the baby to the orphanage.

A FAMILY FOR KATHLEEN

With her medical emergency over, Kathleen was safe, but without a family to call her own.

At a chapel service shortly after Kathleen arrived at the hospital, Sullivan, the chaplain, told the story of the miracle baby.

Among the worshippers was a Navy officer, Marvin Cords. After the service, Cords approached the priest and asked about adopting Kathleen. The priest took him to the hospital.

"When I first saw her, she had a wound dressing that just about covered her entire body," Cords said.

At the time, Cords and his first wife, Sally, had already adopted three children, but they had talked about adopting a Vietnamese child. He hired a Vietnamese attorney and started to track down Kathleen's birth certificate.

Weeks passed, but still no birth certificate came from the nuns at the orphanage. At this point, Cords sought help from Sullivan, who did a little priestly arm-twisting.

"He told the nuns, 'Get a birth certificate for that child, or you'll never get another nickel from anyone at this hospital,' " Cords said.

Days later, Kathleen had a birth certificate.

After more government red tape and delays, including having to get a waiver signed by then-South Vietnamese President Nguyen Van Thieu, Cords brought Kathleen to America.

"She was shy, but very, very stubborn," said Sally Gibson, her adoptive mother. Mostly, the family lived on military bases around the country.

Kathleen recalls that the children, including two more who were adopted later, were summoned to dinner by the ringing of a ship's bell. The six adopted children created a multicultural rainbow of ethnic heritages: African-American, Native-American, Vietnamese and Caucasian.

Kathleen remembers that when they lived in South Carolina, some of the kids on the school bus taunted her African-American brother. The rest of the Cords kids jumped to their brother's defense, and the name-calling ended that day.

LOST AND FOUND

About 12 years ago, Epps started to get serious about searching for her roots. "I figured once I found somebody from the hospital, they could tell me where I came from," she said.

In June 2002, she left an entry in the guest book of a Vietnam veterans Web site: "I'm looking for any staff and/or military personnel who may have been at Third Field Hospital in Saigon, 1969. Anyone who may have remembered a small Vietnamese girl brought in by helicopter. Her whole village was killed by Viet Cong . . . I have very few names and no memories except the year and the place. Could you please contact me, if anyone knows anything? Thanks!"

A few weeks later, Ed Russell, a retired federal employee living near Philadelphia, saw the entry. Russell had served as a chaplain's assistant to Sullivan in Vietnam, but left the country in May 1969, and had never heard the story of Baby Kathleen.

In July 2002, Russell visited Walter Reed Army Medical Center in Washington, D.C., where there are archives of the U.S. medical forces from the Vietnam era.

He found a story published in a Florida newspaper in 1969, written by war correspondent Helen Musgrove. It was titled "Miss Ecumenical." It was the story of Kathleen's baptism.

Russell sent an e-mail to the woman who'd left the notice in the guest book. "Finally, I had found somebody who might know something, but I didn't want to scare him off," Epps said. "A couple of e-mails later, I told him I was that Kathleen."

The Florida story gave the names of Donna Rowe, the former Army nurse, and Richard Hock, the former medic.

Rowe was the key, but they had no clue where to find her.

Russell kept up the Internet search, though, and found an Army nurses' Web site, where an October 2002 Atlanta Journal-Constitution story had been posted.

MISSING LINK LOCATED

Last October, Rowe told the story of Baby Kathleen to filmmakers shooting "In the Shadow of the Blade," a documentary about medical rescues.

"To think that we saved this little scrap of a thing," said Rowe, now a real estate broker in Marietta. "I thought I would never see her again."

Russell told Epps about Rowe's story in the newspaper. Then, Epps contacted Cheryl Fries, the creative director of the documentary, who led her to Rowe.

After that, a torrent of information poured in, filling the blanks of Epps' past.

"I had to tell Cheryl to let me rest for a few days, it was so overwhelming," Epps said.

The news that Kathleen had found them was no less of a shock to the veterans of the Third Field Hospital. Neither Hock nor Rowe had known that for the past 20 years, they have lived within a half an hour's drive from each other.

About a month ago, Hock came home and found a voicemail from a woman who wanted to talk to him about Vietnam.

He doesn't like talking about much of his wartime experience, but he called back. A woman called out for someone else to come quickly to the phone: "Kathleen."

Hock knew exactly what the call was about.

Once the story started coming together, the filmmakers decided to reunite Kathleen with her rescuers for the documentary. Fries said it was too powerful a story not to tell fully.

"This is a story about humanity in the middle of war, about good people in a bad situation," she said. "Kathleen's future exists because good people in American uniforms cared."

On Monday, Epps will fly by Huey helicopter into Fort Sam Houston near San Antonio, where many Army nurses trained for Vietnam.

Alderson had planned to pilot the Huey, but he died last week of pneumonia at a Virginia hospital.

A substitute for Alderson, one of his co-pilots in Vietnam, will be flying the Huey. Rowe, Hock and Warren will be on the ground, guiding it to a landing.

Epps will be bringing more than herself to the reunion. Along with her adoptive parents, she will bring her husband, Billy, and their three daughters, Mary-Ann, 8; Jo-Jo, 6; and Sean, 5.

They live in Downieville, Calif., a town of less than 500 people in the historic gold rush area of the Sierra Nevada Mountains.

A sketch of the Epps' family life includes a blue-collar dad and stay-at-home mom, and a house where bears come to climb in the backyard trees.

Billy Epps said the reunion will help his wife and his daughters "fill in some missing parts of the family history." "I always thought this was an incredible story," Billy Epps said.

As Donna Rowe prepared to come to the reunion to celebrate the story of Kathleen Epps, she was touched by an Iraqi wartime tragedy.

She got a call from a man who works frequently for her, the dad of Diego Rincon, of Conyers. His son, an Army private, was killed in Operation Iraqi Freedom.

Once again, Rowe found herself comforting a family shattered by war. "I thought that part of my life was over," she said. "That's why Kathleen's story needs to be told now."

For Hock, Kathleen's story is one that transcends the brutality of war, a Vietnam flashback that brings joy rather than dread.

"It's about this baby who had the will to survive and who did. She flourished and became a beautiful woman with a beautiful family," he said. "It's the great American dream all over again."

Bill's notes: I wrote this story as one of my first columns for the Akron Beacon Journal Sunday Magazine. I tried to seek out people whom I thought the readers might like to meet. Certainly, a man who can find humor in the topic of death fit into that category.

I N THE IMMORTAL words of the Glib Reaper, "Death is not an easy thing to live with."

While most of us deal with death by whistling past the graveyard, Joe Bernard likes to try out his new one-liners – like that one – in the morgue.

"The dead people are my best audience; they can't walk out on me," he said.

Bernard is the assistant director of the anatomy laboratory at Northeastern Ohio University College of Medicine and a mortician for several private funeral homes. He embalms about 400 bodies a year, and he must introduce medical students to the practice of dissecting cadavers.

Does all this work among people who will never play again make Joe a dull boy? Hardly.

"Dealing with death so close, God, you learn to love life!" Bernard said.

Bernard makes respect for the dead the first rule of his work, but he is also not afraid to use humor to dispel the morbidity and fear that is often associated with the tasks he must perform.

A sign on the door labels his office "State Hospital For The Terminally Weird". Beside a tray of bones, he keeps a notebook with issues of a comedy newsletter.

At medical school events, Bernard is often the master of ceremonies.

He's also not afraid to break the stereotype of the professionally grim undertaker, in order to help his medical students develop a healthy working relationship with death.

For example, when the students are beginning their dissecting assignments, Bernard may walk through the room humming, "I've Got You Under My Skin".

Or, when it comes time to start working in the cranial area, Bernard may do something like produce some preserved cow eyes and sing, "I Only Have Eyes For You".

If a male student in a hurry to change finds the pants in his locker have their legs sewn together, or if one of the laboratory jars is found to contain a pop-out snake, chances are the glib reaper has struck again.

Bernard said he has loved humor since he was a child, and his grandfather would take him to the classic comedies at the movies. He still has a poster on his wall with scenes from W. C. Fields and The Three Stooges comedies.

"I just love to laugh," he said.

But humor is also a tool Bernard uses to teach compassion.

In his work at the medical school, he must take students who are already highly stressed from their other studies and help them master a realm of work that embodies some of the deepest human dreads.

"The tension is there. They have a scalpel in their hand, and they have to cut into a person, and a dead one at that," he said.

Bernard said he tries to make the students realize they are dealing with more than just a corpse. "I tell them to remember this was someone's loved one," he said.

Usually, by the end of the school term, the cadaver "goes from a body to a person" in the minds of the student doctors, he said.

Some of the students use their cadaver's real first name, and some invent life histories, he said.

Training like that helps the students develop the humanity to treat their living patients with kindness, he said.

After each school year, the work on the cadavers is done, and they are cremated. The students in Bernard's labs then hold a memorial service for the people who have donated their bodies for the advance of medical knowledge.

Sometimes, the students will write poetry for the service. Some of them will cry for the people they knew only in death.

Bernard also meets some of the people who are making plans to donate their bodies to the medical school, and he tries to show them the dignity of this choice.

Once, he said, a sickly old man came to inquire about the donation program. The man's feelings of worthlessness and of being a burden seemed to be eased by the notion that his death could serve a purpose, Bernard said.

At the end of the conversation, the old man asked that his ashes be placed in a garden, saying, "Maybe I'll come back as a rose."

For himself, Bernard said, his work among the dead makes him better able to savor more fully his life among the living.

When he must embalm someone who died shortly after his or her retirement day, Bernard reminds himself to take that fling he'd been putting off.

When he sees a child's body in his morgue, he makes it a point to give an extra hug to his own little girl.

A sign on his office wall gives Bernard's philosophy for living with the dead: "It is hard to die and it always will be...We must view death not as a dreaded stranger but as an expected companion to our life. We must learn to live with an appreciation of our finiteness, of the limits of our time on earth."

Bill's notes: An editor at the Boston Globe, a paper for which I had done some freelance assignments, called me and said he'd heard of a nearly totally paralyzed former Marine, who was a patient at a Miami hospital. The man, Howard Cordes, was trying to find a legal way to die. I went to the hospital, walked in without permission or telling anyone what I was doing, and eventually found his room. At first, he didn't want me to write his story. But I asked him if I could just talk with him a while, and he agreed. Then he said I could come back later, when his wife would be with him. They gave me permission to do an interview for the story that follows. It ran simultaneously in the Globe and the Miami News.

BOSTON GLOBE, NOVEMBER 2, 1974

MIAMI — YESTERDAY was Howard Cordes's 56th birthday. He wishes he hadn't made it.

Cordes, who was the 1933 Vermont Golden Gloves boxing champion, has lain in a hospital bed for the past three years, totally paralyzed from the neck down by a skiing accident and fighting for each breath.

He has gone so far as to put in writing his request for permission to die, but the system just can't process that kind of paperwork.

"I'm not a man anymore. I want to be a companion to my wife, do things with her, but I can't do anything," he said, with tears streaming down his face.

His wife, Helen, had to wipe those tears away for him. But Howard Cordes is no vegetable, and that may be his heaviest burden in the day-to-day tragedy he lives.

He is aware of all that is missing from his life. He is mentally alert and can see and hear well.

With the aid of a tracheotomy tube in his throat, he can also talk.

He would not be so despondent if he were simply a quadriplegic, but a severe respiratory dysfunction keeps him tied to his bed in the Miami Veterans Hospital. Mrs. Cordes lives by herself in nearby Hollywood.

Only his head is visible above the hospital sheets pulled over his useless body. His skin is ash-colored and his eyes are puffy, but his words and their thoughtful tone show he is in control of his reason.

Periodically, Cordes said, his muscles must have spasms induced in them to prevent complete atrophy.

"It's like a rope being wrapped around my neck and pulled through my torso and shoulders," he said. "They're a blessing and a curse. I'm either stiff as a board or limp as a noodle."

Even in normal conversation, he breathes heavily, and experiences mild coughing fits that rob him of breath and leave him red-faced and gasping for air.

Cordes said he has technically suffocated several times, but the quick responses of his attendants have always cleared his passages in time to start him breathing again.

At one point several months ago he actually signed a "mercy will", stating he did not wish his life prolonged without due cause. However, hospital officials told him they had no legal authority to allow him to die.

"I could pull the tubes out, I guess," Cordes said, "but that wouldn't be death with dignity, that would be tortuous."

Still, he said, he thinks of that alternative at times. When he signed the "mercy will," he was under the impression that euthanasia is legal in Florida. It is not. But after he signed, the director of an organization lobbying for the legalization of euthanasia put out a press release ascribing to Mrs. Cordes many statements supportive of his cause — statements which she said she did not make.

An area newspaper ran a story based on the release, which had Mrs. Cordes lashing out at the Veterans Administration's policy for treatment of incurable cases. "We don't want to say anything against the VA," Mrs. Cordes said. "We're government people, and this is a government hospital. We don't want to be exploited."

Cordes said he felt it would be "disloyal" of him to be the focus of a crusade for euthanasia as long as it is illegal. He even worried that his death would mean that the government funds already spent to keep him alive would "go down the drain."

Since he has been at the Miami VA institution for the past year he said, he has improved. Before he came, his lungs were so bad he could

BILL OSINSKI

not speak and was forced to stay connected to a mechanical respirator in order to keep breathing.

Here, at least, he receives what he feels is first-rate attention. His daily therapy begins with his body being tilted down and his back pounded so that the fluids accumulated in his lungs overnight can be drained.

A set of controls using space-age technology allows him to do things like elevate his bed or turn on the television by blowing into a plastic tube.

He is being trained in other skills, but mostly he just lies there. "I have to be turned over on my sides often, because I keep getting bedsores," he said.

It is the mental anguish caused by this nearly total loss of activity that Cordes says makes his wish for death. For a man who was a marine, an avid skier and huntsman, this is the hardest part to live with.

After seeing combat duty in World War II, Cordes became an agent for the US Immigration Service. He had been with the service 32 years and was in charge of its office at John F. Kennedy airport in New York, when a skiing accident in the Berkshires in early 1972 left him in his present state.

The Cordeses have four grown children living in the Northeast and California. Mrs. Cordes said she had her husband in a private medical center until hospitalization coverage ran out.

Her daytime hours are spent at her husband's bedside, talking with him or reading to him. Neither she nor her husband knows why he is still alive.

She said there are only a very few persons who have suffered such severe paralysis and survived for any length of time.

With his stability and the caliber of treatment he is receiving, Cordes said, his doctors may be able to keep him alive "indefinitely."

When asked if he had any chances for improvement toward some kind of a fulfilling life, Cordes said his doctors are "very hopeful." As he said the word "hope," his face twisted into a smile, the only smile he managed during the conversation.

Hope is a very rare commodity for Howard Cordes.

Bill's notes: As a writer, you hope your words and your work touches the people you write about and the people who read your stories. This story showed that my hopes had been realized in the case of Howard Cordes. Not only had many readers been touched to the point of writing to Cordes and offering help, but the outpouring of support literally changed Cordes' life. I was deeply gratified.

BOSTON GLOBE, SEPTEMBER 19, 1975

MIAMI — TEN months ago Howard Cordes didn't want to reach his next birthday.

Today he hopes he'll live to be 100.

A former boxer and marine, Cordes, 56, has been almost totally paralyzed from the neck down since a skiing accident nearly four years ago. The inability to move and sometimes to breathe made him wish for his own death.

He told the Globe in an interview last November, "I'm not a man anymore."

But Howard Cordes has changed his mind. Living is once again appealing. His paralysis remains, but he can look ahead to his release from the Miami Veterans Administration Hospital within the next few months.

After that, he and his wife Helen will embark on a cross-country drive to visit their three daughters in California and a fourth in Michigan. The fullness has returned to a face that was sunken, and he has learned a new breathing technique that helps prevent the throat congestion that often made it difficult for him to speak.

"I guess I was a little selfish," Cordes said of his earlier death wishes. "It was just that sometimes I'd think about what the odds of recovery are and say, 'What's the use?'"

In response to the story published earlier about him, Cordes said, he received hundreds of encouraging letters, many from church groups and some from as far away as Germany.

"I never knew there were so many kind people in the world," he said. "They encouraged me to keep my faith and offered to pray for me. I guess I never really gave up hope."

Cordes, who had 32 years of service with the US Immigration Service and was at one time the officer in charge of the J. F. Kennedy International Airport immigration office, credits the staff at the VA with much of his physical recovery.

They have outfitted him with an electric wheelchair with controls in a small red rubber ball, which he can operate with slight movements from his middle finger. He undergoes daily physical and hydrotherapy, and the mental miracle of his recovery has been aided by the ability to spend the weekends with his wife in their Hollywood home, he said.

Cordes is still subject to periodic spasms that wrack his body and choke off his breath, and he will probably have a tracheotomy tube in his throat for the rest of his life.

Still, the day is not too far off when the doctors at Veterans will have done all they can for him, and he'll be released. "The government will pay for nursing home care for three months, but after that, I'm on my own," he said. "And that's my only dread."

When he said this, his wife Helen reassured him, "You're coming home."

"I've had a good life," Cordes said. "I was always active, and the children were all grown before this happened. I guess that's how I've been able to pay the price I've had to pay. The accident was no one's fault," he says philosophically, "it was just one of those things."

Bill's notes: Older men are often inclined to reminisce about the good old days. Not many, though, go to the lengths of building a covered bridge to bring a favored childhood memory back to life. Al Purcell did just that, taking a pile driver to all that nostalgia stuff.

ATLANTA JOURNAL CONSTITUTION, SEPTEMBER 29, 1996

P EOPLE OFTEN LET even their best memories fade into the time-dusted corners of their minds.

Al Purcell rebuilt his in his front yard.

When he was growing up in the northeast Georgia mountains, there was a covered bridge at the entrance to his grandfather's farm. He spent some of the best days of his young life around that bridge.

The river pooled upstream to form a swimming hole for him, his cousins and their friends. At nights, they would build a campfire and fish. And the kids could climb into his grandfather's scuppernong vines for a free snack.

"Living didn't come easy back then, but it sure was a great place to grow up," Purcell said. "I can remember sitting up in those vines, having all the scuppernongs I could eat."

The covered bridge was more than a pretty spot in the hills. For him, it was a symbol of family. "You know, we visited a lot back then," he said. "Country people like to visit."

Purcell left the mountains to work as a switchman and in the accounting department of a large railroad company. About 17 years ago, he bought a piece of land in rural Coweta County, near the town of Roscoe, and set about remaking some memories.

He lived in an Airstream trailer while he built his home. On the wall of his family room, he hung the plow that he and his father and brothers used to work their cotton fields.

He drained a swampy area in front of the house and dammed the little creek that flowed into it to form a fishing lake. But the key element from those days at grandpa's farm was still missing.

"I always wanted a bridge," he said. "That was my most cherished memory."

So, since he was the son of a carpenter and a self-described "country boy who appreciates hard work," Purcell started work on his own covered bridge about three years ago.

He selected and cut the pine trees he would use, then had them sawed into lumber. After the lumber aged for about a year, he was ready to start the real work, which would take another two years.

To provide the base support for the bridge, he sunk eight-foot sections of telephone poles for pilings. He set the poles into holes he'd dug, then slammed them down into the earth by using a pile driver of his own design — a 75-pound section of steel pipe. He covered one end and welded handles onto the sides, so that he could lift it up and pound it down onto the pilings.

He built the floor of the bridge sturdy enough so that he could ride his farm machinery over it. He used a front-end loader to place the trusses for the roof.

Purcell's covered bridge has two windows on its lake side. That way, people can fish from the inside of the bridge if it's raining.

But now that Purcell has his own lake, he said he finds that he fishes less often. "The herons catch more fish than I do," he said.

At 62, Purcell is semi-retired. He raises cattle on his land, but not much for income as for his enjoyment of farming and ranching.

One of his favorite diversions is the view from his front-porch rocker over morning coffee. He has kept a large section of his land in near wilderness condition, so he can take a walk in the woods and feel like he's not so far removed from the mountain streams that he could drink from as a boy.

And in the Al Purcell natural museum of memories, there is a place for the sweet taste of youth. Not far from his covered bridge, he's cultivated a fine growth of scuppernong vines.

Bill's notes: There was an outpouring of help for the Warners from readers of this article. In a few days, more than $60,000 was contributed. One of the homeless activists quoted in the article volunteered to serve as a counselor and money manager for the family. I remember how Icelda's 13-year-old son cared for his mother, helping her to get to the hospital when she was ill. She did not ask me to do this story; I chose her at random from families living at the motel. She is one of many, and all of their needs are great.

ATLANTA JOURNAL CONSTITUTION, DECEMBER 19, 2004

T HE FAMILY IN Room 160 is homeless in suburbia.

For the past four months, Icelda Warner and her five children have lived in one room of a pay-by-the-week motel in Norcross.

She and her 15-year-old daughter each share a single bed with one of her younger sons, ages 5 and 6. There is barely enough leftover floor space for her two older sons, ages 13 and 11, to sleep in donated sleeping bags.

She has no car, so she takes a bus to her job as a waitress at a Waffle House. She works mostly the midnight shift or on weekends. Tips are not so good on the late shift, but that's when her daughter can baby sit.

She has kept her family together despite a previous eviction, despite the child support payments that never come, despite all the time they spend together in their 16-by-16-foot home.

"I don't think we can go anywhere but up from here. We've hit rock bottom," Warner said.

Rock bottom may be a scary place, but the Warners are not alone there. A recent survey by Gwinnett social service and church agencies estimates there's a need for more than 1,100 emergency shelter spaces in the county.

Actual spaces available: zero. There is no emergency shelter for homeless families in Gwinnett County.

So instead, the homeless must find someplace to go or find the money for short-term housing, such as extended- stay hotels. That's not so unusual for suburban counties across the country where growth has outpaced the planning for a social safety net.

In metro Atlanta, for example, there are a total of eight emergency homeless shelters for families in DeKalb, Carroll, Rockdale, Cobb and Clayton counties, according to a survey by the Marietta-based Georgia Coalition to End Homelessness.

Many of them tend to be small and rely primarily on private donations, like the Ministries United for Service Training in Cobb County, which has 44 beds.

"There is a general perception that these are affluent areas and the homeless don't exist in places like these," said Claas Ehlers, development director for a national network of churches called Family Promise that provides shelter for homeless families.

Ellen Gerstein, executive director of the Gwinnett Coalition for Health and Human Services, said that echoes in Gwinnett. "They think we're rich in Gwinnett County. The worst part of the issue is our denial due to the image of affluence," she said.

Homelessness also takes a different form in the suburbs. Most homeless families in the suburbs are people who can't pay their rent because of financial hardship.

"They're people just like you and me. They're our neighbors. If we don't help them, success may not live here anymore," said Gerstein, referring to Gwinnett's slogan.

Gerstein has been lobbying for 10 years for the creation of a homeless family shelter in Gwinnett. In recent years, the emergency referral hotline operated by her agency has seen a "tremendous increase" in calls from families in need of housing, she said.

PINNING DOWN THE NEED

Getting a fix on just how much need is in the county is an important step toward providing better services. The United Way is funding a study to be conducted by the Salvation Army on the feasibility of building a homeless family shelter in Gwinnett.

Deb Roberts, area director for United Way of Gwinnett, said she hopes the study will generate accurate data on the number of families living in "last resort" situations like motels and on families who have found refuge by crowding into apartments with friends and relatives.

That's one of several efforts under way. Others include:

> Three social workers with Gwinnett schools who are focusing on helping more than 500 homeless children, a number that has grown steadily in recent years. The children are offered tutoring and assistance with materials and bus transportation.
> The Gwinnett County Task Force for the Homeless, a coalition of church groups and motel operators, which is raising money for a homeless-family shelter.
> Family Promise, which will begin a Gwinnett program in early 2005. Homeless families will get overnight living space at churches and assistance in finding more stable living conditions.
> Love in Action Outreach Ministry, a nonprofit group founded by former assisted living center operator Bobbi Pack, which has gotten a special use permit and placed an option on a Norcross building for use as a homeless shelter, but doesn't yet have the funds to open it.

Clarence Moore, youth pastor at the Atlanta Vineyard Church in Norcross and a cofounder of the Gwinnett County Task Force for the Homeless, said when a family falls into homelessness, it's often very difficult to climb out.

Once evicted, a family would typically need to save enough money to pay first and last month's rent, as well as security and utility deposits, in order to get into another apartment. That often amounts to up-front payments of about $2,000, he said.

This breeds what Moore calls a "mentality of desperation."

Warner knows what that feels, looks, sounds and tastes like. It tastes like the who- knows-how-old bakery products scattered around her family's room — bread and pastries left by church people at the motel's front desk.

It sounds like the voice of the doctor who told her she couldn't go back to work for five days after having pneumonia.

It looks like spinning blue lights on police cars sent to her motel to evict another family.

It feels like the walls are always closing in.

DRAWN BY FALSE HOPE

Warner ended up in this small hotel room after she left the father of her youngest two children in Florida nearly two years ago, after he abused her.

She moved into her mother's already-full house in New York, but she couldn't earn enough to afford her own place there.

Someone, she can't recall who, told her jobs were abundant in the suburbs of Atlanta. So in early 2004, her sister drove her and the children to Gwinnett.

She thought she had enough money to last about six months, and by that time, she figured, she'd surely have a decent job. She figured wrong.

She didn't realize how hard it is in this county to get to work if you don't have a car. She assumed, incorrectly, that even without a car, there would be bus service that would take her where and when she needed to go.

She also counted on court-ordered child support payments that did not come. They moved into an apartment, but by July, her money was gone and they were evicted.

She had found a job at a Waffle House that she could reach by bus, but not in time to stay in the apartment. Her attempts to find an emergency-assistance agency that might help them were unsuccessful.

The shelters that operate were for either abused women or abused children.

She was just broke, and she refused to separate her family. "I found out that if you're homeless in Gwinnett, there's no help for you," she said.

The Warners have lived in two motels, but Warner still considers herself homeless. "Having a roof over my head with six people in one room is not having a home," she said.

She works nights and gets home by bus just in time to get the four oldest kids off to school – a county school bus makes a pickup in the motel parking lot — and settle in to rest with her 5-year-old son.

She earns enough to pay the $151.51 weekly rent. Her food-stamp allotment is $640 a month, but it doesn't always last that long. Any illness — like the pneumonia — puts job and room in jeopardy.

Despite that, like so many who can't make a rent payment in Gwinnett, Warner is hopeful. "One way or another, we're going to stay together, and we'll be all right."

Bill's notes: Atlanta was the landing place for many of the refugees from Hurricane Katrina. Larry Sims came with a story of courage and survival. He became a hero when the moment demanded it, but later on, he couldn't quite get his life together. He and his wife tried to settle in Atlanta, but their marriage failed, and he moved away.

THEY WERE LEFT behind in the rising brown lake that was once New Orleans' 9th Ward — and it was up to them to find a way out.

After the levees failed, 25 people clustered precariously in the rafters of their small wood-frame houses. Safety awaited on the second floor of the apartment house across the street — but only one of them could get there.

Larry Sims swam to the high ground and prayed for a way to get his family and neighbors there too. He was the only one of the group who could swim, and the waters in the street were already about 9 feet deep.

"I just knew that if I didn't do something right now, me and my family and friends was going to die," Sims said.

Just then, a punching bag floated by. Heavy punching bags, the 4-foot-long kind boxers use to practice their body blows, are not a common sight in ordinary times in the 9th Ward. They are not recommended for use as lifeboats, but then, nothing was going according to the manuals that day, Monday, Aug. 29, the day New Orleans drowned.

Sims, a 37-year-old truck driver, knew instantly what to do with the punching bag, and why it appeared at just that moment. "God brought that punching bag right to me," said Sims, who told the story last week at the Norcross hotel where he and his family are staying after they were evacuated.

He snatched the bag and swam across the street with it. One by one, he got the trapped people across. He swam and pulled the punching bag while each person clung to it.

Most of the trips were made calmly, with Sims reassuring his passengers that everything was going to be all right. He told them things like, "I'm not going to let nothin' happen to y'all," he said.

One elderly woman refused to leave her deathtrap of a house, so Sims had to drag her out and then coax her into hanging on to the bag. Another elderly woman was too disabled to hold the bag, so Sims put her on his back and walked and swam her across.

He picked up a roofing nail in his bare foot on that trip, and it was days before he'd get a tetanus shot. A neighbor, Kariste Carruth, saw Sims swimming back and forth. She and her two children, a two-year-old and a five-month-old, and a few neighbors had ridden out the storm in their attic.

She climbed down from the bookcase they'd used as a ladder — there were no openings to the attic, so a neighbor pounded one out with a hammer — made it to her porch and called out to Sims. "We're here! We're here!" Sims came and got them as well.

Tracy Sims, Larry's wife, said she had started to panic before Larry's ferry started up. Their 9-year-old son, Darren, claimed he wasn't scared while his dad was pulling the punching bag across the street, though he did admit that waiting in the darkened attic was spooky.

Diamond, the Sims' 7- year-old daughter, thought the punching-bag ride was fun; at one point, she even let go and tried to paddle herself.

The punching-bag ferry was only the beginning of their evacuation ordeal. Sims shepherded the group throughout the three days and two nights that it took them to escape from the 9th Ward.

He doesn't call himself a hero, but the people he saved certainly do. "He's a big hero. He's the man," said Kimberly Roberts, a friend of Sims and one of the trapped people who followed him out. "He saved all of us."

BILL OSINSKI

Sims and about half his group were brought to Norcross from an Alexandria, La., shelter by a coalition of Gwinnett and Louisiana church people and other volunteers

After they reached the two- story building, the first priority was food and water and formula for Carruth's young children.

Sims does not own a car, and any cars he might have used were under water. Tracy Sims remembered that one of their neighbors had a small rowboat. Larry swam to where he thought the house had been, found the boat and paddled it back, using a plank he'd found.

Strangely, he wasn't exhausted, he said, but he was soaked. Tracy had brought a small bag of clothes with her, and Larry changed into one of Tracy's dresses, the only dry clothing that would fit him.

Then he went out foraging. Sims knew he was breaking the law when he broke into a grocery store to get food and supplies, but said, "I'd do it again. It was for my family."

That first night, the group found a grill on the apartment's terrace, and they cooked a barbecue dinner.

The next day, Carruth went outside. She tried to flag down a Coast Guard patrol boat.

The men in the boat said they couldn't take any passengers. "We're looking for dead people," they told her.

Sims went on another foraging run and then started the hunt for dry land. The waters had receded to the level where most of the group could wade, and they reached a beachhead of sorts, where state wildlife officials were running a ferry to the Superdome.

Priority passengers for the small shuttle boats were the elderly and the sick. Sims and all but two of his group waited for hours, but when it started to get dark, the shuttle boats stopped running.

One of the rescue workers told them to try to get into a nearby naval facility. By the time the group had slogged its way to the installation, it was night.

As they approached, they heard the clicking sounds of guns being cocked and someone called out from the walls of the installation, "Don't come any closer, or we'll shoot." Carruth said her 2-year-old daughter didn't comprehend the warning. "My baby started running up to the building. I had to pull her back."

Where were they supposed to go? Sims tried to keep his people's spirits up, telling them, "As God is my witness, I'm gonna get y'all through this."

He knew they were only a few blocks from a high school building, so he led them there by flashlight, declared the deserted building an emergency shelter and broke in. The school still had some water in its tanks, enough for some of the group to use to clean up.

There was no barbecue on that second night, but they did manage to bring some bread and other staples in their boat.

On the third day, Sims made up his mind that it would be their last in New Orleans. He took the boat and went to a furniture store where he had worked as a driver. The front of the building had caved in, so he found a ladder and used it to climb over the debris and get to the store's loading dock.

There, Sims found a van. The water in the streets was low enough for him to drive back to the high school, blowing the van's horn as loudly as he could when he arrived.

Everyone was loaded into the back of the van, and Sims laced some thick cloth strips across the open back end to prevent anyone from sliding out.

They made a stop at the Superdome, where Tracy Sims found her 79-year-old father, who'd gone there before the hurricane hit.

"For two days, he'd been thinking we were dead," she said.

Her father wanted to stay where he was, but the others were eager to put New Orleans in the rearview mirror.

Sims said a man tried to buy his commandeered van, but Sims wasn't going to make that kind of deal, "not for any amount of money," he said. He fired up the van and headed north.

Three weeks later, on Friday morning, the levees failed again, bringing an encore of floodwaters to the 9th Ward. Sims said it's almost overwhelming to contemplate all that has happened to his hometown. "It makes my heart weep," Sims said.

Bill's notes: Moonshining is the stuff of legend in Appalachia. The men who made it were outlaws, so we don't often hear them tell their stories. So, it was fun to sit down with Ralph Presley, who found a way to distill his tales of his moonshining days into a retirement job.

ATLANTA JOURNAL CONSTITUTION, OCTOBER 1, 2000

F ORGET ALL THAT "Thunder Road" stuff. When it comes to moving fast-cured whiskey, slower is better.

"You can't outrun them Motorolas (police radios)," said Ralph Presley, who's spent about two-thirds of his 58 years dabbling in the fine art of making moonshine.

Presley wasn't in the outlaw business for the adventure of it. Making moonshine was about being able to feed your family if you lived on the Conasauga River in rural Whitfield County.

And you didn't bother trying to sell to your neighbors in those days, because "there wasn't $3 in the whole county," he said. "That was the only thing to do back then. Just about everybody done it, and everybody knew it."

So, when he got a load together, some of his own label and some he'd bought from friends who ran stills, he'd just make out like he was a country boy heading for the city, which he was.

He'd put a horse in a trailer, then pack in 60 or 80 gallons of 'shine around the horse and cover the contraband with hay.

He also could squeeze another 20 to 30 gallons in a box in the camper shell of his pickup and let a few dogs sit on the box for the ride.

Then it was a nice, safe, speed-limit drive to Atlanta or Knoxville or Nashville. Nashville was the best, because a Nashville run usually meant a weekend of partying and a couple of nights at the Grand Ole Opry.

In all those years, there was only one time when the law busted up his still.

Presley is strictly a retired moonshiner these days. He travels the world, helping to set up heavy machinery the Dalton area carpet mills sell to foreign textile firms.

Now, his copper still and wooden "thump bucket" are used only for legal entertainment purposes. He sets up his white lightnin' apparatus for display at the twice-yearly Prater's Mill festivals held in Varnell, not far from his home near Dawsonville.

He'll be telling his tales of mountain life in the old days at next weekend's Prater's Mill Country Fair. And his tales are about as tall as the hills. Presley can't remember a time when he wasn't roaming the mountains. His daddy farmed some, traded mules and made some moonshine on the side.

As a boy, Presley would take off after chores were done on Saturdays with a pack of tea cakes his mother made and stay in the hills until supper-time Sunday. At about age 12, he was given a shotgun and stationed as a lookout while his father's friends were making whiskey. He was supposed to fire the gun if the law came, so the distillers would have time to run for it.

Once, the law blew up a still operated by a friend of his. Presley walked up the road to see what the commotion was, and a couple of lawmen stopped him. Instead of arresting him, they sort of deputized him to help them bring out the confiscated whiskey.

Well, for every gallon Presley carried out of the hollow, he stashed one along the way, so the moonshine wasn't a total loss.

Another time, one of his cohorts, a fellow named Clyde, was sampling too much of the product, got too careless and was bitten by a rattlesnake. Presley did what he could, cutting near the wound and sucking the venom out. Clyde seriously needed a doctor, but he wouldn't go. "He throwed down that old rattlesnake and said, 'Give me a gallon of that liquor,'" Presley said.

Clyde decided to hole up in the basement of the cabin where they were making moonshine. "Every morning I went down to the basement to see about Clyde, and every morning I knew he was going to be dead,"

Presley said. "But he was alive, so I'd just take him another gallon of whiskey."

Clyde lost a good part of his leg muscle, but the homemade snakebite medicine worked.

For a good while, Presley made whiskey with an old man named Cal. When they got ready to move a load, they'd take it out of the hills and hide it in a storage space of the church Cal attended, until they could ship it out.

"That old man, we'd make liquor all Saturday night long until about 8 Sunday morning. Then he'd leave, go up to his house and take him a bath, put on clean overalls and a shirt and put his Bible under his arm and go to that same church every Sunday morning and Sunday night.

He'd come back and help make liquor in between time. Then on Monday, I went back and loaded it up, and out I cut with it," Presley said. In those times, Whitfield County was dry, and Presley and his friends were big contributors to the radio preachers, who'd rail against the evils of drink whenever the liquor issue came on the ballot.

Finally, though, the county went wet, and that was just about the end of the moonshine business.

A lot more than moonshining has changed in Presley's part of Whitfield County. Now there are big brick houses on the same land where once nobody had two nickels to rub together. And there's a Wal-Mart not 10 miles down the road.

Presley's not too keen on some of the new neighbors. They're too fast to slap up "Posted" signs on the woods where he used to roam, and they're way too fast to call out the law whenever his mules wander out onto the road.

Of course, Presley has changed some with the times, too. He keeps a cell phone tucked into a pocket of his overalls. But he hasn't lost his taste for unstamped liquor. "I wouldn't give a drink of copper-made whiskey for a whole pint of legal," he said.

Bill's notes: My favorite part of this story came after its publication. During our phone conversation, Julia Child actually invited me to attend the New Year's dinner she planned to serve in the South of France. "Oh, darling, you simply must come," she burbled. Sounded like a plan to me. I wrote up a trip proposal, arguing that being there when the Kentucky bootleg ham was carved would make a wonderful story. My boss disagreed — but he kept the proposal I'd written as a classic example of reportorial chutzpah.

LEGRAND, KY. — It is slightly purple, slightly illegal and wrapped in plain brown paper, and its last known hangout was a Hart County outbuilding. But it will soon be simmering gloriously in the South of France.

Bootleg Kentucky country ham has hit the big leagues of haute cuisine. The journey that started in J. T. Mitchum's smokehouse about 90 miles south of Louisville and will end on Julia Child's holiday dinner table is not really such a long one, in terms of a gourmet's appreciation of authentic victuals.

"They're really unique. They're not like anything else," Ms. Child said in a recent telephone interview from her Boston home. The renowned chef and cookbook author was referring to home-cured country hams and explaining why she wanted one for the entree of the New Year's Day dinner she plans to serve at her second home in France.

Palates educated in the nuances of pate should have no problem appreciating a farm-bred ham, she said. "There are an awful lot of people who just adore this sort of thing," Miss Child said.

Beyond the taste, there is an element of adventure in eating a home-cured ham. Mitchum's pink-fleshed beauties probably include about two or three violations of the Pure Food and Drug Act per pound — and Mitchum cures some heavy hams.

None of which lessens Miss Child's zest for the ham. She said she previously prepared a home-cured ham supplied by Bill Neusome, of Princeton, Ky., and was eager to try another. She added that she may cook the ham according to an old recipe supplied by Horse Cave resident Tom Chaney, who helped arrange for her to receive Mitchum's ham. "I cook anything I'm interested in," Miss Child said.

That sentiment can be well appreciated in rural Hart County. "There ain't nothing legal about it," Mitchum said of the way he makes hams. Federal processing standards are just not compatible with the old-fashioned way of curing hams, he said.

Rather than comply with regulations for commercial ham processors, he said, he prefers to cure just a few hams for himself and friends. Not many people besides Mitchum still do it the old way. "You can't find a real country ham in the country anymore," Mitchum said. "There's no way you can cure a country ham in the kind of building the government wants you to have."

If a man's smokehouse conformed to federal specifications regarding concrete floors, controlled ventilation, and sealed walls, you might be able to play a good half-court game of basketball inside, but you couldn't cure country hams, he said.

To Mitchum, the smokehouse flavor is achieved only when the smokehouse can allow the natural factors to enter the curing process. The cracks in the smokehouse walls provide for the right circulation, he said, and it takes the uncontrolled heat of a summer day to pull the grease out of a ham. And who needs concrete when the good earth soaks up the drippings better?

Another thing that sets Mitchum's kind of ham apart from most processed hams is the fact that Mitchum's hams lose weight during the cure; say about 12 pounds for a ham that started out at 40.

That alone would probably disqualify his curing as a commercial venture, because most processed hams will retain nearly all their original weight, he said. But the big difference is in time and technique. Mitchum starts with fresh hams in December, and they're not ready for eating until the next holiday season.

In that time, it takes a lot of tender loving care to transform a hog hindquarter into a country-ham feast. Mitchum starts by rubbing the ham with sugar as a curing agent and then covering the sugar-coated ham with salt, which helps pull water and packing-house chemicals out of meat.

That curing step lasts for about four weeks, during which the salt layer must be patched if it is broken by dripping grease, he said. Then he smokes the meat for about four days, using a fire made from hickory and sassafras wood.

The ham is then covered with a mixture of black pepper and borax, covered with a paper bag and left to hang in the smokehouse until holiday time. It is the borax mixture that promotes the purplish mold that coats Mitchum's hams, but that coating is an effective barrier to spoilage during the hot summer months.

The natural de-greasing of the hams also makes the meat more vulnerable to decay, he said, because the grease can cause the bag to stick to the ham and thus promote an attack from ham-spoiling organisms that Mitchum calls "skippers."

To prevent this, he said, the bags must be regularly replaced when they become grease soaked. "It's just like changing a baby's diapers," he said. All that takes a lot of time, especially when you have farmland to tend, Mitchum said. But "that's what you have to go through to have a good country ham," he said.

Though he used to crave the ham himself, his favorite pork item now is "fried middlin' (bacon section) and green onions," he said. He cures hams more as a hobby and as a means of preserving the farm skills of his ancestors.

Mitchum said he remembers the days when nearly every part of the hog, up to and including the skin from the sow's ears, was used to make food for a farm family. Now, as then, the premier part of the pig is the ham.

Mitchum's hams would have remained a Hart County secret, however, had it not been for some cocktail-party chatter earlier this year in Boston. Miss Child said she met Lexington resident Harold Cottrell, a Harvard alumnus, at a Harvard commencement-time party.

The topic turned to Kentucky cooking, and Cottrell said he knew how he might secure an authentic country ham. Cottrell called Chaney, Chaney told Mitchum, and when Cottrell returned to Boston recently, he had a ham in tow. He also carried the baked ham recipe recorded by Chaney's deceased mother, who had been a home economist.

Miss Child said she was intrigued by the recipe. For those who might want to try to duplicate the Julia Child New Year's Day entree, the recipe calls for covering the ham with a heavily spiced dough and simply baking it, fat side up, for about five hours at 375 degrees. The dough is made from four cups of flour, one cup of brown sugar, two tablespoons of crushed cloves, two tablespoons of cinnamon, two tablespoons of dried mustard, one tablespoon of black pepper and enough water to make a stiff dough.

Chaney said the recipe will work with any ham but creates a piece of folk art when used to prepare a genuine country ham.

Bill's notes: I always loved finding stories about sophisticated people in small towns. This article was an especially memorable example. Patrick Terrail had left a world of haute cuisine and Hollywood glamor to find satisfaction in running a small café in Hogansville, Georgia. Years later, Terrail did me the great kindness of obtaining a reservation for my wife Eileen and I at his family's famed restaurant in Paris, La Tour D'Argent. We were given a table with a view of Notre Dame plus a private tour of the wine cellar. Thanks again, Patrick.

ATLANTA JOURNAL CONSTITUTION
MARCH 26, 2000

HOGANSVILLE OR HOLLYWOOD, it's still Oscar night, and Patrick Terrail is still the host of the big party in town. Tonight, Terrail will open his restaurant in an abandoned gas station on Hogansville's Main Street, Gaby's Cafe and Bistro, for a black-tie dinner party for local Oscar watchers.

It will be a different crowd from those in the 1970s and 1980s, when Hollywood's A-list celebs and movie moguls gathered for a fittingly glamorous end to their Oscar night at Terrail's old place, Ma Maison.

There will be no Frank Sinatra. No Catherine Deneuve. No Elizabeth Taylor. No Cary Grant. No Jack Lemmon (Ma Maison regulars, all). In those years, the late super-agent Irving "Swifty" Lazar would book Ma Maison for the after-Oscar party, and invitations among *le tout* Hollywood were coveted nearly as much as the gold statuettes themselves.

Once inside, seating patterns were everything. "You couldn't table-hop," Terrail said.

Tonight, the ambience at Gaby's will be elegant but a bit more relaxed. Terrail will bring in a television so his guests can watch the show. The place will be full, just like Ma Maison used to be. But with just seven tables, there isn't much room for mingling, although it has a counter left over from a previous incarnation as a pizza joint.

One thing that won't be different is Terrail's approach to making a memorable evening for his guests. "Every guest is, to me, a star," he said. "It doesn't matter whether you're in Hogansville or Los Angeles. People want to be entertained when they go out."

Terrail, wearing his trademark carnation, will be devoting his personal attention to both the cuisine and the clientele.

He was raised in the highest traditions of the fine dining experience. Among other restaurant and hotel properties, his family operated La Tour d' Argent, one of the oldest and most honored restaurants in Paris.

He came to the United States for university training and ended up in Los Angeles, where he found a rather bleak cuisine scene.

"Back then," he said, "most people in LA. didn't know basil from parsley."

Terrail moved to fill the void by buying a decidedly undistinguished wooden building on Melrose Avenue in Hollywood. He transformed it into Ma Maison, opening in 1973.

To this day, Terrail isn't certain how or why the restaurant became the place to see and be seen. It was located near several major studios back when they were the center of the movie industry.

Friday lunches at Ma Maison soon became de rigueur. Getting reservations at Ma Maison wasn't easy. First, you had to have connections to even secure the phone number, which was unlisted. The parking lot often resembled a Rolls-Royce dealership.

Terrail knew his customers well enough to know who was inside by a quick scan of the license plates in the lot. Terrail's favorite memories of those days, plus some of his favorite Ma Maison recipes, are collected in his recently published memoir, "A Taste of Hollywood."

Sometimes wistful but never indiscreet, Terrail tells how his restaurant became Orson Welles' unofficial office, how he once "saved" Burt Reynolds' life and how Elizabeth Taylor nearly shut the place down just by coming in.

Some of Terrail's old friends give testimony to the Ma Maison mystique in the book: Sherry Lansing, studio executive: "Ma Maison was more than a restaurant It was a club. It made me feel special. I miss it"; David Melnick, producer: "Patrick, in addition to being an extraordinary restaurateur, was also one of the wisest diplomats in Los Angeles." Liz Smith, syndicated columnist: "I'll never forget Ma Maison's green carpet and the Rolls-Royces outside. Hollywood glamour personified."

But the foundation of the restaurant was service and cuisine. Terrail made stars of his chefs, most notably Wolfgang Puck.

But trends being what they are, Ma Maison's run was nearly over by the mid-1980s. "Andy Warhol said everyone gets his 15 minutes of fame," Terrail said. "I had 15 years."

About six years ago, Terrail was diagnosed with cancer of the lymph nodes and told he had only months to live. He sold Ma Maison and joined in an ill-starred hotel-restaurant venture. After his cancer went into remission, confounding the medical experts, Terrail took on a consulting assignment for a liquor distributor before the 1996 Olympics. That brought him to Atlanta, where he met the woman who would become his wife, Jackie.

Shortly before they were married, a friend and former customer at Ma Maison, John Jones, asked Terrail to visit Hogansville, where Jones had some development projects. Terrail was charmed. Hogansville reminded him of a backlot set at one of the old Hollywood studios.

But it's less than an hour to Hartsfield International Airport, which means he can be anywhere in the country in a few hours. And after his financial and medical struggles, he appreciates the lower cost of living.

Much has changed in Hollywood since the heyday of Ma Maison, Terrail said. Today's stars just don't have the presence of the stars of yesteryear with some exceptions, including Smyrna native Julia Roberts he said.

And Hollywood now is run more by bean counters than by movie makers, Terrail said. As times have changed, Ma Maison's atmosphere of clubby glamour is no longer what the beautiful people seem to want, Terrail said.

About two years ago, he opened Gaby's, named for his mother. Terrail offers a menu of modestly priced but carefully prepared fare, with a few signature items from the old days at Ma Maison, including the chicken salad and cheesecake.

He plans to open for dinner on Friday and Saturday nights. When customers see framed stories about Ma Maison on the walls, they often ask Terrail how he wound up in a little cafe on Main Street. His response: "Hogansville is in the middle of nowhere, but next to everything."

Terrail travels regularly and works as hard as he cares to. And while Gaby's is a long way from Ma Maison, especially on Oscar night, he said it doesn't matter. "I used to be married to my restaurant," he said. "Now I'm married, and I have my restaurant as a girlfriend."

Bill's notes: This was a classic stick-it-to-the-man story. I had fun watching Philip Gilpatrick strike a blow for anyone who's ever been bullied by a utility company. I guess that's why it ran on Page One.

FORT LAUDERDALE NEWS, APRIL 30, 1976

FORT LAUDERDALE, FL — Philip Gilpatrick gave Ma Bell 47,658 pennies for his thoughts. The pennies weren't bad, but Gilpatrick's thoughts were.

Gilpatrick, a Fort Lauderdale hair stylist for Saks Fifth Avenue, settled his disputed phone bill yesterday by dumping nearly a ton of adulterated copper onto the counter of the downtown Southern Bell offices.

"It's my way of showing my aggravation," Gilpatrick said, as he shoved the bags, boxes and rolls of pennies through an opening in the plastic counter partition toward a bewildered clerk.

At first the Southern Bell officials bristled. They wanted Gilpatrick to wait until they had counted the pennies before they issued a receipt. After surveying the mountain of pennies, however, they decided to take Gilpatrick's word and that of the six banks where he'd amassed the pennies and restore service to Gilpatrick's disconnected phone.

The first act of this "50,000-Penny Opera" began several months ago, when the phone company ordered Gilpatrick to pay an additional $140 deposit for his private phone, he said. His original deposit was slightly more than $125, he said.

The phone company justified the hike because of what they called "erratic payments," Gilpatrick said. Gilpatrick conceded that his phone bill is not always paid precisely on time but claimed that was only due to his business travels, which take him out of town about half of each month.

"I've had continuous service for 13 years here," Gilpatrick said, "and I've paid more than $48,000 in phone bills. I guess they did this because I paid them too much money."

Gilpatrick balked at paying the additional deposit, and the battle was joined. Next came a series of fruitless negotiations with the phone company, interspersed with a letter-writing campaign by Gilpatrick to various phone company bigwigs and public officials.

Meanwhile, two months-worth of unpaid phone bills were being tacked onto Gilpatrick's account. The combined bill for the service charges and extra deposit reached $476.58 before Gilpatrick agreed to pay up last week, he said.

He wrote out a check for the service charge portion, he said, but the-phone company demanded immediate payment of the deposit, too. Gilpatrick said he received a final notice from the phone company that threatened the cutoff two days before the due date on the bill.

Miffed at this latest turn, Gilpatrick stopped payment on the check he had written. His phone was promptly disconnected, he said. "It's really sad that this could happen to anybody," he said.

With no phone but plenty of hostility, Gilpatrick set out to retaliate. He said he got legal counsel and an opinion from the U.S. Treasury that the phone company would have to accept payment in pennies.

Then he made the rounds of six area banks and loaded up a car trunk with what Treasury officials estimated was about 2,000 pounds of pennies.

Then he unloaded his loot on Ma Bell. A.Y. McConnell, Southern Bell district manager, was called in to watch the parade of pennies.

Although McConnell said he could not comment specifically on Gilpatrick's account, a deposit increase in a case such as Gilpatrick's is "only good business judgment, when something like returned checks are involved," he said.

Gilpatrick's latest correspondence from Southern Bell's corporate offices states that his $140 deposit will be refunded after a "period of time" when Gilpatrick has shown that he will pay his phone bill regularly. Until that unspecified "period of time" passes, Gilpatrick said, he intends to show up on the 15th of each month at the phone company's office with a car trunk full of pennies.

Bill's notes: I never learned how this sad story ended. After it ran, I gave Debby Intili bus money to help her get out of Miami.

MIAMI NEWS, JANUARY 15, 1976

A 22-YEAR-OLD NEW JERSEY woman who says she was trapped into selling her baby for $1,200 has returned to Miami to find her son Joey and help prosecute the child broker.

Debby Intili says she signed the hastily typed agreement to sell the boy in a Miami motel last April. The child then 18 months old, was taken away by a male accomplice of the broker, who kept telling the child, "Mommy's coming. Mommy's coming."

Intili pocketed the cash and left for New Jersey. "I know people will say, 'How could she do a thing like that?'" Intili said. "But at the time I did it, I didn't know what was going on. I figured it was the best thing for my son. I was in a state of shock."

"For a while I couldn't even think about it without crying. If I could have waited another day, I never would have signed. I didn't even know there was such a thing as placing your child in foster care," she said.

Intili claims a 49-year-old Canadian woman served as broker in the deal. She said the woman is currently being held in the Broward County Jail without bond in connection with another alleged baby-selling scheme.

The woman, who has not been charged in the Intili case, has been under a Dade State Attorney's office investigation of black-market baby-selling rackets. Martin Dardis, the chief investigator for that office, said Intili is assisting them in their investigation, and the people who now have little Joey have violated the law by participating in a conspiracy.

Dardis said the child is believed to be living with a wealthy couple in Long Island, New York.

Joey was born in 1973, about three years after Debby married Joe Intili, a plumber from Rahway, New Jersey. She was 17 at the time of the marriage.

When the child was about a year old, Debby Intili left her husband, took Joey, and came to the home of her mother and stepfather in Hollywood, Florida.

She got a job as a waitress, but she and her mother argued about the best way to care for Joey, she said.

Later, she was introduced to the woman who became the baby broker. The woman invited her to come to live in the woman's Fort Lauderdale townhouse, she said. There was a brief mention of adoption during that first meeting, she said.

The baby broker identified herself to Intili as a social worker with a private practice and as a guidance counselor for youths with drug abuse problems.

In April, Intili told the baby broker that she would sign the adoption papers. A little later, the baby broker and a man she introduced as a Miami attorney picked up Intili and the baby at the house of Intili's mother.

Intili said the documents she signed stated she had given up all rights to Joey and had received no money for the adoption. However, she had, in fact, received $1,200, she said.

Less than a month later, back in New Jersey, Intili received a call from the baby broker, who said the adoptive parents were complaining, because Joey was being "very nervous." The women said a man would visit Intili with more papers.

A day later the man and Intili met in Elizabeth, NJ. Mrs. Intili said the documents he carried had the official seal of Nassau County, N.Y. She signed them.

In early May, Intili went to Mineola, L.I., but found no adoption records bearing her son's name. So, she came back to Florida and told her story to authorities.

The question of custody of Joey Intili will be decided by the courts.

Bill's notes: All sorts of media rush to disaster zones, but most leave soon after the storm passes. In 1998, a series of monster tornados ravaged once-beautiful suburban neighborhoods. The trees that had earned Atlanta the name "city in a forest" were toppled like so much kindling. I convinced my editors to allow me to show how the people on one small street accepted the loss and fought to recover. It became a series called "The Cul-de-sac Chronicles". The parents of one of the resident families, Joe and Gretchen Conboy, were personal friends of mine. A huge pine tree had crushed their bed; but, thank God, the whole family was on vacation when the tornado hit. I convinced them to trust me to tell their story. On the day I described in this article, it was almost as hard for me to watch as it was for them. In an hour or two, one front-end loader reduced their "forever" home to landfill.

THE ATLANTA JOURNAL-CONSTITUTION, JULY 4, 1998

T HEIR HOME WAS chewed into matchsticks and bricks, but he saved the red dress he gave her on the night he proposed.

Nearly three months after the tornado exiled Joe and Gretchen Conboy and their five daughters from their Dunwoody home, Demolition Day arrived this week. The iron-toothed bucket of the front-end loader stopped at a bedroom closet that had been blocked off since the storm.

The Conboys scavenged the debris for the last of their treasures they could reclaim: the dress, her sewing machine, his father's camera, and the set of Hot Wheels cars he's kept since he was a boy.

A few hours later, the family home was ready to be hauled to a dump. "Everything we were emotionally attached to, we got out," Gretchen Conboy said, managing a tearful smile. "Today, we're going to stop looking at the old house, and look forward to the new one."

A STRESSFUL PROCESS

As difficult as it was for the Conboys, the demolition of their home was, in a way, a hopeful sign for their storm-devastated neighborhood. "In a sick sort of a way, I guess this is progress," said John Seckman, the Conboys' next-door neighbor.

Four of the eleven families that lived on their cul-de-sac, Windon Court, were displaced by the storm. Only one has been able to return.

Just before the recent demolition of their home on Windon Court in DeKalb County, Gretchen Conboy and her husband, Joe, were able to go inside and rescue a few prized possessions. Just as no one on Windon Court was ready for the tornado, no one was ready for the aftermath of months of often-stressful dealings with insurance companies and government agencies. "It's been an emotional roller coaster," Gretchen Conboy said, "and for the first two months, there were more downs than ups."

When a house is a total loss, as theirs was, arriving at a settlement with the insurance process is literally a brick-by-brick process. Every detail must be examined; for example, adjusters cut a door of the Conboys' house in half, to establish whether it had been made of regular pine or fir pine, Gretchen Conboy said.

The settlement bid document was 54 pages long, she said. "It's an incredible process, an organizer's dream," she said. "But if you don't get consumed in the process, it won't come out the way you want it to."

AN IMPERFECT SETTLEMENT

Joe Conboy said his focus was to "keep everybody calm" during the negotiations. He also wanted to make sure the insurance adjuster knew he was dealing with people, and not just another case.

Even so, it was an ordeal. In the end, Joe Conboy said, there were a few points he might have disputed, but he decided to accept the settlement and start the rebuilding. "We got to the point where we decided, this is enough, this is fair," Joe Conboy said.

On Thursday morning, the last permit was obtained, the last settlement letter was signed, and Conboy called his contractor, transmitting the "go" order for the demolition crew. When he walked out of his office, though, he got hit with a wave of nausea, when he realized he was heading out to watch his home get torn down.

The capricious destruction of the tornado has left the three families who live at the end of the Windon Court cul-de-sac the Conboys, the Seckmans and the Wagners, all at different stages of recovery.

Those three families relocated to the same apartment complex, so their children have been able to maintain their friendships.

PRAISE FOR DEKALB OFFICIALS

John Seckman said he may be nearing a settlement, and he hopes his home will be demolished within the next few weeks. While he understands that the insurance companies must handle the negotiations as a business process, from his point of view the overriding fact is that "we've been thrown out of our homes."

Insurance adjusters at first wanted to try to repair his badly damaged home. "It was like I'd had a car wreck, and they wanted to try to straighten out the frame," he said.

He gave DeKalb County officials high marks for the way they have helped ease the impasses in negotiations between insurance companies and some tornado-displaced homeowners.

For Rob and Karen Wagner, their recovery is stuck in one of those impasses, and the issue of whether the home can be repaired is still unresolved. "The nitpicking is making our lives miserable," Karen Wagner said. They are still far apart on issues like whether their cracked and crumbling chimney can legitimately be claimed as tornado-related damage, or whether the cracks in their foundation can be repaired by filling them with epoxy, she said.

Their insurance company's structural engineer differs dramatically with an engineer they have hired, so last week they had the house inspected by a third engineer recommended by the county. They hope to resolve the disputes within a few weeks, but; for now, she's highly distressed.

"I don't want to waste my life or waste my money; I just want my house fixed," she said.

AN INSTANT MEADOW

Rob Lowenthal, regional public affairs officer for State Farm Insurance, the firm that holds policies on several of the Windon Court families, said he could not comment on the specifics of any of the cases.

However, he added, he realizes that the homeowners are frustrated and have endured major disruptions of their lives.

"State Farm delivers a promise to its people to be there at claims time," he said. "Our claims people are professionals whose job it is to help people get through this."

There is no insurance policy, however, that will cover the loss of friends and community that the people on Windon Court have suffered.

For the three months since the tornado, the short street has served as a transfer point for debris removal. As fast as a pile of dead trees was removed from the street, more was dragged in. The stumps and branches and logs are gone now. But the street that used to be a playground for neighborhood kids is now dirt-covered and mostly quiet.

John and Lisa Seckman had 50 tons of fallen timber removed from their back yard alone. But without the big shade trees, the seeds dropped by birds at their feeder have sprouted into a field of huge sunflowers. "It's God's sense of humor," Lisa Seckman said.

Bill's notes: I love to explode stereotypes. To find a strip joint in the middle of nowhere was one thing, but to find it managed by a little old lady instead of a hairy-chested, cigar-sucking guy made this story a natural for me. It also showed that vice doesn't stop where the city lights fade. Not long after the story was published, the sheriff shut down the Ripcord.

ATLANTA JOURNAL CONSTITUTION, JUNE 18, 1995

ARCADE — IT may be a sign of how thoroughly big-city diversions of the 1990s have filtered down to the small towns, or some might say it is yet another sign that the apocalypse is hard upon us, but there are ladies with no clothes on dancing at the Ripcord Lounge in Arcade.

The Jackson County town is struggling to hold on to its charter as a city and it's about 10 miles from the nearest freeway, but business is great at the Ripcord.

"It's a good, decent club," said Wanda Atkins, the 60-something manager of the Ripcord, who didn't have to add that the operative definition of "decent" has been stretched some in recent years.

Used to be, square dances were the thing out in the country; now, it's table dances.

"Back when I went to clubs," Atkins said, "they were called burlesque and they didn't go this far."

On the outside, the place could be mistaken for a roadside nursery. Atkins has profusely decorated one exterior wall and a walkway with silk flowers, and the parking lot is landscaped with real flower beds and statues of cherubs.

But just inside, there's a picture of two farmer's-daughter-type young women, depicted, fittingly, in a bubble bath.

Atkins said there's not much aside from the location that distinguishes her club from the mega-clubs in the big city. The customers mostly come from nearby cities of Athens, Winder or Gainesville, with a few coming down from South Carolina. The place does no advertising to speak of, she said, but it stays full on weekend nights.

The dancers are similar in background to their counterparts in the big city, she said. They're mothers, divorcees and a few refugees from the Atlanta scene.

When the Ripcord opened about three years ago, there were protests, but the operators of the club prevailed.

"It's there; what can you do about it?" said Mayor Joe Sikes, a lifelong Arcadian.

Considering the trend of court rulings favoring freedom of expression, naked and all, Sikes said it would be a waste of scarce city funds to pursue a legal battle.

Arcade has a history of success in catering to the vices of outsiders, having gained some notoriety as the "Beer Capital of Georgia" after it incorporated in the 1960s and passed ordinances that promoted beer sales at lower prices than in surrounding cities.

But Sikes said, the spread of supermarkets has pretty much wiped out Arcade's price advantage. In one sense, Sikes said, Arcade's having a strip joint instead of a general store is just one of several signs that it's getting harder to leave the city behind.

Arcade's population has tripled during the past decade, to about 1,100 people. And many of them get upset by such citified issues as the city imposing mandatory trash pickup by a city contractor.

"People come out here thinking this is a small town, and they want it to stay small," Sikes said. "But with some of those city things, it's going to be like that wherever they move."

BILL OSINSKI

BRUSHES WITH THE LAW

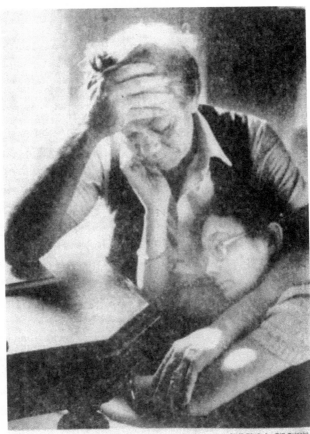

Staff Photo by Bill Osinski

James "Buddy" Graham was consoled at his Elizabethtown home yesterday by friend Carolyn Jo Goodman while he mourned the shooting death in Illinois of his son, Clyde Daniel Graham.

PICTURE OF BUDDY GRAHAM AFTER LEARNING HIS SON CLYDE HAD BEEN KILLED BY POLICE. Photo by Bill Osinski.

Bill's notes: I lived in Elizabethtown, Kentucky, when I got a call from the news desk that a state trooper had been shot and killed. I went to the State Police post and received the basics of the story. When the briefing officer said there had been an eyewitness to the crime, I quickly asked if I could interview him. I was surprised when my request was granted; after all, the killer was still at large, and the witness might be in danger. Not only that, I was given a police driver to take me to the crime scene for the interview. On the way back, the officer stopped at a home where dozens of squad cars had massed for arrests where I saw suspects being threatened with shotguns. Later, I would be summoned to testify in court about what I saw. It was uncomfortable for me, but I only repeated what I had seen that night. My testimony helped get the Kentucky State Police Commissioner fired. I also became highly suspicious that I had been used that night to advance the police cover-up of their misconduct. (Some of the background information in this story was contributed by my former colleague, Al Cross.)

LOUISVILLE COURIER JOURNAL,
NOVEMBER 8, 1979

ELIZABETHTOWN, KY — Kentucky State Police Trooper Eddie Harris, 28, of Elizabethtown was found shot to death about 8 last night on U.S. 31 E about three miles east of Hodgenville in LaRue County.

Two suspects were taken into custody early this morning. Their names were not released.

Commander John D. Robey of the Elizabethtown post said Harris apparently had just stopped a speeding car when he was shot. Harris' gun was not drawn, Robey said.

Dispatcher Steve Case at state police headquarters in Frankfort said that the slain trooper asked for backup units after identifying a vehicle as one that may have been involved in an armed robbery in Elizabethtown earlier in the day.

The owner of a mobile home near the scene of the shooting said he witnessed the incident. Phinis Hundley said he was watching television when he saw the flashing blue lights of a police car.

Because the road is relatively straight stretch, Hundley said, "They're always stopping somebody along here."

Hundley said he got up, looked out the window and saw a state trooper standing beside a brownish car that he had stopped. The trooper was holding a flashlight and was apparently searching the inside of the car, he said.

"Then I heard this big pop," Hundley said, and the trooper fell to the road. The driver of the car then pushed open his door and got out, he said. "He just kind of kneeled down and shot him again," Hundley said.

The car then sped off, and Hundley said he went out and saw the trooper lying on the road. "He was bleeding really bad around the head. I knew there wasn't anything I could do for him."

Hundley then used Harris' radio to inform police dispatchers of the shooting. Hundley spent the next several hours talking to police investigators and was still disturbed over the incident around midnight.

"I won't sleep much tonight" he said.

Robey said Harris apparently was shot with more than one weapon, and it is believed that at least two people were involved. Robey said the backup units sent to the scene found an abandoned car believed to have been involved in the shooting about two miles away.

A wallet found in the car was among the factors that led police to stake out a home about a mile south of Elizabethtown on KY 61. The two men were arrested there about 12:30 a.m. as they tried to re-enter the home.

The approximately 25 police officers at the scene of the arrest were visibly angry. Three women occupants of the home were made to lie on the ground in the front yard while the two men were dragged into police custody.

As the officers shoved the suspects into patrol cars, they shouted at them and shoved them slightly. One of the men was jabbed with the butt of a shotgun, but they were not beaten and did not appear to be hurt.

A third suspect was still at large last night. As many as 100 police officers were involved in the search for suspects last night. Canine and helicopter units were being used and officers from the Jefferson County, Elizabethtown and Hardin County departments were called to assist state police.

Harris had been a state trooper for seven years. He was married and the father of three children. A colleague of Harris' said that the slain trooper may well have known who was in the car when he stopped it.

BILL OSINSKI

Harris was described as a hard-working police officer who often discussed the dangers of his job and sometimes seemed concerned about the prospects of being killed in the line of duty. "It seemed like he had a sixth sense about it" the trooper said of Harris.

The spot where Harris was killed was only about two or three miles from the rural LaRue County home where he grew up. His death marks the second fatal shooting of a state trooper in the area in the past three years.

In 1976 Trooper William Pickard was shot and killed in LaRue County while trying to serve a warrant.

There had been other reports that the vehicle stopped by Harris may have been involved in an armed robbery yesterday at a drug store in Caneyville, about 60 miles west in Grayson County. However, officers said they had no information connecting the incidents.

Wales Montgomery, 42, of Leitchfield, was accidentally shot after the robbery attempt at Caneyville Drugs late yesterday afternoon. According to a spokesman at the Leitchfield Police Department, Montgomery and Gay Hazle, owner of the store, were outside the rear of the store shortly after 5 p.m. when two men drove up asking to have a prescription filled.

Hazle had just closed the store, but he let the men inside, according to reports received by police. When one of the men pulled a gun, Montgomery emerged from a back room with a gun. Police reports said a scuffle ensued, and Hazle ran across the street to get Sol Allen, a Grayson County constable.

When Hazle and Allen returned to the store, the men had fled apparently without taking anything and Montgomery was on the floor, according to the police spokesman. Montgomery, apparently mistaken for one of the would-be robbers, was then shot in the upper left leg, the spokesman said.

Bill's notes: On the day Clyde Graham, the suspect in the killing of the State Trooper, was shot to death in an Illinois motel room by a Kentucky State Police officer, I was assigned to go to the Graham family home. I had previously done a similar story at the home of the trooper whom Graham was accused of killing a month earlier. I was struck by the similarity of the two households. Grief makes no judgments; it hits families equally hard, whether the victims wore a badge or fought the law. While I talked with the Graham family, there was a moment when Clyde Graham's father Buddy was embraced by his girlfriend. I had no time to ask permission, but I captured the moment with my Nikon F2. It was a moving photograph, if a bit out of focus. The newspaper's publisher, Barry Bingham Jr., had the picture enlarged, and it hung on a wall outside his office for years. I stayed on the story for more than two years, until I was able to report that Clyde Graham had been shot in the back.

ELIZABETHTOWN, KY. THE hand that fired the shot that killed Kentucky State Police Trooper Eddie Harris on Nov. 7 simultaneously signed Clyde Graham's death warrant, Graham's family believes.

"The police said they'd kill Clyde if they had to put a gun in his hand," James "Buddy" Graham, the father of the fugitive suspect, said yesterday.

The elder Graham spent the day with relatives and friends, consoling each other over their loss, a scene similar to those in the households of Eddie Harris' family the day after the trooper was killed.

In both settings, grief seemed stronger than the bitterness over the violent deaths.

Graham said he wished that the $30,000 that had been offered for his son might go to Harris widow. "I never learned to hate and I don't want to now," Graham said. "I don't want blood for blood."

A televised news bulletin stilled the conversation in the Graham household. When the bloody details of Clyde Graham's death from police bullets at an Illinois motel were broadcast, the family's resentment over the way police have treated them spilled out in a torrent of tearful recriminations.

"There ain't no telling what they did to him before he died," cried Carolyn Jo Goodman, a friend of Buddy Graham's.

When the television announcer used the name of the trooper believed to have shot Clyde Graham, Ms. Goodman said she remembered that officer saying that Clyde wouldn't come home alive.

"He said he'd do it," Ms. Goodman said of the police officer, who she said questioned her during the investigation. "He made that promise."

At least a half-dozen others gathered in the Graham home nodded in agreement when Ms. Goodman said she never felt that Clyde would live to see a courtroom.

During a press conference later yesterday at the Elizabethtown state police post, post commander Capt. John Robey declined to discuss the assertion that police revenge entered into Clyde Graham's death, except to deny it.

"There's nothing we could say to anyone who would believe that," Robey said.

Graham had been the prime suspect in the Harris shooting investigation ever since the night of the slaying, when police found an abandoned car containing Graham's wallet about a mile from the scene.

Ms. Goodman and members of the Graham family all said Clyde was not the type of person to be involved in the brutal murder with which he was charged. "He was quiet, easygoing. He never went out drinking, he never caused nobody no problems," she said.

He had had minor scrapes with the law, including a burglary conviction for which he received a suspended sentence, but Ms. Goodman also recalled that he'd been stopped for speeding last September in Bullitt County and nothing other than a traffic ticket resulted. (Harris was killed after he stopped a speeding driver.)

Clyde worked irregularly as a home-repair contractor, and his only ambition was to be a farmer, she said.

"They'll never convince any of us that he did it," she said, referring to the charge against Clyde.

Clyde's brother, James David Graham, said Clyde didn't have the stomach to shoot his own dog, after the animal had been run over by a car and seriously injured. "I was the one who had to shoot the dog," James said.

The only person in the Graham household who had held out hope that Clyde would return was his father. "I expected to hear from him anytime," Buddy Graham said.

The only people he did hear from, though, were callers who thought they had a line on his son's whereabouts. Graham said he followed those tips into Pennsylvania, Indiana and Missouri, in a fruitless search for the fugitive.

"I went all over hell looking for him," Graham said. "I wanted to help the boy; that's all I was interested in."

The father said he was also searching to settle his own mind about his son's guilt. "Once I looked him in the eye, I'da known," Graham said.

Even without hearing Clyde's story, Graham said his son would have stood a chance in court. "I wanted him to come to trial," Graham said.

Though Clyde Graham won't get a day in court. Buddy Graham, James Graham and Charles McLain, a family friend, will.

They were arrested the night of Harris' death, in a tense scene at the Graham home, when dozens of police officers were straining to keep themselves under control. The two Grahams and McLain, charged with resisting arrest and disorderly conduct, were later released on their own recognizance.

James Graham, who was hospitalized two days and said he suffered internal injuries during the arrest, is still upset about the way his family was treated that night.

"They dragged me into the bedroom by my hair," he said. "Then they put a shotgun to a 4-year-old's head to try to get me to tell where Clyde was.

Buddy Graham counseled his son to try to put away his hostility. "None of that will bring Clyde back," he said.

Of his own feelings, the elder Graham was uncertain yesterday. "I'm just trying to get myself collected," he said.

The time since Clyde became a fugitive has been difficult, he said, but almost all his friends in the community have been supportive. Yesterday afternoon he was still trying unsuccessfully to call the Effingham, Ill., funeral home where his son's body was taken.

He was also undecided about what would happen to the two pigs in his back yard; the animals were to be used to help start Clyde's farm.

But the most difficult thing to deal with, he said, was the knowledge that his son's death will only perpetuate the questions about what happened when Harris stopped a speeder on a lonely LaRue County road a month ago.

"Nobody will ever know now," Buddy Graham said.

Bill's notes: After the publication of this and other articles I wrote contesting the official police version of the two killings, police supporters staged a protest parade in downtown Elizabethtown. There were two flatbed trucks in the parade, one with a coffin with my name on it, and the other with a coffin with the name of Barry Bingham, Jr., then the publisher of the Louisville Courier Journal. My bosses offered to put me and my family in a hotel, but I didn't want that. On my way to cover an event at the State Police barracks, State Police Sgt. Eugene Coffey, Clyde Graham's executioner, was standing near the sidewalk leading into the building. As I passed him, Coffey silently spun the open cylinder of his .375 handgun.

ELIZABETHTOWN, KY. KENTUCKY State Police Commissioner Kenneth Brandenburgh has declared the Eddie Harris-Clyde Graham case closed. But according to some key state witnesses, his recently released report on the killings is incorrect or incomplete in several areas.

An independent review of the details of the case has developed two major areas of conflict with statements in the Brandenburgh report on the events surrounding the Nov. 7 shooting of Trooper Harris and the subsequent shooting of Graham, the prime suspect in Harris slaying:

* State police Sgt. Eugene Coffey, the officer who killed Graham at an Effingham, Ill., motel, testified at a coroner's inquest that he had been told that Graham had an automatic rifle, a pistol and ammunition in his motel room. Brandenburgh's report names four people who gave Coffey that information.

When interviewed by The Courier-Journal, however, two of those people said they told Coffey the exact opposite, that Graham had no guns. The third person named in the report denied ever speaking to Coffey or having any information pertinent to the case. The fourth person couldn't be located by The Courier-Journal.

* The Brandenburgh report says Graham told four people that he had killed Harris and it names two of those people. According

to the report, the two said they heard Graham's admission of guilt during a conversation in their New Haven home on the night of the Harris shooting.

One of those people told The Courier-Journal that he was drunk at the time and wouldn't have been able to identify the fugitive in his home that night as Graham or to testify about the conversation. The other said that since making his original statement to police, he has become convinced that the fugitive he talked with wasn't Clyde Graham.

On another aspect of the case, the placing of Clyde Graham at the scene of the Harris shooting, the Courier-Journal's review has developed information that wasn't included in the report. The only witness who has identified Graham as the driver of the car that Harris stopped before he was shot was a woman in a car that passed by just before the shooting.

The Courier-Journal interviewed all four women who were in the car; one woman confirmed she could identify Graham and the other three said they couldn't. There is also an area of possible conflict between the women's recollection of the timing of events and that of the only other witness at the scene.

When asked about the variances from his report, Brandenburgh said there is documentation to back up the facts as stated in his report. "If somebody wants to change their story at this point, there's nothing we can do about it," Brandenburgh said.

He said he didn't wish to comment on the specifics of the accounts in this story, because his report is currently being reviewed by Kentucky Attorney General Steven L. Beshear. A spokesman for Beshear's office said last week that a report on Beshear's review should be given to Gov. John Y. Brown Jr. in about a month.

Attempts were made to reach Coffey for comment, but a state police spokesman said he was on vacation.

THE GRAHAM SHOOTING

Moments after Graham was shot, Coffey knelt over the body and said he thought Graham had been reaching for a gun, according to an Illinois police officer quoted in Brandenburg's report.

No guns were found in Graham's room, but police did find a knife in his back pocket. The report said four people told Coffey that Graham had guns in his room. The sources of that information listed in the report are Ronald Gene and Gerald Durall, two Elizabethtown men who accompanied Coffey to Effingham, and Debra Douglas and Jackie Redmon, described in the report as friends of Graham's.

However, both Duralls told The Courier-Journal that they told Coffey the exact opposite — that as far as they knew, Graham had no guns. The Duralls have been indicted for hindering the apprehension of Graham.

Special Agent John Moomaw, the Illinois police officer in command the night Graham was shot, is also named in the report as saying he had been told that Graham was armed. In a recent telephone interview with The Courier-Journal, Moomaw said he was given that information by one of the men from Kentucky but not by Coffey or his partner, Lt. Ellis Ross.

Both Duralls denied giving such information to Moomaw, and the Duralls were the only others who had gone to Illinois with the Kentucky policemen.

The third listed source of the weapons information was Debra Douglas. In an interview with The Courier-Journal she denied talking with any Kentucky police officer between the times Harris was shot and Graham was shot. "I couldn't believe it," Ms. Douglas said when she learned she had been named in the report. "I've never said nothing. Nobody ever asked me nothing."

The only connection she said she has with the case is that she is a friend of a woman who works in the same Indianapolis business as two women in the Graham household. Ms. Douglas said she and her friend and the two women associated with the Grahams were arrested on drug charges in Indianapolis the day after Harris was shot.

Brandenburgh's report makes note of the arrests, but it doesn't mention that the charges against all the women were dropped the next day.

The fourth source of the weapons information is listed in the report as a Jackie Redmon. No one by that name could be located by The Courier-Journal, but a Hodgenville-area man named Louis Redmon, who said he had talked to Coffey about the Graham case, was found.

In an interview with The Courier-Journal that man gave three different answers to the question of whether he had supplied such information. First, he said he might have; then he said he didn't think he did, and then he denied it outright.

In a supplement to Brandenburgh's report — a document that was a response to earlier charges of police' misconduct reported in an article in The Courier-Journal — Coffey told a state police officer investigating the charges that he, Coffey, had interviewed only three people during the Graham case. The three were the Duralls and another man not connected with the weapons information.

Brandenburgh's report also says that the Duralls told police that Graham told them he would never be taken alive. However, Gerald Durall also said that before Graham was shot Durall told Coffey that he would be able to go to Graham's room, explain that the area was surrounded by police and persuade Graham to surrender.

Coffey dismissed that approach, saying, "It's my job to apprehend him," Durall said.

After Graham was shot, both Duralls were brought from the police station to the motel to identify the body, even though identification of the suspect was the reason given in Brandenburgh's report for Coffey's going to Graham's door.

THE CASE AGAINST GRAHAM

Within half an hour of the Harris shooting, police found an abandoned car that witnesses identified as the one Harris had stopped. Graham's wallet and fingerprints were found in the car. In Brandenburgh's report the account of Graham's movements after the shooting is based mostly on a statement given police by James Othell Potts, a New Haven man who is under indictment for hindering the apprehension of Graham.

Potts' statement begins by identifying the man who came to his door about midnight on Nov. 7 as Clyde Graham. Potts also said the man told him he had just shot someone. Those details from the statement were used in Brandenburgh's report.

During a recent interview with The Courier-Journal, however, Potts recanted those parts of his statement saying he was under extreme duress when the statement was taken. "I would've said anything they wanted me to say," Potts said, referring to the police. "They just put it down the way they wanted it, and I signed it."

Potts went to the Elizabethtown State Police barracks to give the statement, after police had received several tips that he might have aided a fugitive. Potts said he had been drinking heavily before he went to the police post and had taken eight nerve pills.

When he got to the post, he said, police gave him a pint of whiskey, which he drank as he gave his statement. During a preliminary hearing on Potts' case, several police officers testified that Potts was given whiskey at the station.

Potts now says he doesn't believe the man who came to his door that night was Clyde Graham. Someone did come, Potts said, and Potts' son, James Jr., let the man in. Potts said the man was dressed in an Army fatigue shirt and light pants, and he noted that the original description put out by police said Graham was wearing a light shirt and dark pants at the time of the shooting.

The man did say he had just shot someone, Potts said. The fugitive was unarmed and said, "If I had a gun, I'd shoot myself," according to Potts. Potts said he gave the man some food and a change of clothes. He also said he cut his visitor's hair that night. In Brandenburgh's report the only mention of Clyde Graham's hair having been cut was at the Illinois motel two weeks after the shooting.

At the time, Potts said, he thought the man might have been Graham. He said he didn't personally know Clyde Graham and the fugitive was a young man with long hair, which matched the police description of Graham.

However, Potts said, the man who came to his home had a missing front tooth. After the body of Clyde Graham had been taken back to the Graham home. Potts said he received permission from the family to inspect it. The corpse had a full set of natural teeth, he said.

Based on his statement to police, though, Potts was arrested shortly after he gave his statement and was charged with hindering the apprehension of Clyde Graham. Potts had to put up the title to his home to make a $20,000 bond in the case, and the matter hasn't come to trial. He was indicted by the Nelson County grand jury last March, but the trial isn't scheduled until November.

Brandenburgh's report says that James Potts Jr. asked the fugitive if he had shot the trooper, and the man answered affirmatively. When the younger Potts was interviewed by The Courier-Journal, however, he said he was drunk when the man came, and he couldn't make a specific identification.

He said he gave his statement identifying Graham because he felt intimidated by police investigators, who he said threatened to bring other charges against him unless he cooperated. "I would have said anything I could to get them to leave us alone," James Potts Jr. said.

The other two people who heard the alleged admissions from Graham aren't named in the report.

THE HARRIS SHOOTING

The official account of the events of Nov. 7 begins shortly after 7:30 p.m., when Harris pulled out of a side road about four miles north of Hodgenville to stop a car that was traveling north on U.S. 31E.

There was another car traveling just behind the car Harris was after. The second car contained four women on their way to New Haven. All four women gave depositions to police on what they observed in the next few minutes.

Recently, they also gave their accounts to The Courier-Journal. Their names weren't released in the police report, and they asked that their names be withheld from this article. The women's car stopped as the police car pulled over the first car, then the women's car slowly passed by.

All the women said the policeman was still inside his car when they passed. Two of them said they thought the driver of the first car was getting out of his car, but the other two said they thought the driver stayed inside.

One of the four women said she was able to identify the driver of the first car as Clyde Graham after she had seen Graham's picture on television and in newspapers. The other three women, however, said they weren't able to make a specific identification of the man in the first car.

Two of the women who said they couldn't make an identification said they recalled that the woman who identified Graham was sitting in the seat behind the driver which would have given her the worst view. But the woman who identified Graham said she thought she was sitting in the rear seat on the passenger side.

There is agreement among the women on the sequence of what they saw after passing the two cars. They all said the same car that was stopped by Harris caught up with them at or near the top of a steep hill on the same road.

The top of that hill is 1.1 miles from the scene of the shooting, and this is what suggests a conflict between the accounts of the women and that of the other witness, a man who lived in a nearby trailer named Phinis Hundley.

As excerpted in Brandenburgh's report, Hundley said he watched the policeman get out of the car and walk up to the first car. The trooper stood by the driver's door for "a couple of minutes," according to Hundley's account in the report. He said he then heard a shot and saw the trooper fall. The driver of the car got out and shot the trooper again, Hundley's account said.

The women all said the first car caught up with them when they had barely traveled a mile. The driver of the women's car said she drove slightly below the 55-mph speed limit after she passed the two cars.

"They couldn't have done any talking," one of the women said, referring to Harris and the occupant of the first car.

Hundley, who also was interviewed by The Courier-Journal, said the driver drove off "like a bat out of hell" after the shooting, meaning he could have caught up with the women and still have had the conversation.

Bill's notes: Buddy Graham tricked everyone into thinking he had had his son's remains cremated. But after Attorney General Steve Beshear (who later became Governor) began his investigation, Buddy Graham cooperated with the exhumation. Kentucky State Police Commissioner Ken Brandenburgh was fired for his efforts to cover up the police misconduct in the case. Eugene Coffey died of a heart attack before Beshear's investigation. I was summoned to testify at Buddy Graham's federal trial on charges he aided his son's escape. His defense was that he was only trying to avoid what eventually happened – Clyde's death at the hands of Kentucky police. The jury acquitted Buddy Graham after deliberating only 20 minutes. After the court was adjourned, Graham's lawyer extended his hand to me, and I shook hands with him. My boss scolded me sternly.

LOUISVILLE COURIER JOURNAL, SEPTEMBER 3, 1981

FRANKFORT — FUGITIVE murder suspect Clyde Daniel Graham was shot once in the back, and that fact was "deliberately concealed or not discovered as a result of gross incompetence" by some Illinois officials and at least one Kentucky State Police trooper, Kentucky Attorney General Steven Beshear has concluded.

Beshear also said that "nothing approaching a struggle" occurred between Graham and the Kentucky State Police sergeant who shot him. Both findings were included in a final report released yesterday on Beshear's 16-month investigation into the killings of Graham and Kentucky State Police Trooper Eddie Harris in 1979.

And both findings directly conflict with reports issued by the Kentucky State Police including one written in March 1980 by former Commissioner Kenneth E. Brandenburgh and an Illinois coroner's inquest.

The earlier reports claimed that Graham struggled briefly with the officer and was shot twice in the front of his body. Beshear's report says that Graham was shot once in the chest and once in the back.

Moreover, the Beshear report claims that a state police raid on the Graham home near Elizabethtown on the night Harris was shot "rapidly became uncontrolled." And he said the police used "excessive force" during that raid while arresting James D. "Jimmy" Graham, Clyde Graham's brother.

Brandenburgh's report had exonerated his men on that night as well as on the night Graham was killed. Beshear's report terms Brandenburgh's study "cursory and incomplete."

Gov. John Y. Brown Jr. asked Brandenburgh to resign last Oct. 10 because of his handling of the Graham case.

Graham was the prime suspect in the slaying of Trooper Harris on Nov. 7, 1979, on a rural road in LaRue County. And Beshear's report, released at a news conference in the courtroom of the state Supreme Court, does restate one of the primary findings of previous investigations — that Graham murdered Harris.

After an intensive manhunt, Graham was shot and killed on Dec. 7, 1979, by Kentucky State Police Sgt. Eugene Coffey at the Villa Inn motel in Effingham, Ill.

Coffey testified at a coroner's inquest the following month that he and Graham wrestled briefly, that Graham reached for a pocket later found to contain a knife, and that he shot Graham twice in the front of his body.

Coffey's version of where Graham was shot was corroborated by the coroner and a pathologist in Effingham. The coroner's jury ruled after a hearing that took less than an hour that Graham's death was justifiable.

Coffey died of a heart attack last October before he could be confronted with evidence that there was no struggle and that he had shot Graham in the back, Beshear said yesterday.

Beshear's investigation was requested by Brown after news reports, primarily by The Courier-Journal, continued to question the findings of Kentucky and Illinois officials.

Besides finding evidence of misconduct by Kentucky State Police, the Beshear report also raises questions about the actions of the Illinois State Police, Effingham medical officials and the FBI.

The lone action recommended in the report is for the establishment of an independent unit, either inside or outside the state police, to investigate complaints against the agency.

State Police Commissioner Marion Campbell declined to comment on the recommendation other than to say he had already created an internal investigations unit.

Beshear said he doesn't believe that criminal charges will be filed or that grand jury investigations will be conducted in the case in Kentucky.

But he said Illinois Attorney General Tyrone Fanner assured him yesterday that the findings will be studied carefully in that state. The report has been submitted for review by Brown, Campbell and state Justice Secretary Neil J. Welch, as well as the governor and attorney general of Illinois and police and medical officials there.

During yesterday's news conference, Beshear said he hoped the credibility of the Kentucky State Police would not be "permanently tarnished" by those parts of his report that appear to reflect negatively on the agency.

Beshear said that, in two subsequent cases in which state police officers have been killed, the force's conduct during searches for and arrests of suspects has been highly professional.

One effect of the Graham case, he said, has been that police officials are now "cognizant of the ability of some people (police officers) to get out of hand. That's what happened here."

The report did not satisfy Graham's father, James E. "Buddy" Graham, who attended the press conference. Graham insisted that his son was innocent of the murder of Harris. The section of the Beshear report that supported the conclusion that Clyde Graham was Harris' killer was "part of the old Brandenburgh report," Graham said.

The report's findings of misconduct on the part of the police only substantiated claims that he and his family have made since the time of the incidents, he said.

THE GRAHAM SHOOTING

Acting on information from informants, Coffey and Kentucky State Police Lt. Ellis Ross went to the Villa Inn motel in Effingham. While in the motel office, Coffey and Illinois State Police Lt. John Roberts discussed how they would approach Graham's room.

E.M. "Pete" Estrada, the motel operator, said in a deposition to Beshear's investigators that Roberts first suggested that he make the arrest and Coffey back him up. Coffey responded, "No, I'll do it, but first we got to figure out how to do it."

Roberts also gave a deposition and stated that he wasn't sure how the decision was made, but he maintained that he was in control of the arrest procedure.

Nevertheless, it was Coffey who opened the outer door to Graham's room and knocked on the inner door. Coffey made several statements about what happened when Graham opened the door:

* At the inquest, Coffey testified: "He (Graham) started backwards, he raised an object in his left hand and went for his rear pocket with his left hand. In a brief struggle in an attempt to subdue him, I saw I could not do so, and I fired two shots and he fell."

* To Illinois police investigators, Coffey stated: "I first attempted to restrain him and he was still attempting to remove an object from his rear pocket, I was put in fear of my life. Having my service revolver in my right hand, I fired two shots."

* The Brandenburgh report stated that Coffey "grabbed his right arm, but Graham jerked away and continued to reach for his right pocket. Coffey then fired once and when this shot did not knock Graham down, Coffey fired again, at which point Graham went down."

The Beshear report concluded from statements of several witnesses outside the motel room, however, that there could not have been any struggle between Graham and Coffey.

Coffey remained outside the doorway as he fired the shots, holding the outer screen door in his left hand and the gun in his right, the report stated.

The Beshear report concluded that Coffey must have known that one of his shots entered Graham's back, but that Coffey never made that part of his statements.

Coffey had also stated that be believed Graham was heavily armed at the motel. Beshear's investigators interviewed the four people whom Coffey had listed on an internal police memo as the sources of that information.

BILL OSINSKI

Three of the four denied giving Coffey any such information, and the fourth could not be located, the report stated.

Also, two Illinois police officers gave statements quoting Ross as not believing that Graham was armed, the report stated.

One of the officers, state police Cpl. Al Morton, said he recalled Ross saying the information that Graham was armed was not true.

The other officer, Sgt. Donald Gillespie of the Effingham City Police, said he recalled Ross saying that he (Ross) did not believe that Graham was dangerous or that he would use firearms against the police.

In his statement to Beshear's investigators, Ross denied making such statements.

No guns were found in Graham's room, but a small knife was removed by police from Graham's rear pocket. Beshear's investigators were unable to establish that the knife was Graham's.

A picture of the knife found with Graham was shown to Ronald Gene Durall, a police informant who had helped Graham escape to Illinois.

Durall said the knife in the photo was not the knife he had seen in Graham's possession. Jimmy Graham also told investigators that the knife was not his brother's.

Graham's death was officially ruled a justifiable homicide by every agency that investigated the matter.

Beshear said, however, that his investigators became suspicious when they received photographs of Graham's body from Illinois police files. The photographs were taken to forensic pathologists, who expressed the opinion that one of the wounds on Graham's back was an entry wound.

But, because it was believed that Graham's body had been cremated, no action was taken right away.

Later, after an investigator found out that the body had not been cremated, Beshear ordered that Graham's body be exhumed early this year.

The body was removed from a Louisville cemetery, and a second autopsy was performed by Dr. Frank Cleveland, a medical examiner in Hamilton County, Ohio.

After the second autopsy, Cleveland was able to confirm that Graham had been shot once in the back and once in the chest.

In a deposition concerning the autopsy, Cleveland said he did not know how the shot in the back could have been missed in the first autopsy.

"I do not understand how Dr. Frank, in doing the examination and having the fresh body to examine, how in the one instance he could recognize that the gunshot wound on the front of the body . . . was a gunshot entrance wound and failed to recognize that the wound on the right side of the back of the body also was a gunshot entrance wound."

Some tests were impossible to perform in the second autopsy, because of the decomposition of the body. Cleveland was able to estimate, however, that Graham was shot both times from a distance of two feet.

Cleveland also developed an opinion, based on the trajectories of the bullets, that the first shot hit Graham in the chest as he turned away, and that the second hit him in the back as he was falling.

The Beshear report also criticized the procedures of Illinois police in securing some of the evidence, particularly the shirt that Graham was wearing when he was shot. That shirt cannot be found, the report stated.

The FBI came in for some criticism for its part in the search for Graham. The report states that agent Don Bottles was present during the planning meetings for the Effingham trip.

The day before the trip, the report stated, Bottles alerted FBI agents in Indianapolis to search local motels after it was thought Graham might be hiding there.

But no similar alert was put out by Bottles when he found out Coffey and Ross were going to Effingham, the report stated.

POLICE MISCONDUCT

About 40 to 50 police raided the Graham home near midnight on the night Harris was shot. The Beshear report concluded that the raid "rapidly became uncontrolled."

The report also concluded that police used excessive force in arresting Jimmy Graham. It did not make a conclusion in the case of the two other men who were arrested, Buddy Graham and his nephew, Charles McLain.

In August 1980 a federal court jury in Louisville acquitted Buddy Graham on charges of harboring his son. Police conduct during the raid was a central issue in that trial.

But Buddy Graham and McLain were convicted in Hardin District Court in November 1980 of resisting arrest in connection with the incident. Jimmy Graham was acquitted.

Police officers have stated that they raided the house because they believed Clyde Graham was there.

The accounts of the early parts of the incident roughly coincide. The three men and three women inside the Graham home emerged in response to police orders. All except Buddy Graham obeyed instructions to lie on the ground, according to police.

The resisting-arrest charges stemmed from police allegations that Buddy Graham tried to prevent himself from being handcuffed. Then, according to police, a scuffle broke out, and McLain rose to try to help Graham.

The Grahams claimed the three men were all beaten by police.

Testimony from emergency room physicians showed all three had suffered blows from blunt instruments. The most severely injured was Jimmy Graham, but no police officers testified that he had done anything to resist arrest, the Beshear report stated.

Dr. Marilyn Hicks, who examined Jimmy Graham, stated that he had suffered "severe blunt trauma about the head and face" and that the wounds must have been caused by "numerous blows."

The Graham family members present during the raid filed a civil-rights complaint with the U.S. Department of Justice shortly after the incident. There has been no official response.

During the press conference, Beshear said that it would be difficult to prosecute any of the police officers for the incident at the Graham home.

The Grahams have not been able to identify any officers who might have been involved in the beatings, he said. "If we can find out who it was, somebody ought to be blamed and punished," Beshear said.

He said the Brandenburgh report exonerating the state police "points up the inherent problem of agency personnel investigating their own agency."

Bill's notes: I had never been to Logan, Ohio, until I was assigned to cover the Dale Johnston double murder trial. When I drove up to the courthouse, I was astounded to see a long line of people waiting outside. This was on one of the coldest days of the year; the temperature was below zero. As the trial went on, I realized that most of the spectators who scrambled for seats in the courtroom wanted to hear stories more scandalous than the ones on their TV soap operas. Also, they wanted someone to pay for the murders that had petrified them. They got their conviction, although almost every bit of the state's testimony in that courtroom turned out to be lies.

LOGAN — THE spectators come to the Hocking County Courthouse in the coldest hours of the coldest days of the year.

For their troubles, they get a day's rights to a piece of crowded pine bench, where they hear things that scald their small-town sensitivities.

Some bring crocheted cushions, so they can be more comfortable while they listen to the tale of two young lovers who were murdered, mutilated and dismembered.

The story includes accusations of terrible things that went on inside the trailer on Trowbridge Road. In the home the young woman left two months before she was butchered, there was routine nudity, times when her stepfather masturbated in front of her, and other times when he committed incest with her, witnesses have testified.

And there has been even more: an important prosecution witness who had to be hypnotized before he could recall the events he would testify about; a close relative of the female victim who has developed amnesia; and repeated charges that local investigators bungled the case.

No wonder that the orange cards that gain the holders admission to the trial of Dale N. Johnston are the toughest tickets to obtain in the Hocking Valley.

Johnston, 50, is charged with the October 1982 murders of his stepdaughter, Annette Cooper Johnston, 18, and her fiance, Todd Schultz, 19.

Testimony in the 2-week-old, nonjury trial could end today or Saturday, after which a verdict will be rendered by a three-judge panel.

Ten days after Miss Johnston and Schultz disappeared, their torsos were found floating in the Hocking River. Testimony on the results of their autopsies, which had been sealed until the trial, showed that the genitals had been removed from both torsos.

Their skulls and limbs were found partially buried in a cornfield that banks on the river. The causes of their deaths were six .22-caliber gunshots to Schultz's body and two to Miss Johnston's.

Schultz's torso was heavily slashed, and there were cross-shaped cuts on his abdomen, the physician who performed the autopsy testified.

Prosecutors have accused Johnston of murdering the couple because their relationship had apparently ended an illicit affair he began with his stepdaughter when she was 10.

Several witnesses have testified that Miss Johnston had told them that Johnston had coerced her into having sexual relations with him. Defense attorneys have vigorously contested the incest testimony. They also contend that Johnston was baling hay at his farm on the day the couple disappeared.

Also, they have contended that Johnston's arrest came after local investigators deliberately overlooked evidence that might incriminate other suspects.

Johnston's attorneys will not reveal whether their client plans to take the stand. However, Johnston's son, Dale R. Johnston, is expected to testify; and defense attorneys' cross-examination questions have suggested that Miss Johnston's revelations of incest may have been connected to relations with her stepbrother, rather than her stepfather.

There has been nothing like the Johnston case in Hocking County, local observers say, since a hatchet-murder case in the late 1800s.

So, area residents are going a long way to get a seat for what is literally the trial of the century.

"I came here at quarter after five in the morning a couple of days ago, and there were already eight people in line," said one spectator, a woman who has attended every trial session. "I don't have any husband or kids to cook and clean for, so I can come and go as I please," she said.

She is one of about five spectators who have gotten passes every day, she said. Most of the people who come to the courthouse in the predawn hours are there out of simple curiosity, she said.

Every day, about 75 passes to seats in the small courtroom are given out on a first-come, first-served basis. Sheriff's deputies report that the ticket line forms every day before 6 a. m.

One day, there were twice as many people in the line as there were passes available, one deputy said.

They all pass a first-floor bulletin board, where one of a jumble of flyers promotes a social service agency with the warning: "Domestic violence is reaching epidemic proportions."

Most people who get a pass spend the whole day squeezed into their spot in the courtroom, since only a few people turn in their passes at the noon recess. Everyone going into the spectators' area must sign for their pass and go through a metal detector.

There are several signs around the courthouse warning that anyone who brings even his pocket-knife to the screening area risks being turned away. The crowd is mostly middle-aged or elderly women, but there usually is a sizable representation of both younger and older men.

It isn't hard to hear whispered verdicts being returned in the spectators' section; but these people do not have to take into account, as the judges must, the legal doctrine of reasonable doubt. Defense attorneys have attempted to inject that notion into nearly every aspect of the state's case, which consists of a few pieces of circumstantial evidence and a lot of hearsay.

There is no murder weapon or dismemberment tool in evidence. Prosecutors have not been able to pinpoint the place where the killings occurred.

Castings of boot prints taken from the cornfield have been matched by state expert witnesses to a pair of boots taken from Johnston. However, other experts called by the defense have challenged the validity of the match.

In addition, investigators from outside police agencies called by the defense have testified that local investigators may have mishandled evidence at the crime scene and may have ignored potential evidence that might have pointed away from Johnston.

A state witness testified that on the day the couple disappeared, he saw a man who resembled Johnston angrily approach a couple who resembled the victims and order them into his truck. But that witness gave his statement to police under hypnosis, and an expert witness testified for the defense that the statement was taken in a questionable fashion and that the hypnosis may have clouded the witness's recollection.

Much of the testimony has centered not on the killings but on what went on inside the Johnston home.

Accusations that Johnston often went about his home nude came from Logan Police Department investigators who interviewed Johnston after the couple disappeared. These same investigators testified that Johnston was cooperative, giving consent to a search of his home and giving police pictures of Miss Johnston to aid in the identification of the bodies.

The pictures, which were entered into evidence, were taken of Miss Johnston by her stepfather when she was 13. In two of the pictures, the girl was nude; in one of those she carried a rifle and an ammunition bandolier and in the other she clenched a knife in her teeth.

Johnston's wife, Sarah, testified that she was unaware of any occasions of Johnston masturbating in front of her daughter. But on the question of whether she was aware of an incestuous relationship between her daughter and Johnston, Johnston's attorneys invoked the marital privilege and Mrs. Johnston was not required to answer.

She did acknowledge saying to Johnston on the day after the disappearances that she didn't care if he had raped Annette, she just wanted Annette back.

The incest allegations came during testimony from several friends of Miss Johnston and from Todd Schultz's mother, Sandra. The allegations were based on conversations the friends had with Miss Johnston.

Mrs. Schultz said the couple had lived in her home for the two months prior to the killings. On the day they disappeared, she said, Miss Johnston became upset and left the house. Todd followed her, and the couple walked off together in the direction of the Hocking River, she testified.

Bill's notes: I will never forget the terrifying echo of the cheers from the lower floor of the courthouse, when the townsfolk learned that Dale N. Johnston had been found guilty of the brutal murders of his stepdaughter Annette Johnston and her boyfriend Todd Schultz. They wanted their guilty verdict, and they got it. But I could not believe that three judges could agree that Johnston was the killer. I had come to Logan at the outset of the trial, expecting the State of Ohio would certainly not put a man on trial for murder, unless they had solid evidence against him. The evidence presented at the trial was anything but solid. I did my job, wrote the story on the verdict. But I knew that an innocent man had been railroaded to death row.

L OGAN — DALE N. Johnston has been convicted of crimes the state termed "the ultimate form of incest."

The 50-year-old handyman's face retained the set and color of concrete as he was pronounced guilty of murdering his stepdaughter Annette, with whom he'd admitted having sexual contact, and the young man who was going to take her away.

Seconds after the verdict was read late Saturday afternoon, the hush inside the courtroom was broken by cheers from the scores of people lining the corridors of the Hocking County Courthouse. Some spectators had come to the building as early as 2 a.m.

They cheered again moments later as Johnston was led back to jail.

Saturday's verdict represented the legal resolution of the crimes that have stunned this small southeastern Ohio town since Oct. 14, 1982, when the torsos of Annette Cooper Johnston, 18, and her boyfriend, Todd Schultz, 19, were found floating in the Hocking River.

Both had been shot to death, and then their bodies were dismembered and mutilated. Their limbs and skulls were buried in a cornfield near the riverbank.

Members of the Schultz family, sitting in the first two rows of the courtroom to hear the verdict, made obvious, though restrained, shows of emotion.

"Justice has been done," said Sandra Schultz, Todd's mother, as she parted from a sobbing embrace with a relative. But she added, "It can't bring Todd and Annette back."

The three-judge panel that presided over the trial took less than two hours to deliberate.

Defense attorneys apparently took that as a positive sign for their client, as they appeared quite relaxed while the parties and spectators filled the courtroom to await the verdict.

Defense attorney Thomas Tyack silently mouthed "What!" when visiting Judge Joseph Sirigliano of Lorain County read the verdict.

Later, Tyack declined to comment on the verdict, except to contend that the defense had established grounds for reasonable doubt of the charges.

Johnston, who could receive the death penalty, will not be sentenced for several weeks. He will undergo psychiatric evaluations and a presentencing investigation first.

Hocking County assistant prosecutor Fred Mong, who presented the state's case, said after the verdict, "From a legal point of view, the system has worked." But Mong said the crimes still represented "a tragedy, a personal loss for everyone."

The impact of the murders on the town has been somewhat exaggerated, Mong said. "The community's going to continue to go on as a community and be as normal as it ever was," Mong said.

About 200 pieces of evidence were introduced during the nearly three-week-long trial. But when the testimony ended, the defendant had no verified alibi (except for his wife's testimony), and the prosecution had no murder weapon nor a definite murder location.

Johnston took the stand Friday and testified that he was home with his other stepdaughter, Michelle, when the killings occurred. Michelle testified that she had developed amnesia and could not recall anything about the evening of October 4, when the couple disappeared. She was able to recall, however, the events of the morning and afternoon of that day.

There was expert testimony that stated Michelle's amnesia was induced by a trauma, and Mong asked in his closing argument, "What traumatic event did her eyes behold?"

Having only circumstantial evidence linking Johnston to the crimes, the state put the lifestyle in the Johnston home on trial. From the outset, the prosecution worked to establish Johnston's sexual obsession with his stepdaughter as the motive for the crimes.

Johnston admitted to having "sexual contact" once with Annette when she was 11 or 12. He also said the family members would sometimes go nude in the home.

Several prosecution witnesses, however, gave testimony that indicated the problems ran much deeper than Johnston admitted. They said Annette told them she'd been raped by her stepfather.

In his closing argument, Mong hammered on the theme of the illicit relationship. "Incest, like rape, is not a sexual occurrence, it is one of abuse, dehumanization and violence," Mong said. "The ultimate form of incest is murder," he said.

The ultimate violence in this case was precipitated by an argument over a car, Mong said. Johnston had bought a car that was supposed to be a present for Annette, but he kept it for his wife's use.

It was one of several actions he took to try to get her to come back home, Mong said. Annette had left the Johnston home and moved in with the Schultzes about two months before the murders.

Annette and Todd needed a car of their own, because she worked and Todd had just lost a job and faced the prospect of looking for work in other cities.

In reconstructing a version of the confrontation that led to the shootings, Mong theorized that Annette told her stepfather something like: "This is it! Give me a car, leave me alone, or I'll tell them what you're really like."

Defense attorney Robert Suhr presented an entirely different scenario during his closing argument. He contended that it was "ridiculous to believe," as the state contended, that Johnston would have committed the murders at his secluded trailer and then brought the body parts back to a field quite near town for disposal.

The murders, and what followed, were done in the cornfield, Suhr said, and evidence ignored by the state points to ritual slayings. "Someone killed them, and later, a person or persons returned to the area. They were cut up, perhaps in some kind of ceremony, perhaps not," Suhr said.

To support this theory, Suhr cited several pieces of evidence: Todd's torso had wounds that may have been inflicted by design a cross-shaped wound with ray-like marks coming from it, all under a wound made in a horizontal line. Annette's hands had seven fingernails missing, and the limbs and skulls were buried in seven spots arranged roughly in a semicircle. The dismemberment wounds were made in a "chop-chop, stab-stab" fashion, possibly indicating that several people were involved in the process; and the apparent lack of hemorrhaging could indicate that the wounds were inflicted some period of time after the shooting.

BILL OSINSKI

Bill's notes: Wickline refused to grant an interview for this story. My point in doing this profile of him was that he should have been investigated for the killings of Annette Johnston and Todd Schultz, but the local police were adamant in their insistence that Dale Johnston was the killer. Wickline was certainly in the area and actively committing crimes at the time of the Logan murders. Also, he was practiced in the dismemberment of human corpses. After the truth came out and I started re-investigating the case, I learned that Logan police definitely knew Kenny Linscott, the admitted accomplice, and they deliberately steered away from him. Linscott and the killer, Chester McKnight were both hangers-on of a local organized crime group, which almost certainly knew of Wickline. If Wickline had any answers to these questions — which I believe he did — he took them to his grave. In 2004, the State of Ohio executed him for the murders of Chris and Peggy Lerch.

H E LEARNED MEAT carving in a prison slaughterhouse and later was convicted of applying his state-taught skills to the disposal of the bodies of his murder victims.

William Wickline Jr.'s macabre methods were, to some homicide investigators, the mark of a professional killer — carve up the victim, bag the body parts, scatter the bags where no one will look. No corpse, no crime.

Yet others believe he engaged in human butchery partly for sport.

But whatever forces propelled Wickline's knife, several law enforcement agencies are trying to establish his credentials as a serial killer of nonpareil savagery. He has been convicted, indicted, or named as a suspect in five or possibly six homicides in which the victims were dismembered, decapitated or both.

And some police investigators believe that list could be expanded to include two killings for which another man has already been convicted.

During his youth in the middle-class community of Reynoldsburg, just east of Columbus, Bill Wickline was little more than a suburban bad boy. He began his crime career by egging his high school principal's car.

But by the time he'd grown into a six-foot-three-inch bull-necked man, police records show he had graduated to drugstore burglaries, pimping, running a narcotics house, and then on to postgraduate crime: murder, and beyond.

His exploits have earned him stints in at least six state penal institutions. During one confinement, he took some college-level psychology courses; during another, he was taught to be a butcher.

He has since been convicted of the dismemberment murders of a young couple involved in drug trafficking, and he was indicted in West Virginia in the contract killing and decapitation of an overly ambitious drug dealer.

He also is suspected of a possible contract killing in Florida, in the disappearance and possible murder of a known gambler and in the murder of a youth who may simply have been in his way.

"He was the most dangerous criminal I've ever run across in this state," said a West Virginia police detective.

Wickline, 34, now spends his time on Ohio's death row, seeking legal ways to avoid execution in the electric chair. But while he waits, police are trying to determine just how many people he may have killed.

In addition to the six killings to which Wickline has been linked in some fashion, detectives in a Columbus-area police department believe he should be investigated for a possible connection to two other dismemberment murders — the 1982 killings of 19-year-old Todd Schultz and his 18-year-old girlfriend Annette Johnston, whose body parts were found in and near a cornfield in Logan.

In 1984, Miss Johnston's stepfather, Dale N. Johnston, was convicted of those killings. He and Wickline now both share a death-row address.

In October, the Beacon Journal published a series of articles that raised questions about the police conduct in the investigation of the Logan killings. At that time, police sources said that Logan investigators never seriously considered any suspects other than Johnston and that they doubted the killings could have happened in the manner alleged by prosecutors.

With or without the Logan murders, though, the list of Wick-line's suspected victims makes for a long-running serial.

The list grew primarily from the investigation of the murders of the Columbus drug dealers, Chris and Peggy Lerch. Police informants in that case told investigators about other killings Wickline had spoken of.

Columbus police then checked with other police agencies to determine whether the informants' information matched actual or suspected crimes.

Thus, the following list of Wick-line's suspected or known victims was developed:

* Chris and Peggy Lerch. According to testimony in the trial, the following story evolved: Chris and Peggy Lerch were a young couple heavily involved in drug trafficking in the Columbus area. On Aug. 14, 1982, they argued with Wickline over a $6,000 drug debt.

During the argument, Lerch boasted that he had had sex with Wickline's girlfriend. After the argument, Wickline asked Lerch to come with him to the upstairs bathroom to help him fix a clogged tub drain.

While Lerch was looking into the tub, Wickline slit his throat. He then apparently decided Mrs. Lerch would have to be eliminated as a possible witness, so he strangled her while she slept.

One of Wickline's girlfriends testified against him, claiming he threatened to kill her unless she helped him by holding Mrs. Lerch's legs while he strangled her.

According to the girlfriend's testimony, both bodies were decapitated and dismembered in the bathtub; body parts were placed in plastic garbage bags and left in trash dumpsters around Franklin County.

Almost two years passed before Wickline was indicted. The bodies of the Lerches were never found. Besides the testimony of Wickline's girlfriend, the case was supported by evidence that included Mrs. Lerch's wedding ring, which Wickline had apparently kept.

* Charles Marsh. A known drug dealer, Charles Marsh was found murdered in his bed in Parkersburg, W.Va., on Nov. 11, 1979. His hands had been handcuffed behind his back, and he had been strangled with a telephone cord. His head had then been cut off and placed on a night table beside the bed.

The killer had taken the time to comb the hair on Marsh's severed head. Medical examiners determined it had been severed with one cut, or at most two, indicating the killer was a skilled butcher. West Virginia police investigated the case extensively for about five years, without being able to identify a suspect.

But the investigation led police to believe the murder was a contract killing, and the decapitation was added as a warning to others in the drug trade who might be considering expanding their territory, as Marsh had tried to do.

Also, police developed information from sources early in the investigation that the killer was someone who had been a meat cutter while in prison, where he had earned the nickname "the Butcher."

After Wickline was indicted in the Lerch case, Columbus and West Virginia police shared information, and Wickline was indicted in late 1985 for killing Marsh. No trial date has been set for the Marsh case, pending the outcome of Wickline's appeal in the Lerch murders.

*   Tony Muncie A 14-year-old resident of the eastern suburbs of Columbus, Tony Muncie disappeared in October 1983. His body was found two days later along a highway in Delaware County. His death was caused by stab wounds in the back. His arms had been severed at the shoulders and elbows. His legs and head had been partially severed from his torso.

Investigators could not establish any drug involvement on Muncie's part, but they did obtain information that he may have been killed simply because he refused to get away from a drugstore that Wickline intended to rob. Police said Wickline is a suspect in the murder.

*   Tory Gainer. Tory Gainer was well-known to police as being heavily involved in illegal gambling operations in central and southeastern Ohio. He disappeared in 1978 or 1979, and though no missing-person report was ever filed, police believe he was murdered.

Informants told Columbus police Gainer was killed and dismembered, and his body parts were left in different landfills around Fairfield County. Police consider Wickline a suspect in the possible homicide.

* Unknown victim. Informants told Columbus-area police that Wickline may have accepted a contract to execute a man in Florida in early 1983. Police then contacted Dade County (Miami) police, who confirmed that in January 1983, the body parts of a man had been discovered in a canal in a rural section of the county.

The man, whose identity still has not been determined, had been stabbed to death, then decapitated and dismembered. A Dade County detective said that the medical examiner who assisted in the investigation had suggested police consider looking for suspects among the hog farmers of the area, because of the obvious knowledge of butchery displayed by the killer.

"He really knew what he was doing," police said they were told by the medical examiner.

* Possible Logan links. The killer of Miss Johnston and Schultz dismembered and decapitated his victims — the same fate suffered by victims in the cases in which Wickline is believed to be involved. Unlike the cases already linked to Wickline, though, there was an added element of mutilation in the Logan murders: the sex organs of both victims were cut away and never found.

Also, a three-judge panel convicted someone else — Dale N. Johnston. Prosecutors portrayed Johnston as an insanely jealous stepfather who had had an incestuous relationship with his stepdaughter Annette and who went into a jealous frenzy over her plans to marry Schultz. The prosecution focused on the situation within the Johnston household, so no evidence on the murdered couple's lifestyle or any possible drug involvement was presented at trial.

Despite the verdict, some Columbus-area homicide detectives have said that they still believe Wickline should be a suspect in the Logan murder.

The notion that there could have been two such sadistic killer-butchers operating at the same time in the same area of Ohio stretches coincidence too far, one detective said. Only rarely is a killer capable of the behavior exhibited in these murders, police said.

Wickline was living just a few miles from Logan when Miss Johnston and Schultz were slain. According to a friend of Wickline's, he left Columbus after the Lerches were killed in August 1982, and he moved to a trailer in a rural community just north of the Hocking-Fairfield County line.

Wickline continued living an active outlaw life after he moved to the Logan area, and police sources claim he was part of a burglary ring that specialized in breaking into drugstores, then dealing the stolen narcotics. The same sources confirmed the ring was active in the Logan area.

Wickline's last arrest, in January 1984, occurred about 15 miles from Logan, in Nelsonville, where police arrested him during a thwarted drugstore burglary.

Miss Johnston and Schultz were known to have friends in the Buckeye Lake area of northern Fairfield County, an area among the first where police were dispatched to search for the two after they were reported missing.

Wickline also frequented that area, stashed stolen goods and drugs there, and had friends and relatives in the same area, friends of Wickline said. Wickline demonstrated the proclivity and expertise for committing murders like the ones in Logan.

Law enforcement officials from three different agencies said that dismembering his victims was more than just an efficient means of body disposal for Wickline. "He really seemed to enjoy it," one investigator said. "It was like a sport to him."

Officially, the Johnston case is before the state appellate court, from which a ruling on Johnston's motion for a retrial is expected within the next month or two.

Logan Police Chief Steve Barron said he could not comment on the case, because it is still being adjudicated. However, he said he would be willing to discuss the case with any legitimate police investigator. "Anytime a police officer has information on a crime in my jurisdiction any crime I want to talk with him," Barron said.

Under the provisions of Ohio's home-rule laws, however, crime is largely a local matter. Issues such as when to close or reopen an investigation and whether to cooperate with other police agencies in a multijurisdictional investigation are decided solely by local authorities.

The Ohio Bureau of Criminal Identification and Investigation, the state's criminal investigative agency, acts only to assist local law enforcement agencies and acts only at the request of the local agencies. Jack McCormick, a Columbus lawyer who headed the bureau for about 10 years, said legislative attempts to change that system have failed repeatedly.

Bills aimed at giving the agency more investigative authority, he said, are always met with concerted lobbying opposition from organizations representing local sheriffs, prosecutors and police chiefs. "It won't change in your lifetime or mine," McCormick said.

KILLER'S PORTRAIT

In his youth, Wickline was regarded as a good student and potentially an outstanding athlete. Although he was a member of the wrestling team for a while in high school, he never lived up to his athletic promise, and he did not earn good marks in his high school classes.

Public school officials in Reynoldsburg recall him as having affectionate, even doting, parents. Though he was not a flagrant troublemaker, some of his best friends were. There was some suspicion he might have been involved with drugs during his school years, but he was never charged.

The worst offense he was caught in was egging his high school principal's car. Wickline and an accomplice cleaned up the car the next day, even waxing it as an unrequested bonus.

A friend who has known Wickline about 15 years, but asked not to be identified, said he did not become a criminal straight out of high school. "He was more like a flower child," she said. "He had maybe two pairs of jeans and some T-shirts, and hair down to the middle of his back. He was anything but a charmer."

His first arrest came in 1971, when he was 19. He was arrested at least nine more times in Ohio between then and 1984. During that period, he served time in state prisons in Columbus, Mansfield, Chillicothe, Orient, and London.

Typically, Wickline would enter a guilty plea and do his time when caught. One investigator remembered that Wickline didn't seem bothered by the prospect of returning to prison — it gave him time to concentrate on pastimes such as lifting weights.

At one time, he took some college-level courses while in prison, saying he wanted to become a psychologist. Police and friends agree on one point about him: His intelligence set him apart from the run-of-the-mill criminal. "What makes him so dangerous is that he's so smart," a woman friend of Wickline's said. "He had everything going for him."

Though his arrests include drug and prostitution-related charges, his specialty was burglary. In this pursuit, he was also a pro, knowing if he never carried a gun during a break-in, he couldn't be charged with the more serious armed-robbery felonies.

But during a decade spent more inside prison than out, Wickline became more and more deeply involved with what one friend of his called the "prison mainstream", those groups of inmates who use fear and violence to control most of the illicit activities within prison populations.

"Once you get in the mainstream, you don't get out," the friend said.

Another close friend of Wickline's — not the one who testified against him at the trial — said she, too, saw a change in him. "Each time he got more serious," she said, speaking of his demeanor after he was released.

His turn to major-league violence came after a temporary breakup in their relationship, she said. While Wickline was in prison, she went off with another man. She said she was abducted, but Wickline thought she went willingly.

Not long after this, in November 1979, Wickline was released, and the Marsh killing occurred.

"After that, he was never the same," the woman said. Wickline developed an affinity for knives and a reputation as a man not to be crossed.

One prosecuting lawyer said it was practically impossible to offer any potential witnesses deals attractive enough to convince them to testify against Wickline. "They were terrified of him," the prosecutor said.

A ruggedly handsome man, Wickline maintained relationships with several women, and even after the relationships were broken off, he retained some sort of attraction to them.

The girlfriend who testified that Wickline threatened to kill her remained loyal to him for another couple of years. She tried to make bail for him after his arrest in Nelsonville and went there to pick up his impounded car.

Another former girlfriend said Wickline threatened her on at least two occasions, but she still loved him. "Nobody ever says anything good about Bill," she said.

She maintained Wickline could do all kinds of drugs without losing control. "It was only when he was drinking scotch that he'd go crazy," she said.

But another former friend of Wickline's said sex, drugs and some bizarre forays into the occult were all enmeshed in Wickline's lifestyle. At times, the friend said, Wickline was involved with a group that engaged in animal-sacrifice rituals in which a male member of the group would use his chest as a human altar on which the animal was sacrificed.

But does all this make Wickline a better suspect than Dale Johnston in the case of the Logan killings?

Investigators in three different police agencies said they believed the question of Wickline's possible involvement should be investigated further.

One police investigator and one prosecutor, however, said they didn't think Wickline committed the Logan murders. They said, based on the cases in which they investigated Wickline, he was strictly a professional killer.

Thus, the sexual mutilations of the Logan victims would not be characteristic of Wickline; also, there was no drug angle brought out in the Logan case.

Columbus lawyer Don Woolery, who represented Wickline at his murder trial, said he was convinced Wickline did not murder Schultz and Miss Johnston, but he added that he could not divulge why he was so certain.

Woolery charged that some police investigators might be trying to clear their books of some unsolved crimes by trying to blame Wickline.

One friend said she had put the question directly to Wickline, after she heard of the Logan murders, asking: "Have you been out playing again?" But Wickline denied he was involved, she said.

Wickline also has denied that he was involved in the two murders he was convicted of, as has Johnston. Nevertheless, some police investigators are haunted by the possibility that one man may have committed all of them. For now, though, the state of Ohio plans to execute them both.

Bill's notes: This article was the first in a series in the Akron Beacon Journal challenging the guilty verdict against Dale N. Johnston. The paper allowed me to work off and on for almost two years on this series, even though the murders and the trial were nowhere near our circulation area. That would be next to impossible in today's newspapers; in fact, there's no way I would be assigned today to cover a murder trial 200 miles away.

But our pursuit of the truth was rewarded. More than a year after this series, the appellate court threw out the guilty verdict, along with most of the prosecution's key "evidence". The decision was a scathing indictment of the police, prosecutors and trial judges in the case. Johnston was released from death row, and although local prosecutors tried to bring him to trial again, they were forced to drop the charges. They were able, however, to make sure Johnston lived under a cloud of presumed guilt for the next 25 years.

In 2006, the real killers confessed. Chester "The Molester" McKnight, a prison inmate with a history of assaulting women walking along the same railroad tracks one county to the south, admitted that he killed Todd and Annette, after luring them into the cornfield on the promise of drugs. When Todd tried to stop McKnight from sexually assaulting Annette, McKnight shot him to death; and when Annette screamed, he shot her. The couple had just met McKnight an hour or so earlier, when they went to the home in West Logan of Kenny Linscott, a local drug dealer.

Essentially everything the state had presented at the trial had been lies.

McKnight and Linscott were indicted on two counts of first-degree murder. McKnight plead guilty and was sentenced to an additional 17 years in the prison of his choice. In what I characterized as the "deal of the millennium," Linscott plead guilty to one count of corpse abuse and was released that same day.

The case became the basis for my non-fiction book "Guilty By Popular Demand".

AKRON BEACON JOURNAL, OCTOBER 27, 1985

LOGAN, OH — On the day before the night of October's first full moon, the moon they call the Corn Moon, two young lovers quarreled, then went walking on the C&O Railroad tracks near the Falls Mill bridge over the Hocking River.

Night fell, but they didn't come home.

Eight days later, a member of a search party saw what appeared to be a pig carcass in the river. Police searching the riverbank two days later found the torsos of Annette Cooper Johnston, 18, a runner-up in the Miss Parade of the Hills contest, and her fiance, Todd Schultz, 19.

Most of the rest of their remains were found two days later in seven graves in a cornfield slightly downriver from the bridge.

It has been three years since that grisly discovery, and almost two years since Dale Nolan Johnston, Annette's stepfather, was arrested and charged with shooting, butchering and then burying the two young people.

The state's case against Johnston was strong enough to persuade three judges to send him to death row.

But others, including police investigators, say the case is still too weak to resolve their doubts.

The murders unsettled the foundations of community life in Logan, the small-town county seat of Hocking County in a mined-out sector of Ohio's coal country. Prosecutors had evidence of inhuman behavior, evidence they were able to reinforce with hearsay testimony of unspeakable evil.

The prosecutor called the murders "the ultimate form of incest."

Here are the state's contentions:

* Johnston lived as a sexual libertine in a trailer on Trowbridge Road in the hills about 12 miles outside Logan. But he went beyond casual nudity in the household, even to the point of masturbating in front of Annette, fondling her and having sex with her.
* On Oct. 4, 1982, Johnston's jealousy over his stepdaughter's informal engagement to Schultz went out of control. He abducted them on the streets of Logan and took them to his trailer, where he shot them.
* After the killings, Johnston severed the limbs, heads and sex organs of the victims. Then, in an effort to divert suspicion from himself, he took the body parts to a cornfield a few blocks from Schultz's home in Logan. He buried the limbs and heads in the middle of the field and dumped the torsos into the Hocking River.

However, some elements that scenario don't fit, according to three investigative sources. The investigators, who worked for different police agencies at the time, discussed the case on the condition their names would not be used, because the verdict against Johnston is under appeal. Here are the defense contentions:

* There may be more evidence pointing to the cornfield than to the trailer as the murder scene. Police had to make three lengthy searches of the Johnston property to come up with a few pieces of disputed evidence. The instruments used to kill Schultz and Miss Johnston and cut up their bodies were never found.
* The only witness who placed Johnston with the victims on the day of the murders was a friend of the Schultz family who changed important details of his statement, causing one investigator to dismiss him as a potential witness. The testimony of this witness came after he was hypnotized by Logan police, who used methods termed improper by a defense expert.

BILL OSINSKI

* The state's investigators decided almost from the beginning that Johnston was the suspect and disregarded any evidence that did not support the case against him. A number of witnesses have filed affidavits saying they had information that pointed away from Johnston, but it was ignored by police

Prosecutor Christopher Veidt said he could not discuss specifics of the case, but he did say he was confident all leads had been investigated. He said the validity of the charges had been confirmed by the verdict and by the refusal of the same court to give Johnston a new trial.

The motion for a new trial is now before the 4th District Court of Appeals in Scioto County. Because of the appeal, Hocking Common Pleas Judge James Stillwell, who presided at the trial, said he could not comment about the case.

ADDITIONAL EVIDENCE

Sheriff Jimmy Jones also declined to discuss it, but he said those who question the verdict are not aware of all the evidence.

Some material, particularly juvenile court records of statements by Johnston's other stepdaughter, Michelle, who was 16 at the time of the killings, was examined by the judges in chambers.

"Some people will say, 'How could a father do something like that?'" Jones said. "What they don't realize is that it happens every day,"

Logan Police Chief William Barron rebutted criticism of the state's case in general and, in particular, criticism directed at police Detective James Thompson. "I stand behind the case and I stand behind him," Barron said. "He's a damn good detective; he wouldn't be here if he wasn't."

The Johnston case was the second homicide investigation led by Thompson in his 10 years on the Logan force, Veidt said; but Barron said Thompson had been involved in several other homicide investigations.

Defense attorney Robert Suhr said there never was a fair investigation, but only a concerted effort to build a case against Johnston. Because of the sensational nature of the crimes and the fear generated in the community, Suhr said the defense team, including Thomas Tyack of Columbus, decided to waive Johnston's right to a jury trial and have the case heard by a panel of three judges.

The defense believed it would be impossible to obtain an unbiased jury in Hocking County, he said. Judge Stillwell had indicated to the attorneys that he would make every effort to select a jury in the county and would not be inclined to move the trial, Suhr said, so the defense decided Johnston's chances would be better in front of judges.

Not only did the state succeed in convicting Johnston, Suhr said, but the entire Johnston family has been kept under a cloud of suspicion.

According to Suhr, prosecutors implied during the trial that Johnston's wife, Sarah, and stepdaughter, Michelle, were at least aware of the killings. "It was a really vicious kind of a thing," Suhr said. "They totally tried to destroy a whole family."

Last month, Mrs. Johnston was involuntarily committed to a state mental hospital. The judge who signed the commitment order, Frederick Mong, was the assistant prosecutor who presented most of the state's case at Johnston's trial. The commitment was changed to a voluntary one in mid-October.

MOTIVE

What follows is an examination of some of the major elements of the case.

Claims of incest against Johnston had been made by Annette Johnston, according to four prosecution witnesses. They testified that Annette had confided to them that she had been raped by her stepfather.

Todd Schultz's mother, Sandra, testified that Annette had told her she had been raped by her stepfather and that he sometimes masturbated in her presence. Two high school friends testified that Annette had made a similar complaint to them; and a teacher who interviewed Annette when she was a candidate in the Parade of the Hills beauty pageant testified Annette wondered whether she should tell the pageant judges that she had been raped by her stepfather.

Dale and Sarah Johnston moved to Hocking County from southwest Ohio in the mid-1970s, not long after they were married (a second marriage for both). Johnston testified they picked the isolated site on Trowbridge Road because they wanted to raise Sarah's daughters, Annette and Michelle, and Dale's son, Dale Ray Johnston in a country atmosphere; and part of their lifestyle was casual nudity in the home.

Snapshots taken at the home and introduced into evidence showed Annette, as a girl of about 13, naked or half naked. In some of the shots she wore cartridge belts around her shoulders.

In August 1982, the day after Johnston became angry at Annette and Todd for changing clothes in the same room, Annette moved out of the trailer, according to prosecution and defense witnesses. She moved into the Schultz home in Logan.

The state contended his stepdaughter's departure sparked jealousy in Johnston. There was testimony Johnston told her dentist he would no longer pay her orthodontia bills and that he asked her employer to fire her, both actions allegedly intended to make her dependent on him again.

The Johnstons also were withholding a promise to give Annette a Buick Skyhawk Mrs. Johnston was using to get to her job as a receptionist at a doctor's office in Logan. Prosecutors theorized that on the day of the killings, there was an argument at the doctor's office among Mr. and Mrs. Johnston, Annette and Schultz over the car.

After the argument, prosecutors speculated, Johnston drove Schultz, Annette and Michelle to the trailer. Once there, Annette may have threatened to tell more people about Johnston's relationship with her, which may have caused Johnston to start shooting.

Prosecutors theorized Johnston took the body parts back to Logan to bury them in the cornfield, rather than try to hide the corpses somewhere near his trailer, as a move to divert suspicion.

Johnston testified that he loved his stepdaughter, helped her raise and show her horses, and supported her in her plans to marry Schultz. He denied that he had masturbated in front of Annette, touched her improperly or had an incestuous relationship.

He did admit, under questioning by defense attorneys, that there had been one incident of unspecified impropriety when Annette was about 12. However, when prosecutors had the opportunity to cross-examine Johnston, they asked him no questions about the nature of his relationship with Annette.

WIFE'S STORY

Mrs. Johnston's testimony supported her husband's version of their home life. She said Annette visited the trailer several times after she moved out and that the family had normal, friendly conversations.

She said Annette and Schultz also visited her at the doctor's office several times. There was no fear in Annette of a jealous stepfather but there was something wrong with her, Mrs. Johnston said.

Always meticulously neat as a girl, Annette had let her appearance become disheveled and she had become moodier since leaving home, Mrs. Johnston said. Annette said at least twice that she was considering returning home, Mrs. Johnston said.

In an affidavit filed in support of the motion for a new trial, Virginia Blume, wife of a doctor who works in the same building where Mrs. Johnston worked, said she heard Annette say she was tired of the fighting in the Schultz home and she wanted to return to her parents.

"She wasn't happy there" in the Schultz home, Mrs. Johnston said.

OCT. 4, 1982

Annette was in a good mood when she came home to the Schultz house on Henrietta Avenue that afternoon; she had received high marks on two tests in computer programming courses at the junior college.

Otherwise, it was an unremarkable Monday.

Annette fixed herself a sandwich and a glass of milk at 2:45 or 3 p.m. Todd Schultz had eaten a light lunch earlier. They went to his bedroom upstairs.

About 4 p.m., Schultz's mother saw Annette walk out of the house. Mrs. Schultz went upstairs to tell Schultz that Annette was leaving by herself. Schultz sprang from his bed, bolted out of the house and caught up with Annette.

She had been walking toward town, but when Schultz joined her, they talked a while, then changed directions and headed for the railroad tracks that ran beside the cornfield.

Several people said they saw Schultz and Miss Johnston as they walked. Some of those sightings are disputed, but there's no dispute that after the evening of Oct. 4, no one saw them again until 10 days later, when their mutilated torsos were found in the Hocking River, beside the cornfield near the railroad tracks.

Melody Morehouse had driven into town after watching her favorite soap opera, which ends at 4 p.m. As she drove past the Home Tavern, on the fringe of a small industrial area, she recognized the two walking in the street. She blew the horn of her pickup truck, waved and saw them walk toward the trestle bridge where the railroad crosses the river.

The tracks, the cornfield and the river form a triangle of seclusion not far from some of the busiest parts of Logan. The cornfield covers about 25 acres inside the triangle.

It's not easy for anyone on the outside to see what might be going on inside the triangle, which was why it was known as a place where people could go to shoot a gun or have a skinny-dipping party or make love.

The field is fringed by trees, underbrush and rocky slopes along the river, and the railroad is on an embankment perhaps six feet above the field.

At the western intersection of the river and the tracks, near the Falls Mill bridge, anyone can walk into the area along the riverbanks. At the eastern intersection, there is a path near the trestle that goes down by the river at the edge of the cornfield.

And there is a gravel driveway that goes over the tracks and up to the edge of the field.

The tracks divide Logan from West Logan. On the West Logan side, Homer Street runs parallel to the tracks. About 20 homes on Homer have back yards next to the railroad.

Debbie Bourne, who lives on Homer not far from the trestle, testified that at about 4:40 p.m. she saw a couple whom she later identified as Schultz and Miss Johnston walking on the tracks, heading toward a section known as West Logan.

Another prosecution witness, Scott Cauthon, testified that at about 4:30 p.m., he was walking on the tracks as a shortcut from West Logan into Logan. He said he passed a couple he later identified as Schultz and Miss Johnston. He said the couple left the tracks and walked into the residential area of West Logan.

DISPUTED SIGHTING

The most disputed sighting of the couple was reported as occurring between 5:30 and 6 p.m. in Logan. This time, the two allegedly were seen being abducted by Annette's stepfather.

Steve Rine, a state worker, testified that he was driving down Front Street, slowing down for a stop sign; when an angry confrontation caught his attention. Rine said a slim, gray-haired man angrily shoved a young woman, then a young man, into an orange car.

In court, he identified the young people as Schultz and Miss Johnston, and the older man as Johnston. Rine said there were two other people in the car and gave vague descriptions that roughly matched Annette's mother and her sister.

Before he testified, Rine was hypnotized twice by Detective James Thompson. The defense objected to Rine's testimony, contending his memory might be tainted by the hypnosis.

The court at first ruled that Rine could testify only to what he remembered before he was hypnotized. But the court later ruled that the defense's questioning of Rine had strayed from the guidelines, so all restrictions were removed.

Rine testified that he first told his story to police at the Schultz home, about a week after the bodies were discovered. Rine was visiting at the home with his then-girlfriend, a relative of the Schultzes.

Rine told two investigators from the Hocking Sheriff's Department that he might have some information in the case. However, one of the investigators, Rodney Robinson, testified that he quickly dismissed Rine as a potential witness.

Robinson said Rine at first said a van or pickup was used in the abduction, but when Rine went back over the story later, he said the vehicle was a car. Rine also said he had not seen anyone well enough to make an identification and he was unsure of the date and time of the sighting, Robinson testified.

Another officer decided what Rine probably saw was the roundup of two youths who had run away from a foster home, according to Robinson's testimony.

Schultz's mother said in a recent interview she thought Rine's testimony was being unfairly questioned. She said she thought he was hesitant to go into detail during his initial questioning because she was present. "It was a very awkward situation," she said, referring to her position as a parent of one of the victims.

Under cross-examination, Rine said after one of the hypnosis sessions he had said the people involved in the abduction were biker types. He had also stated one person who was involved in the abduction was a tall, young man with long brown hair and a droopy mustache.

He also had described the vehicle used in the abduction as a van or pickup.

ATTEMPTED REBUTTAL

The defense attempted to challenge Rine's testimony by calling Dr. Bruce Goldsmith, a clinical psychologist from Columbus who was recognized as a hypnosis expert.

Goldsmith testified he had reviewed tapes of the hypnosis sessions and the interviews were improperly conducted and, in addition, there apparently were erasures in the tapes.

Police questioners planted information in Rine's memory, Goldsmith testified.

Goldsmith said in a recent interview that the hypnosis sessions were "very poorly administered" by police officers who had questionable credentials for such testing. "It was a travesty that the judges didn't even bother listening to the tapes," Goldsmith said.

During the trial, Stilwell said he and the other judges had no intention of listening to the tapes. Goldsmith said such deficiencies seemed increasingly serious in light of the importance of Rine's testimony to the rest of the state's case. "It was the foundation for the whole house of cards," Goldsmith said.

Two other prosecution witnesses testified they saw members of the Johnston family in town on the afternoon of Oct. 4.

Holly Simmons said that while she drove near Front and Gallagher Streets, she saw a man resembling Johnston stop a pickup truck that resembled the one Johnston drove.

Eugene McDaniels, who was repairing the building where Mrs. Johnston worked, testified he entered the building about 7 p.m. to ask Mrs. Johnston why the lights were on. He said he stayed only a few moments, just long enough for Mrs. Johnston to explain that the doctor was having evening hours.

McDaniels said he noticed three teen-agers in a hallway in the office building. He identified two as Miss Johnston and Schultz; he described the other person as a young girl taller than Miss Johnston, suggesting the girl could have been her sister, Michelle.

Defense witnesses the doctor for whom Mrs. Johnston worked and one of her co-workers testified that her orange Skyhawk was in the doctor's parking lot until the 5 p.m. dinner break and during the 7 to 9 p.m. office hours.

Mrs. Johnston testified she left the office shortly before 5 p.m., picked up Michelle at a medical clinic in Logan and went home. Mrs. Johnston had a light dinner, then went back to the doctor's office, arriving shortly before 7 p.m. for routine evening office hours.

Neither she nor her husband nor Michelle saw Annette or Todd Schultz that day, Mrs. Johnston testified.

STATE'S CASE ACCEPTED

Dale Johnston was convicted, meaning the judges accepted the state's version of the events. It also means they accepted the following chronology:

* Johnston drives his pickup into Logan and leaves it to join his wife and Michelle in the orange Skyhawk shortly after 5 p.m.
* Johnston finds Annette and Todd walking on Front Street and abducts them between 5:30 and 6 p.m. The group stops at the office where Mrs. Johnston works. They have an argument about possession of the car.
* Sometime between 6:30 and 7 p.m., the workman sees Todd, Annette, Michelle and Mrs. Johnston in the building.
* Sometime between the workman's sighting and the arrival of the doctor and his patient for a 7 p.m. appointment, Johnston comes back to the office in his pickup truck, which he had left earlier, presumably near the spot where the abduction occurred. He again forces Todd and Annette, to go with him, this time to his trailer, where he shoots them.
* After participating in the abduction of Todd and Annette and in the subsequent argument, Mrs. Johnson spends a routine two hours at her office, then goes home and helps cover up the murder of her daughter.

The timing of these events becomes important in light of the testimony of Patrick Fardal, chief forensic pathologist for the Franklin County coroner's office. Fardal performed the autopsies, and he testified that the contents of their stomachs indicated Schultz and Miss Johnston had eaten a light meal about two hours before they died or had eaten a heavy meal about four hours before they died.

According to the state's case, the only meal Todd and Annette ate that afternoon was the sandwich and drink they had at the Schultz home before 3 p.m. They allegedly were killed sometime after 7 p.m.

The prosecutors asked Fardal whether digestion could have been slowed by stress, and Fardal said that could be possible.

However, the defense contends the autopsy evidence on stomach contents more closely matches a scenario in which the two were killed in the cornfield somewhere between 5 and 6 p.m.

MONDAY: A look at the physical evidence.

Bill's notes: I first became aware of the Nuwaubians and their leader Dwight York, while I was in Putnam County, interviewing a woman for another story. "Have you seen our Pyramid People?" she asked. I drove out State Road 142, a two-lane blacktop through a largely unpopulated sector of the county. I negotiated a curve in the road and found myself staring at a collection of pyramids, sphinxes, and statues of Ancient Egyptian deities. I'd found Tama-Re, the Egypt of the West. I soon learned the land had been settled by a secretive community of blacks, mostly from Brooklyn, calling themselves the United Nuwaubian Nation of Moors. Who were these people, and what were they doing in rural Georgia? To find answers, I went to Brooklyn, to the former home base of York's group, previously called Ansaru Allah Community. I was traveling with a copy of an FBI intelligence report that stated York's group had been involved in a series of major crimes, including the assassination of a community activist who tried to oppose them. I traded a copy of the report to Brooklyn homicide detectives, who gave me access to the files on the activist's murder. I wrote a story in which I quoted a NYPD Detective as naming a former thug connected to York as a suspect in the re-opened murder investigation. I thought I had solved a 20-year-old murder mystery. Before I left New York, I celebrated at a fancy restaurant and told my story to the bartender. He was amazed and congratulated me effusively. Unfortunately, the bartender was not my editor. Back in Atlanta, the managing editor neutered the story and buried the connection to the assassination somewhere in the middle. I was devastated, but one of York's discarded concubines read the article and wrote an anonymous letter pleading for help to protect the children of Tama-Re. Still, it would be another four years before York was finally arrested, exposed as one of the nation's worst sexual predators, and sentenced to 135 years in the federal "Supermax" prison in Colorado.

ATLANTA JOURNAL CONSTITUTION, SEPTEMBER 20, 1998

EATONTON — THE "Master Teacher" and his followers left a tough Brooklyn neighborhood in New York five years ago for 400-plus acres of Putnam County cow pasture and piney woods.

They dropped their connections to Islam and their Muslim garb. They changed their group's name from Ansaru Allah Community to the United Nuwaubian Nation of Moors.

The leader, a 53-year-old New Jersey native who was born Dwight York, changed his name from Isa Muhammad to Dr. Malachi Z. York. And the part of their new home base that fronts the highway between Eatonton and Shadydale is elaborately landscaped with icons of their new identity: statues of Egyptian deities, pyramids, an obelisk and a sphinx.

Yet their move to this small dairy farming county of 14,000 has not been free of legal and cultural clashes. The group has an annual Savior's Day festival in late June coinciding with York's birthday, when thousands of adherents and curious outsiders gather at the farm, coming from around the country and from several nations.

Mostly, they stay to themselves on the property they call Egypt of the West, but in public hearings over matters such as the commercial rezoning of the farm and their operation of a nightclub without a permit, hundreds of their members have filled the main county courtroom.

York vehemently denies his group is a cult. He prefers to call it a fraternity, specifically Lodge 19 of the Ancient Mystic Order of Melchizedek. But some in Putnam County see cult-like signs in the group's deference to York as its pre-eminent leader; in its requiring new members to make a secrecy pledge and fill out an application that contains questions about their sex life, their bank accounts and their willingness to break ties with the outside world; and in claims in Nuwaubian publications that soon there will come a day when more than 100,000 members will be transported by spaceship to another galaxy.

Beyond the cult issue, other questions have arisen concerning York's past. He has acknowledged he spent three years in a New York prison in the 1960s for assault, resisting arrest and possession of a dangerous weapon.

And in the past few months, a 1993 FBI intelligence report has surfaced, and it describes the New York version of the group as a front for a wide range of criminal activity, including arson, welfare fraud and extortion. The report also links a former member of the New York group to the unsolved 1979 killing of Horace Greene, a community activist who was opposing the group's expansion.

The Nuwaubians have leveled charges of racism, conspiracy and harassment at some officials in Putnam County, where about one-third of the residents are black. In response, county officials and black leaders have expressed concerns that York and the Nuwaubians, nearly all of whom are black, are trying to stir up racial hostility and build their political power so they can dominate local politics or set up a separate government.

York denied the criminal allegations and claimed the surfacing of the report is part of an effort by opponents in Putnam County to discredit him. "I see the game," York said. "They don't want a positive black image here. They're making me out to be a monster. I'm not a monster."

Victor Grieg, who has been a spokesman for the group, said the Nuwaubians "came to live in peace." However, he added, "The good ol' boys are not accustomed to people of color controlling their own lives."

County Commissioner Sandra Adams-Prevost said she resents the Nuwaubians' claims of racially motivated harassment. "My main concern is the divisions they've caused in the community, black and white," said Adams-Prevost, who is black. "Because they can't get what they want, it's racial."

York acknowledges he is trying to build political power, partly by encouraging some followers to move to the area and register to vote. "We want our own county, our own fire department, our own hospital," York said. "That way, we won't have to deal with the racism."

The stretch of Ga. 142 between Eatonton and Shadydale seems an unremarkable road until it passes what looks like a large-scale model of the ancient Egyptian City of the Dead. An estimated 100 to 150 people live in a collection of about 15 double-wide trailers in a treeless section of the property.

York, who owns the land, lives in a modern home set back off the road. "This is our paradise, this is our Mecca, in a sense," said York, who is described in the group's publications as the Master Teacher. The Nuwaubians are, for the most part, urban black people who have come to Middle Georgia to establish York's farm as the base for their renewal of an ancient culture.

Although Nuwaubian publications have said the plan is to turn the property into an Egypt of the West, York recently said he does not intend to make it a tourist attraction, that he only wants to operate concessions to raise money for the group.

County officials estimate that up to 500 people living in Putnam County are affiliated with the Nuwaubian group. In some Nuwaubian publications, York is described as the embodiment of a being from the planet Rizq. Followers believe that a select group of 144,000 will be transported by spaceship to another galaxy.

Other group literature states that York is a descendant of Ben York, the black crewman who accompanied the Lewis and Clark expedition; still others depict him as Chief Black Eagle, a reincarnated leader of the lost tribe of Yamassee Indians.

In real life, he joined the Black Panther Party after his prison stint and later in the early 1970s formed a black nationalist group on the streets of Brooklyn. York said his main pursuits outside the group lie in the field of popular music, where he has been a performer and a producer.

York said he resents any comparisons of the Nuwaubians to infamous cult groups such as those who followed Jim Jones in Guyana or David Koresh in Waco or Heaven's Gate, the mass suicide cult in California that also was awaiting a spaceship.

"We're no suicide cult," he said. He stressed that people who become affiliated with the Nuwaubians never are required to turn over all their possessions and cash to the group's coffers or to him personally.

People can inquire about the Nuwaubians through Internet sites or through bookstores in dozens of metro areas around the country and in most larger cities in Georgia. In some of the stores, classes are offered in Nuwaubian teachings and language, which York devised and named Nuwaubic.

To join the fraternity, applicants must sign a secrecy pledge and fill out a 10-page application. Questions on the application form include: Do you have ties in the world that you feel you cannot break? (Explain). Do you have a bank account? Where? Amount in account? How many times do you have sex a week? What are your feelings about homosexuality? Do you have a communicable disease?

York contends the Nuwaubians' are not out to subvert any established religions. "We believe in all the holy books," he said. The tenets of the Nuwaubians' beliefs, often referred to in group publications as "right reason," are taken mostly from the 39 scrolls, which are tracts totaling about 1,800 pages and written by York.

In the tracts, York draws from Christian, Jewish and Islamic traditions, mixing them with ancient Egyptian history and mythology. Some of the characters in the scrolls are recognizable from Bible stories, but the illustrations depict the characters with dark skin and Egyptian features.

York said he selected the land in Putnam County for his site because of its proximity to the Indian rock formations known as Rock Eagle. In the first few years after moving to Putnam County, the group generally kept a low profile, but recently that has changed.

BILL OSINSKI

Sheriff Howard Sills said the group has demonstrated a pattern of "a seemingly willful indifference to the law and local ordinances." In addition, he said, some of the group's publications and members have said they are part of a separate sovereign nation.

Mostly, the run-ins have been in regard to zoning and building disputes or traffic violations that have escalated into confrontations leading to arrests, he said. But Sills said he thinks the prospect of violent confrontations is real and that he has requested federal help in investigating and monitoring the group. He said he has not received an official reply.

In April, Sills padlocked a building on York's farm that was being operated as a nightclub called Club Ramses. The building had a permit to be used only as a storage facility. The Nuwaubians were fined $45,000 for the violation, which they are appealing. Sills filed a civil suit against the group to keep the closure in effect.

A recent consent agreement provides for the club to remain closed unless the group gets the proper zoning and permits. Gus Kilgore, pastor of the New Life Outreach Christian Center in Eatonton, said he has opposed the Nuwaubians because he considers some of York's teachings and writings to be anti-Christian.

Kilgore has spoken out against the group on some of his local radio broadcasts and is trying to form an alliance of black and white clergy to oppose the group. "They've come here and are saying, 'Move over and let us have our way, and if you don't let us have it, we'll take it,'" Kilgore said.

The Nuwaubians sometimes have "shown a hostile spirit" in their relations with county residents, Kilgore said, adding that he has received anonymous threatening letters.

It isn't the first time York and his group have generated ill will in the community. One reason he decided to leave Brooklyn and drop all the Muslim trappings of the organization he had built there, York said, was that there was open hostility between his group and some black Muslim organizations. In addition, he said, he had been the target of seven or eight assassination attempts, which he saw as the work of hostile Muslim groups.

The 1993 FBI report, made available to The Atlanta Journal-Constitution by a Putnam County official who asked to remain anonymous, indicates the group generated controversy while based in New York. When asked about the report, an FBI spokesman in New York said it was Justice Department policy not to confirm the existence of such a report or the status of any investigation. The agency is authorized to investigate internal threats to national security through its division focusing on domestic terrorism.

Internal reports on groups such as Ansaru Allah would not be unusual, according to federal and local law enforcement officials, even if the agency never takes any action in reaction to what it learns. The agency apparently never shared its findings with New York law enforcement officials, and no criminal charges related to allegations in the report have been filed against York or any of his followers.

But that could change. In an effort to further investigate the report's allegations, the Journal-Constitution informed New York homicide officials of the report. In addition, the case files of the Horace Greene investigation were reviewed, and some of the people mentioned in that case were located and interviewed.

As a result, the investigation of the Greene killing has been reactivated, and Roy Savage, who was named the killer in the FBI report, is a suspect, according to Frank O'Keefe, a homicide detective in the New York Police Department.

The FBI report described Savage as an enforcer for the Ansaru Allah Community. The motive for killing Greene, according to the report, was that he was resisting the group's efforts to take control of his neighborhood.

Savage now is serving a 98-year sentence in a New Jersey prison for the 1983 dismemberment killings of two of the five women with whom he left Ansaru Allah in 1979, after the murder of Greene.

York said the group has no connection to the killing of Greene, whom he described as a "buddy," though the FBI report described the two as opponents. He said Savage "may have been a member" of Ansaru Allah but never more than a fringe member. York described Savage as a "nut."

Former New York police Detective Bill Clark, who led a cold-case investigation of the Greene killing, said he believed the killer may have been a member of Ansaru Allah. He said he was hindered in looking into the matter by city policies that categorized Ansaru Allah and other black Muslim properties as "sensitive sites."

"Normally, I would've gotten in with them right away and started pulling the men out for lineups," Clark said. Instead, he had to make an appointment just to interview York in the case, he said.

Jack Eutsey, a former police detective in Newark, N.J., said he encountered similar bureaucratic barriers about four years later when he was investigating Savage. Eutsey said he wanted to enter Ansaru Allah to find a woman who had lived with Savage and returned with her daughter to Ansaru Allah after the 1983 killings.

New York police insisted he make an appointment, but Eutsey resisted. "I just garbed up and went in," he said.

Wearing Muslim attire, he got inside and persuaded witnesses to leave with him and testify against Savage, he said.

The FBI report mentions arson and other activity in New York connected to Ansaru Allah's efforts to control city neighborhoods by making merchants hire them as security guards. It says the group recruited women to join so they could sign up for welfare and share their benefits with other members.

York said he is aware of the FBI's surveillance of him and his group. He believes federal agents have targeted him because he has had ties to Sudan, where the United States recently bombed a factory believed to be processing materials for chemical weapons for terrorists.

The name Ansaru is taken from the Ansaar, a Sudanese ethnic group, he said. York said he has traveled to Sudan, and he has a Sudanese ex-wife and two children who live there. However, he noted, his former contacts in Sudan have grown mostly hostile toward him because he no longer is Muslim.

York said he was questioned by FBI agents in 1995 regarding his Sudanese connections. He regarded the interview as a routine screening related to security for the 1996 Olympics. He said he passed a lie detector test and that nothing further came of the matter.

Now that he has been in Georgia for five years, York said he wants to focus on developing the Nuwaubian community. "We're all about trying to save the children," he said.

According to Putnam County school officials, members of the Nuwaubian group have applied to home-school about 150 children. York said the group sees such a step as necessary to protect the group's children from violence and gangs that may be prevalent in public schools.

York said he has decided to encourage more political activity among Nuwaubians in an effort to remove from office the county officials he believes are opposing them. "It's the only way I'll get fair treatment," York said.

County records show that more than 150 voters who have registered in recent years have identified themselves as Moors, a sign that they probably are affiliated with the Nuwaubians. There are about 9,200 registered voters in the county.

Amid the growing controversy, York said he is reconsidering his plans for building an Egypt of the West in Middle Georgia. "I'm thinking I may be going to take my family and go somewhere else," he said.

BILL OSINSKI

Bill's notes: This story was the first time I was able to get an account of one of York's many, many victims into print. For several years, I had known York was a sexual predator of epic proportions, but my paper wasn't about to get ahead of the investigation, not while York was claiming to be a persecuted religious leader. York's indictment gave us the legal cover we needed, and I hurried to Orlando to get this victim's story. The girl who told me her story remained stoic throughout, so I sought to do the same, on the surface. Inside, though, I wondered whether I'd have to excuse myself and be sick. Of course, my story had to be submitted to the newspaper's lawyer, who soothed the nervous editors by saying York was "beyond being libeled."

ATLANTA JOURNAL CONSTITUTION
JUNE 2, 2002

ORLANDO — IT began, the girl said, when the man they all called "The Lamb" told her that submitting to his sexual desires was her ticket to heaven.

She was 12; he was 50 or 51.

Nuwaubian leader Dwight York started summoning her to do cleaning chores in his home on the sect's farm in Putnam county, she said. Soon after that, the encounters with York at the farm where her mother had brought her to live turned sexual, she said. It would continue for about the next 2 1/2 years — sometimes every night — and she obeyed, she said.

Sometimes, other adults and children were present or participating with York in the sex acts, she said.

"If you do this, you'll go to heaven, you'll be saved," she said York told her during their encounters. "I knew it was wrong from the get-go."

Now 17, the girl has broken free of the farm and York's influence.

She has told her story, first to her father and then to a Putnam County grand jury that recently indicted York, now 56, on 116 counts relating to molesting underage girls and boys. Those charges were brought shortly after York's arrest May 8 on federal charges of transporting children across state lines for illegal sexual activity.

The girl is named as a victim in 13 counts of the state indictment and as a witness in four others. She and her father spoke with the Journal Constitution at their home in Orlando.

Putnam County Sheriff Howard Sills, who spearheaded the four-year investigation that led to York's arrest, said he has not personally interviewed the girl or others who testified before the state grand jury. But he said he believes they are credible witnesses. "I think the indictment speaks for itself," Sills said.

"Could all these people be lying? Yes. But could a spaceship land tomorrow in the back of the jail? In the same way, yes." The sheriff said he has "never been involved in a child molestation case where so many people have come forward."

During a recent hearing at which York was denied bond, an FBI agent testified that the government has identified 35 people allegedly molested by York as children. The victims were as young as 4, the agent testified.

'THE STORY IS TOO CRAZY'

The 17-year-old girl is on the honor roll in her high school and plans to go to college. She can speak dry-eyed and matter-of-factly about her experience inside the Nuwaubian group, even laughing at times at what she sees now as a bizarre but difficult experience in the cult-like group.

Ed Garland, York's defense attorney, declined to comment for this story. He has previously suggested that the witnesses against York may have been coached by either their relatives or by police.

The girl denied that she has received any form of coaching. "No one would know how to coach me," she said. "The story is too crazy."

Regardless of what happens in court, the girl's family has been shattered and divided by their associations with York's groups. The girl's mother and one of her older sisters remain loyal to York; the mother continues to live on the 400-acre Putnam County farm that is the base for York's group, the United Nuwaubian Nation of Moors.

York and 100 to 200 of his followers came to Georgia in 1993 from Brooklyn, N.Y., where they had formed a group called Ansaru Allah Community. In New York, the group was Muslim-oriented in ideology, costume and religious practices; while in Georgia, they have adopted practices and garb from ancient Egypt and have decorated their farm with Egyptian- style pyramids, obelisks and statues.

York is referred to as the "Master Teacher" and "The Lamb." In some of the group's literature, York claims to be a godlike being from a planet he calls Rizq.

The entanglement of the girl's family with York goes back to the early 1970s in Trinidad. York went there to establish a branch of his group, the Ansaru Allah Community, which was then based in Brooklyn, N.Y., the father said. He said York's brand of black historical consciousness mixed with observance of Islamic religious practices appealed to him, and he became affiliated with the group, which did not practice communal living in Trinidad, as it did in Brooklyn.

The father married a woman who had become pregnant by York. They raised that child, a daughter, and had six children of their own, including the 17-year-old, he said.

In the early 1980s, his wife took the eldest daughter to Brooklyn to meet York, the girl's biological father who had never supported her, he said. They decided to stay, his wife becoming one of York's wives, he said.

The father said he and his children followed the woman to the Ansaru Allah Community but stayed only a few months. "I couldn't even talk to her," he said about his wife.

Some of the apartments in the complex of apartment houses on Bushwick Avenue were rat-infested, and others had no electricity and open holes in the floors, the father said. The men and women lived in separate buildings, with the women staying in the community and doing York's office work, while the men were sent out to the streets of New York to peddle things such as incense and York's books and pamphlets, he said.

He said he worked and lived in the New York area and kept the children with him. His wife would stay with the family sometimes, but also would return to Ansaru Allah. The couple separated for good in the early 1990s, with the wife taking their four daughters back with her to York, who at that time spent most of his time at his rural estate in Sullivan County, New York.

Their two sons were grown by this time. In 1994, the mother and the couple's two youngest daughters went to the farm in Putnam County; the older two daughters had left on their own.

By this time, York had changed the name of the group to the United Nuwaubian Nation of Moors; most of the Islamic practices and ideology were dropped. And he promised to lead a select group of his followers to a form of extragalactic salvation, the father said.

The girl, who is the fifth of six children, said the living conditions for her and the other children were "very bad." Their doublewide trailer had no air- conditioning, broken windows and cracked plywood floors, she said. Their food consisted mostly of staples, such as oatmeal, rice, beans, carrots and cabbage, she said.

When she was about 12, she and some other girls her age started being called to York's house on the farm. She was told she was to help keep house for York, she said. Some of the women in the group started to ask her sexually explicit questions, such as, "Have you ever been with a boy?" she said.

They told her about some of the sexual things that York might want her to do, she said. After York would have sex with her, he would order her not to tell anyone, especially her mother, about what he did with her, she said. "He said if I told her, she would be punished," the girl said.

So, the girl kept her meetings with York a secret. She said she knew she wanted to leave, but she also knew she'd have to be older before she could manage to find her way out. In the meantime, she worked in York's office, sometimes preparing stories for the Nuwaubian newspaper.

One night in 1999, she sneaked back into York's office and called her father in New York asking him to come to Georgia to get her. "She said something bad had happened to her, but she wouldn't say what," the father said.

The next day, the father and two of the girl's older siblings arrived at the Nuwaubian compound. They were allowed past the security gate because the guard didn't recognize them, he said. His daughter had been watching for them and made a run for the car. Her mother saw her leaving and called to her.

She assured her mother that she wanted to leave, and she did, taking nothing but the clothes she was wearing. A few months later, the father sent a plane ticket for the youngest daughter, and she rejoined him in New York.

He divorced his wife not long after getting his daughters back, and his ex-wife remains on the Nuwaubian compound, as far as he knows. He said he still cannot understand why his wife, an educated woman, remains loyal to York.

After his daughter rejoined him, she was moody, rebellious and reluctant to discuss any details of her life in the Nuwaubian community, he said.

A DESIRE TO TELL THE PUBLIC

But about a year ago, he overheard her and her younger sister talking about how York had molested her. He said he was outraged and shocked, but he was able to persuade his daughter to tell the full story. "It was like his spell over her was broken," he said.

He called the police in Florida, who told him he would have to report the crime to Georgia authorities. Within a day or two, he took his daughter to FBI offices in Orlando to be interviewed by the agents working on the York investigation.

The father said he wants the justice system to deal fairly but harshly with York. He agreed to be interviewed and to allow his daughter to be interviewed for this story, he said, because he wants people to know how his family was damaged.

"York has no respect for humanity. Somebody had to stand up to him," the father said. "And I had to stand up for my daughter." The father said he has contacted an attorney in Georgia for the purpose of filing civil litigation against York. He added that although his daughter has not spoken to him about the details of her experiences with York, he is tormented by visions of her screaming, all to no avail.

"All the time my daughter was screaming, there was no one to help her," he said. "For every scream my daughter screamed, he should spend 10 years in jail."

Bill's notes: For approximately four years, I had to fight to keep writing stories on the Nuwaubian cult. The cult leader, Dwight York, claimed that he was being persecuted by a Cracker sheriff; all he wanted to do was to live in peace with his people on their land. I later learned that York would lead his followers in praying that harm would come to the sheriff (Howard Sills) and to me. York, of course, was lying, but it wasn't until after he was indicted that I was allowed to write this story. One of the big reasons it was published was that one of the paper's editors had a relative who'd been in the cult. It is still hard for me to believe that someone so evil was able to get away with it for so long (35 years). The cult saga became the basis for my non-fiction book "Ungodly".

E ATONTON — FOR more than three decades, Dwight York was a god to his people.

But the way he lived as a man was decidedly unholy, says a group of his former followers.

It didn't matter whether he assumed the trappings of an Egyptian-style deity — as the leader of a group based on a former cattle farm in Putnam County and called the United Nation of Nuwaubian Moors — or whether he claimed to be a descendant of a legendary Muslim warrior prophet leading the Ansaru Allah Community, a group based in a collection of apartment houses on Bushwick Avenue in Brooklyn, N.Y. The contradictions between what York claimed to be and what he was were the same, the former followers say:

While he restricted and controlled the sexual relationships of most of his followers, he practiced total sexual freedom, with any woman, girl or boy he chose, fathering 100 or more illegitimate children over the years.

While he demanded his followers give him unquestioned loyalty and obedience, plus all or most of their possessions, and work long hours without pay, he held them in contempt and considered them fools for believing in him.

While he publicly claimed he was a victim of racial discrimination because he is black, he privately preached racial hatred toward whites.

While most of his followers lived in squalor, he lived in luxury.

York's own arrogance, and a few of the children he sired, are what finally brought his Wizard of Oz-like charade to an end. He now sits in a jail, indicted in both federal and state courts on charges of sexual abuse of children. The 116-count state indictment, which is expected to be expanded in the months ahead, represents perhaps the largest prosecution of its kind in Georgia courts.

Some of those closest to York – the children he exiled, the women he discarded after they bore him babies – played pivotal roles in building the government's case against him.

York's attorney, Ed Garland, was unavailable for comment for this article. However, in a previous court argument, Garland has suggested that witnesses who have participated in the York investigation may have been pressured or coached, either by their relatives or by law enforcement agents.

The former followers interviewed for this article include:

➢ A son of York's who broke with him after learning his father was having sex with his 14-year-old girlfriend.
➢ A daughter of York's who was shunned from the community after she refused his sexual advances.
➢ A woman who was expelled from the community while she was pregnant with her third child by York.
➢ Two victim-witnesses in the child molestation charges and the father of one victim.
➢ A young man who lived at the Putnam County farm for about two years.

All of them asked that their names not be used. Some of them made that request because of their participation in the case, while others said they are concerned for their safety.

During York's bond hearing, an FBI agent testified that at least two of the witnesses reported they have been threatened, either by York or by his supporters.

The followers tell the story of a man who used the promise of salvation for a select 144,000, whom he would choose, mixed in with an ideology of racial pride and pseudo-religious doctrines, to create a cult of followers who had near-fanatical loyalty. But all York was really interested in was the money and the sex, they say.

York's son recalled his father once saying he would dress up like a nun for the kind of money he was getting.

THE EARLY YEARS

Just who, then, is Dwight York? Not an easy question to answer, even if all one wants is the man's name.

Among York's aliases are Isa Abdullah, Isa Muhammad, Imam Isa, Imam Isa Abu-Bakr, Imam Isa Al-Hadi Al-Mahdi, Rabboni, Yashuah, Melchisedek, Yanuwn, Nayya, Dr. Malachi Z. York, Chief Black Eagle, The Lamb, and Baba (the pet name he encouraged his victims to call him).

His group has been called Nubian Islamic Hebrews, Ansar Pure Sufi, Nubians, Ansaru Allah Community, Washitaw Tribe, United Nuwaubian Nation of Moors, Lodge 19 of the Ancient Order of Melchizedek and, most recently, the Holy Seed Baptist Synagogue.

He was born in New Jersey in June 1945. When he was 19, he was convicted of assault, resisting arrest and possession of a dangerous weapon and he spent three years in a New York state prison.

According to his son and daughter, York told of a relative having molested him as a child and of being raped while he was jailed.

After his release, York became affiliated with the State Street Mosque in Brooklyn in the late 1960s, during the peak years of the Black Power movement. He started his own group, first on Coney Island, then in Brooklyn.

The group settled into a headquarters on Bushwick Avenue in Brooklyn. Though it professed to be primarily a religious group, it also promoted the doctrines of black racial superiority and hatred of whites, according to the report of a 1993 investigation of the group by an FBI domestic terrorism unit, as well as to Abu Ameenah Bilal Philips, a Muslim scholar who studied the group.

The original vision for the group, then called Ansaru Allah Community, was that of an orthodox Muslim community, where the brightest of the children would be raised to become skilled professionals, according to York's son. This son is the fifth of six children of York and Dorothy Mae Johnson, also known as Zubadah Muhammad, who is believed to be York's first and only legal wife.

York's son recalled that his father was fascinated with sleight-of-hand tricks. York used to extend his hands over his favored followers, adding a dramatic poof of dust, but the son discovered the "dust" came from trick pills secreted in his father's pockets.

In its early years in Brooklyn, the group was given credit by police and in New York newspaper articles for cleaning up what had been a drug-infested neighborhood. The group expanded to a collection of about 12 buildings and a mosque that York built, and affiliated branches were opened in about a dozen U.S. cities and in Canada, Britain, Trinidad and Jamaica.

York's son recalled that one of his duties when he was an adolescent was to take suitcases full of cash to York's trusted female aides.

According to the FBI intelligence report, however, the expansion was fueled by criminal activity, including extortion, arson and welfare fraud. For example, the report stated, when York's group wanted to buy another building and the owner was reluctant to sell at the price offered, the building was firebombed.

The men in the group were mostly sent out to peddle group literature and items such as incense on the streets of New York, while the women maintained the community and cared for the children.

York was never indicted for any of the criminal activity described in the FBI report. That report was not completed until 1993, and by that time, the days of Ansaru Allah were already growing short.

LEAVING NEW YORK

By the late 1980s and early 1990s, York had started spending much of his time at a rural property in Sullivan County, N.Y., that he called Camp Jazzir.

It was during this time, York's son said, that he started seeing his father's dark side.

There was a select group of girls who seemed to have special access to York, said the son, who was about 14 or 15 then. One day, he said, he discovered a videotape in his father's bedroom that showed his own 14-year-old girlfriend performing sex acts with toys.

The girl admitted that she had been having sex with the older York. After that, the son said, he started to speak out against his father's sexual practices within the community.

York's daughter also had a falling-out with her father.

When she was 18, in the early 1990s, she said, a woman in the community came to her and told her that she was to prepare to have sex with York. At the time, the daughter said, she was a virgin who had been raised by the cult's strict religious codes.

She refused and was soon banished from the community, after being married by York's order to a man hired to teach Arabic to the community's children, she said. York forbade her mother to participate in the wedding, she added.

Soon, York's son and his mother joined the daughter in exile. The daughter recalled having to make trips back to Ansaru Allah to smuggle out some of her mother's clothing and possessions.

The son said his mother became despondent after learning that York had been molesting the children. He said she told him: "We set them up like lambs to be slaughtered by the wolf." She died in 1995.

By 1993, the pressure on York was increasing from the outside, as well as from within.

Besides the FBI investigation, Philips wrote a book on York's group titled "The Ansar Cult." Philips, now a teacher in the United Arab Emirates, described Ansaru Allah as a "heretic, pseudo-Muslim sect."

The book includes interviews Philips conducted with about a dozen former members of the group. They described Ansaru Allah as a place where the ordinary members had insufficient food and slept in overcrowded rooms, often on the floor.

York slept with whomever he chose, while husbands and wives in the community were not allowed to sleep with each other, they said.

York mated men and women as he saw fit, and he determined when and where they could have sexual relations, they said.

The Philips book included a Muslim cleric's decree that no true Muslim should be associated with York's group.

About that time, York dropped all Muslim religious practices and costumes and moved to Georgia.

THE GEORGIA YEARS

In 1993, York paid approximately $1 million for a 400-acre farm in rural Putnam County.

At first, York sought to claim identity with Native Americans. His group's tracts said he had chosen to move to Putnam County because of the county's Native American historic site at Rock Eagle.

Soon, though, the group changed identities again, this time going all-out with an Egyptian motif. York had pyramids, obelisks, and statues of ancient Egyptian deities built, mostly along the part of the land that fronts on Ga. 142. The group assumed the name United Nation of Nuwaubian Moors, and it called the farm the Egypt of the West. There were never more than 100 to 200 people actually living on the farm property, although an undetermined number of people affiliated with the Nuwaubians has moved to Putnam and surrounding counties since the farm was established.

York tried to claim status as a sovereign government for the Nuwaubians. He said he and his followers should be allowed to run their own affairs because of the racial discrimination he was being subjected to.

Inside the cult, things went much the same as they had in Brooklyn, according to the former members. About four years ago, child welfare officials received an anonymous complaint that children were being molested on the Nuwaubian farm.

But no one stepped forward to make an official criminal complaint.

About that time, York's son said, he learned York was continuing to have sex with underage members of the community. Some of the children were ones he remembered from when he was growing up in Ansaru Allah, he said.

Some of those children had grown up and had children by York, he said.

He came to Georgia to confront York, and he said York admitted that he was sick, but he thought he could control his sexual predations, he said.

But the son was not satisfied with his father's explanations, so about two years ago, he moved to metro Atlanta. His home soon became a sort of halfway house for people leaving the Nuwaubian community.

He recalled a time about a year ago when he told the young people staying with him about the hard times he'd had after leaving Ansaru Allah. Some of the girls in the group started to cry, he said, because they'd been told he and the others who left had deliberately abandoned them.

Then the girls started to tell him about the extent of the sexual abuse, York's son said. At that point, he called Putnam Sheriff Howard Sills and said he had information about his father.

The next day, the son met with Sills and FBI agents in Atlanta. He brought with him a young woman who has become one of the key witnesses in the investigation.

At about the same time, York called several of his children together for a meeting in New York, according to the daughter. She said she thought he wanted to make peace, but it turned out that he just needed money.

She said York thought the children, especially his sons, should want what he had, that is, power, money and women. He said he never believed his own rhetoric and that he considered those who did to be fools or idiots, she said.

In a related development around the same time, two women filed separate paternity suits against York in Clarke County.

One woman said she was expelled from the group while pregnant with her third child by York. She said she had been sick during that pregnancy and was charged with malingering, but part of the reason she was expelled was that York knew the child would have serious birth defects and, thus, not be worthy of being claimed. The child, a boy now about 10 years old, is profoundly retarded and has several major medical problems. He is a ward of the state of Florida and lives in a nursing home.

The other woman said she had one son by York when she was 18. But she has also told investigators about molestation by York while she was under age.

These two women and York's son said 100 would be a conservative estimate of the number of children York has fathered.

THE FOLLOWERS

The former members of York's groups interviewed were all asked why they, and people like them, would give so much to a man who, by their own accounts, gave them so little in return.

Some cited York's charisma, his ability to transmit absolute conviction in his arcane, ever-changing ideologies. Whatever York says became part of what they call "Right Knowledge," and everything and everybody else is simply wrong, they said.

There is also a racial undercurrent to some of York's appeal. In a tape showing him speaking to a group of his followers, York calls white people "devils." He advocates the religion he concocted, rather than what he called the secondhand religions passed down by white people.

In much of York's literature, he claims only 144,000 people will be allowed into heaven. Since he is the leader, anyone who wants to be part of that group must follow him.

And since he sets himself up as a god, no one can question him, the followers say. That is how he gets people to accept the miserable conditions and the forced breakups of their families, they said.

It is also a line that he has used to get children to agree to have sex with him, according to one teenager who has testified to the state grand jury. She said in a recent interview that York told her submitting to him in sex was the way she'd get to heaven.

Experts from agencies that monitor cults and hate groups say they have seen these patterns before.

BILL OSINSKI

Recently, the Nuwaubians were placed on a list of hate groups by the Southern Poverty Law Center.

"It's definitely a black supremacist group, a mirror image of white hate groups," said Bob Moser, a senior writer for the center who is preparing an article on York and the Nuwaubians for its magazine.

Moser said he has interviewed former members of the group and has viewed tapes of York speaking privately to groups of his followers.

York gets his followers to follow him blindly because they accept him as a god figure, he said. "Once you accept that Dwight York is special, then you automatically have to subordinate yourself to that authority," he said. "But instead of giving his people opportunity, he takes it away, essentially getting free labor from his followers."

Despite all the religious trappings of York's group, "for him, the bottom line is the money," Moser said.

CARICATURE OF A CULT

Phillip Arnn, senior researcher for Watchman Fellowship Inc., a Texas-based Christian anti-cult organization that maintains files on 5,000 cult-related organizations, said his group has characterized the Nuwaubians as "almost a caricature of a cult."

The group's files on the Nuwaubians included reports of gatherings where cartoon-like figures representing manifestations of beings from outer space were projected around a room, he said.

But there was also a darker side to the group, he said, particularly the often-stated beliefs of the Nuwaubians that only 144,000 people would be allowed to go to heaven and that York would be the one to do the selection.

"That is a classic antisocial, apocalyptic scenario," Arnn said.

Now, the scenario York faces is the prospect of spending many years in jail.

And there is an even sadder legacy for some of the children York is accused of molesting.

Of five children taken into protective custody by the state, four have been found to have sexually transmitted diseases.

Bill's notes: In this trial, more than 50 years ago, prosecutors attempted to punish the woman, and the woman alone, for an abortion. Today, they're still trying. The rapidity with which the jury acquitted the woman speaks loudly about where the general public stands.

BOWLING GREEN, KY. — Marla Pitchford finally rediscovered her smile yesterday, after an eight-man, four-woman jury took less than an hour to clear her of charges of performing an illegal abortion on herself.

"This is the first smile that's been on my face in a long time," said the 22-year-old former college student. Miss Pitchford had spent much of the three days in a losing battle against her emotions, as the details of her broken love affair and aborted pregnancy became the subject matter for her precedent-setting trial.

Miss Pitchford did not take the stand during her defense but spoke calmly and confidently to a crush of journalists after the verdict.

"The nightmare's over with," she said, adding that the support she has received from her family and friends during the legal proceedings has "definitely made me a stronger person." She said the experience has resulted in closer ties with her family, and that sentiment was echoed by her mother, Mrs. Jeanetta Pitchford.

"It's been hard, but it's been rewarding," Mrs. Pitchford said. The mother had sat solemnly by her daughter's side during the trial, and only after the not guilty verdict was announced did the farm wife from Scottsville allow herself some joyful tears.

No woman had ever been criminally prosecuted for performing an abortion on herself, and Flora Stuart, Miss Pitchford's attorney, said the verdict may mean that no other woman will have to face similar charges. The actual verdict was that Miss Pitchford was not guilty "on grounds of insanity."

A psychiatrist and two psychologists had testified that Miss Pitchford was suffering from "hysterical neurosis" last June, when she inserted a six-inch knitting needle into herself, causing the abortion of her 20-to-24-week-old fetus.

A psychiatrist had testified that the abortion amounted to a suicide attempt on her part.

Testimony during the trial showed that Miss Pitchford previously had sought the abortion at clinics in Louisville and Nashville at the insistence of her former fiance, 26-year-old Dwight Mundy, who was a student with her at Western Kentucky University. Their relationship ended after the abortion.

Mundy testified Tuesday as a prosecution witness, only after being indicted as an accomplice and then offered immunity from prosecution in return for his testimony.

The defense never disputed the facts of the case, contending instead that Miss Pitchford was incapable of rational thought at the time of the abortion and that the law she was prosecuted under was never intended to provide criminal sanctions for pregnant females.

The jury seemed persuaded by those arguments. One juror, 21-year-old Mrs. Vickie Porter, sobbed with joy and embraced Miss Pitchford after the verdict was announced. "There's no words for it; I'm so happy for you," Mrs. Porter told Miss Pitchford.

Mrs. Porter said "there was no question" among the jurors that a not guilty verdict should be returned. "We were all unanimous," she said, adding that only one ballot was taken during the deliberations. "I couldn't believe that we all came together so well," she said of the jurors, whose ages ranged from 21 to 70.

All of the jurors were married, and all but one have at least one child. As for the legal process that brought Miss Pitchford to trial, Mrs. Porter said she felt "it never should have come this far."

Assistant Warren County Commonwealth Attorney Tom Lewis, who helped prosecute the case, said there is no plan to appeal the verdict.

BILL OSINSKI

Lewis said Miss Pitchford was brought to trial because her act, in the view of the prosecutors, constituted a violation of the state's abortion statute. However, he conceded, the law may need some reworking. "The statute is unclear, and it's up to the General Assembly to change it," Lewis said.

When asked if he thought such changes will be made, Lewis said, "I certainly hope so."

The case has attracted attention from the national media, and the presiding judge, Warren Circuit Court Judge J. David Francis, said he was caught somewhat off guard by the media blitz.

Good-hearted theatrics were Francis' trademark throughout the proceedings which he often interrupted to make sure that the jury and the news media were provided for as best as possible.

Francis said he could not immediately discern any far-reaching legal precedents that might emerge from yesterday's verdict. Also, he said, he is not sure what specific changes need to be made in the state's abortion statute. "The General Assembly seldom seeks my advice," Francis said, "and if they asked me how to change the law, I wouldn't know what to tell them."

Under Francis' ground rules, the trial never really delved into the moral implications of the abortion issue. In the pretrial phase, he upheld a defense motion to ban the use of any other terminology besides "fetus" in references to the pregnancy of Miss Pitchford.

Lewis skirted those rules during his closing statement yesterday, when he told the jurors that while Miss Pitchford nearly died from the abortion, "the baby did die."

Acting on a strenuous objection from defense attorney Kelly Thompson, Jr., Francis cut Lewis off and admonished the prosecutor to adhere to the pretrial rulings.

Also, during his closing, Lewis attempted to refute the defense contention that the state abortion law does not apply to the pregnant female who tries to abort herself.

"A quack doctor, an abortionist, would be far better at performing an abortion than an untrained pregnant woman," Lewis said. Holding up the knitting needle, Lewis said, "If she wanted to commit suicide, why didn't she plunge this into her heart."

In her closing, Ms. Stuart stressed her contention that justice already had been denied in this case, because the man who collaborated in Miss Pitchford's pregnancy was not around to share the consequences of the abortion.

"That's the way it's always been historically," Ms. Stuart said. "The female ends up with the baby inside her, and the male walks free."

Ms. Stuart compared her client to Hester Prynne, the adultress-heroine of "The Scarlet Letter," who was made to wear a badge for her crime. "Can you as jurors deem any more punishment than Hester Prynne received from the Puritans," Ms. Stuart said, referring to the fact that if Miss Pitchford had been found guilty, she, could have faced 10 to 20 years in prison.

Miss Pitchford said she plans to visit friends in Colorado and may attend another college later.

Bill's notes: The most famous defense attorney in Georgia, Bobby Lee Cook (the model for the Andy Griffith TV series "Matlock"), was set for an expected fiery cross-examination of the prosecution's star witness, Eddie Lawrence, who brokered the shotgun murder of Sara Tokars in front of her two young sons. But the real-life day in court turned out to be as cold as the heart of Fred Tokars, the Atlanta lawyer who ordered his wife to be murdered. Tokars promised Lawrence $25,000 for the murder, but never paid up. I was assigned to try to capture the drama of the moment, but I was more taken with the banality and the methodical tone of the testimony about the extremely shocking crime. I felt unwell throughout the day, probably caused by bad oysters I'd eaten the night before; but I left town sick to my stomach from the testimony about the casual negotiations for the horrific murder. Tokars was convicted. He died in prison in 2020.

ATLANTA JOURNAL CONSTITUTION, MARCH 18, 1994

BIRMINGHAM — THE pivotal confrontation of the Fredric Tokars trial has ended, with a firsthand account of the shotgun slaying of Sara Tokars recalled as just another business deal gone bad.

Admitted murder broker Eddie Lawrence spent most of Wednesday and Thursday on the witness stand. His story was that Tokars hired him to kill Tokars' wife, Sara, and he stuck to it, despite a finger-wagging cross-examination by defense attorney Bobby Lee Cook.

His account of the killing was delivered in the same mellow monotone that he used to describe his other alleged dealings with Tokars — sham corporations, offshore bank deals that never materialized, unfinished construction projects, an abandoned foray into counterfeiting, hanging out in nightclubs hoping to recruit drug dealers into Tokars' alleged money-laundering schemes, and a few unfruitful attempts to break into the Atlanta political scene.

Eddie Lawrence says Fredric Tokars never paid him $25,000 for his wife's slaying.

The cold and methodical testimony seemed matched to the mood in the courtroom. Tokars mostly avoided looking at his accuser; instead. he either fixed his gaze on the jury or made notes on a legal pad. More than half the jurors busied themselves with notetaking also.

Only once during Lawrence's testimony was it obvious the subject was a brutal killing and not just white-collar con games.

When Lawrence recounted his version of the events of the night of Sara Tokars's slaying in November 1992, Fredric Tokars took off his glasses and dabbed a tissue at his tear-misted' eyes.

Mary Bennett, Sara Tokars' sister, struggled to maintain her composure but later broke down sobbing.

But was Eddie Lawrence telling the truth? It's the central question of this federal racketeering trial, not to mention the upcoming murder trial.

The defense team contends the answer is "no." In cross-examining Lawrence, Cook assumed the lead role in the defense team's attempt to convince the jury of that. Cook started politely enough, taking the tone of a waiter at a swank restaurant. "Good afternoon, Mr. Lawrence. I'm Bobby Lee Cook, one of the lawyers for Mr. Tokars in this case, and I'll be handling your cross-examination," Cook said.

But before Lawrence could order anything from the legal menu, Cook transformed himself into a righteous country preacher. Time after time, Cook imparted an accusatory tone to his questions, by switching the modulation of his voice to evangelist level and stabbing his finger into the air for emphasis.

Each time, Lawrence dug in, remaining unimpressed and intractable, like an atheist who'd been dragged into church.

Cook would thrust: "There's a lot you can't remember, isn't there?"

And Lawrence would parry: "I'm not absolutely, positively sure when it happened, but I do know without a doubt that it did happen."

Mostly, Cook attacked Lawrence's credibility by trying to trip him up on what Cook saw as inconsistencies in various statements Lawrence has made.

Some of the questions Cook exploited included: *Was Lawrence planning to pay a legal fee to Tokars with real or counterfeit money? Why did Lawrence lie when police and Tokars' private investigator asked him about the killing? Did Lawrence try to recruit others besides alleged triggerman Curtis Rower to commit the slaying?*

But practically every time Cook attempted to expose inconsistencies, Lawrence responded by restating earlier testimony, and with added emphasis.

BILL OSINSKI

Now, the jury must now decide whether Cook's barbed questions amounted to darts or harpoons.

However, the entire courtroom was chilled by the calculatingly cold way that, according to Lawrence, murder became part of the corporate transactions between a well-known lawyer and his young, moving-on-up entrepreneurial client.

Never in their numerous conversations about killing Sara Tokars was it discussed whether it was a good idea or a bad idea, right or wrong.

Lawrence said he once suggested it might just be easier to let his wife divorce him. But once Tokars vetoed that option, Lawrence carried out his patron's order about as dispassionately as he said he'd done other errands for Tokars, such as fixing the plumbing in Tokars's bathroom or making runs to the bank with drug dealers' cash.

Lawrence said he fit the murder into a day otherwise filled with ordinary chores and minor crimes. Before he and Rower drove to Sara Tokars's house, Lawrence picked up his 8-year-old child at the home of the child's grandmother and dropped the child off with another grandmother.

Also, Lawrence managed to drop in for short visits with two other friends. After the killing, Lawrence said, he made a couple of stops so that Rower could buy himself some drugs. And in the only conversation he said he had with Fredric Tokars after the killing, Tokars said only that the killing was a tragedy and he was going to Florida.

Lawrence said he never got the $25,000 that Tokars had promised him. That meant that Lawrence never paid the $5,000 he'd promised to the accused gunman, Rower, nor the $500 he'd promised to Rower's sister, who helped make Lawrence a suspect.

So, he said, Tokars stiffed him in their last business deal.

TRAIL OF FOLLY

Picture of the author and fellow journalist and drinking buddy Dave Barry at a dive bar in New Orleans during the 1988 Republican National Convention. Photo courtesy of Dave Barry.

Bill's notes: I had a blast covering this presidential campaign, but I repeatedly got the sense that the events I was rushing to and writing about had little or no relation to the governance of this nation. Maybe that's why we get the presidents we get. Still, I met some great folks along the way. Bob Squier, one of the operatives I quoted in this and many other stories, was a great guy — gracious, professional, and insightful. After this story ran, he told me he'd clipped it and posted it on his office billboard, with a note saying, "This guy gets it." I felt like I'd won the Pulitzer.

C ALL IT THE year of Post-it politics.
The presidential campaign that took two years and cost more than $200 million has been detached from the bulletin board of the American consciousness as if it had all been just one of those mildly sticky memos.

"It was almost the election that wasn't there," said Larry Sabato, political scientist at the University of Virginia. "It went quietly into the night on little cat feet, dirty little cat's feet," he said, apologizing to poet Carl Sandburg.

All the strident themes of George Bush's victorious campaign — furloughed murderers on the rampage, the flag being trampled by the Democrats, "liberal" as a curse word — seemed to vaporize the day after the election.

Now that it's president-elect Bush, the talk is all about healing and governing by bipartisan consensus. And so much else that seemed so important during the campaign has been reduced to the trivia-question file: What event captivated the entire political community for most of a year and then became instantly irrelevant the moment it ended? The caucuses of Iowa, State Woebegone.

What formerly front-running, press-hating candidate was last seen as a commentator for an Italian radio network? Gary "Catch Me If You Can" Hart.

Well then, did anything of significance happen while America was choosing the next leader of the Free World?

Some who have observed the long trek say they can see a few milestones as they look back in review at Campaign '88:

* The "de-wimpificatlon" of George Bush. By most accounts, Bush evolved as a tough, effective, campaigner, while Democrat Michael Dukakis devolved into the timorous no-show that people used to accuse Bush of being.
* Another two-by-four between the eyes for the Democratic donkey. Once again, the Democrats demonstrated mule-like intransigence in nominating a candidate out of step with the majority of the electorate; but the experts say the party had best concentrate on defining and selling itself, rather than tinkering again with its nominating process.

"The last time we changed the rules, we almost wiped out the two-party system," joked Democratic consultant Bob Squier.

* Negative campaigning via television advertisements reached new heights, or depths, for a presidential campaign. Mudslinging always has been around, but it's never dominated a presidential campaign before.
* Poll-mania. Public opinion polling, especially by major television networks, proliferated throughout the campaign season. Some saw these polls as manufactured news, particularly when television networks would release their own poll and then broadcast a news story seemingly tailored to confirm the poll's findings.
* The Duke who wouldn't put up his dukes. Somehow, the Democrats managed to trash a real opportunity to regain the White House by nominating a national candidate who displayed an obvious ineptness at and distaste for national politics. Dukakis proved himself a worthy successor to George McGovern and Walter Mondale.

"The one thing that really stuck out in this campaign was the tremendous transformation of George Bush's personality," said Atlanta-based pollster Claibourne Darden. "Nothing else is close. It was a most magnificent turnaround."

Somewhere between his funereal announcement speech in October 1987 and the Republican convention in August 1988, Bush discarded his whiny, high-pitched delivery and the "old maid's flail" that had characterized his public presence, Darden said.

In place of those quirks, Bush developed a "wonderfully concerned frown" and a dynamic ability to make his point, Darden said. It didn't matter that there wasn't much content in the lines Bush delivered to laud vice presidential nominee Dan Quayle for not burning his draft card (one of the few things Quayle was never accused of) and to proclaim that Bush was not a card-carrying member of the ACLU (the furthest thought from anyone's mind); the lines had resonance and impact, Darden said.

"He was almost into iambic pentameter," Darden said. "He was really nailing that stuff. Edgar Allen Poe would have been proud."

During the early phases of the campaign, said Washington-based political analyst William Schneider, the Democrats couldn't wait to take on Bush for the general election. "They were saying, 'If we can't beat George Bush, we'd better find another country,'" Schneider said. Bush effectively reversed that momentum by going full-throttle into an attack-Dukakis mode, he said.

"If the election had been a referendum on George Bush's judgment, Bush would have lost," Schneider said, referring to gaping lapses in judgment Bush exhibited in, for instance, the selection of Quayle and his role in the Iran-Contra affair. "But Bush skillfully changed the election to a referendum on Dukakis' values; and Dukakis couldn't defend his values; he'd never had to," he said.

Of course, the calendar also was kind to Bush. Iran-Contra and the Wall Street crash were year-old news by election time, and the campaign year turned out to be one of peace, prosperity and popularity for Bush's mentor and predecessor, Ronald Reagan.

*   Democrats' dilemma. Much has been made of the dire straits of the Democratic Party, which has now lost five of the last six presidential elections, three by electoral landslides. This time, fingers of blame are being accurately pointed at the party's bad candidate, bad strategy and a primary process loaded in favor of liberal candidates.

But something else, perhaps something more important, needs attention. Hugh Winebrenner, political scientist at Drake University, said, "The Democrats are not looking at the larger questions: What is the Democratic Party? To whom should it direct its appeal? What does it stand for?"

For 1988, the Democrats ran a "schizophrenic" campaign, trying to appeal more to the white middle-class while trusting that blacks and Hispanics would continue to vote overwhelmingly Democratic, he said. "They tried not committing to anything or anyone, and, as a result, they didn't excite anyone," Winebrenner said.

However, before the Democrats move too far to the right in order to attract middle-class votes, he said, they should remember that the fastest-growing segments of the population are Hispanics and blacks. In 20 years or less, the Democrats could forge electoral majorities by emphasizing their appeal to these voters, he said.

Until then, the Democrats would do well to de-emphasize the Iowa caucuses, said the Iowa-based Winebrenner. Liberal special-interest groups have learned how to dominate the Iowa campaigns, so that the most likely result in the future will be what happened in 1988 — a standoff among the most liberal candidates in the field, he said.

Sabato said what the Democrats need most is a thorough reality check. "What the Democrats have to come to terms with is that they represent an ideology that is nowhere near a majority ideology," he said. If the Democrats could break away from their tradition of nominating Northern liberals and open their process up to a candidate from the South or West, they'd stand a better chance of winning, he said.

Merle Black, political scientist at the University of North Carolina, said the increasing tendency of Southern voters to vote Republican in presidential elections shouldn't discourage the Democrats from looking South in their campaigns.

Although Republicans have captured an average of between 57 and 58 percent of the total Southern vote in recent elections, that is still far short of the 75 percent levels enjoyed by Democrats when they owned the Solid South in the 1930s, he said.

Democrats may be tempted to persist in their strategy of concentrating on the populous Northern states because in 1988 they lost some of these states by only a few percentage points, he said. However, he added, it is the Sun Belt states that will be gaining around 20 electoral votes after the 1990 census.

Schneider said the Democrats still will need an effective campaign message, assuming they can define themselves and develop a competitive campaign strategy. "The Democrats need to worry about what theme they can sell to the voters," he said.

While the Republicans eagerly grasped the nationalistic issue of patriotism, the Democrats shied away from nationalistic themes that might have worked for them, such as greedy practices of multinational companies and the threat of foreign competition, he said.

What they were left with was the alleged managerial skills of Dukakis, whom Schneider called "the most themeless politician I've ever seen."

If the campaign of 1988 is remembered for only one thing, that probably will be the profusion of negative television advertisements. The Bush campaign relentlessly aired commercials that depicted Dukakis as an unpatriotic coddler of criminals who was even softer on communism than he was on crime.

"The lesson of 1988, unfortunately, is negative campaigning works," Schneider said.

Advertisements that attack an opponent rather than promote the candidate who pays for them already have become a staple of state-level campaigning, he said. "But this campaign was a breakthrough," he said. "It was the first time in the television history of national campaigns that negative ads dominated the race."

Historically, mudslinging has crept into many presidential races. The opponents of Andrew Jackson, Grover Cleveland and Warren Harding all tried to make sex scandals into campaign issues. But this year, the nation's voters were treated to a heavy televised diet of taunt and counter-taunt between the two final candidates.

"We're going to see more and more of it, until someone can prove that it doesn't work," Schneider said.

Sabato said he was less concerned by the advertisements on television than by the television networks' fascination with their own opinion polling. The polls financed by the television networks and major national newspapers did not necessarily influence the voters too much, he said, but they did influence the election coverage of the news organizations who paid for them.

For example, if a network released a poll showing one candidate losing ground, the tone of its story was that the trailing candidate was a loser, he said. Ironically, the public became more annoyed with the media, television and newspapers included, than with the candidates, he said.

University of Texas political scientist Bruce Buchanan said the result of all this political static on television is that campaigns bear less and less relation to the issues that will confront the eventual winner. Candidates aren't seeking a mandate, he said; winning is their only objective.

Dumping on the Duke.

Squier, who was called in as a consultant to Dukakis during the final stages of the campaign, said Dukakis never realized he was in a fight until he was knocked out. Dukakis stoically tried to stay standing while being hit with a series of gut punches — the Willie Horton furlough, the Pledge of Allegiance issue, the ACLU affiliation, the pollution of Boston Harbor, the pictures of him riding in the tank and the meekly answered question about what he would do if his wife were raped, Squier said.

"Bush was saying, 'Mike Dukakis, you're weak,'" he said. "And because of his silence, people started thinking that he was weak." Squier said the Democrats need to give a combat-readiness examination to their next nominee.

Black said Dukakis never seemed to recover from scurrilous rumors propagated by some Republicans against Dukakis early in the campaign. When the press reported the rumors that Dukakis had sought psychiatric counseling and that Kitty Dukakis had burned an American flag during her college days, Dukakis "went into a tailspin," Black said.

"In some respects, Bush just psyched Dukakis out," he said. Buchanan said Dukakis "wasn't especially good at quickening the pulse, making people like him, even though in every other respect, he was a most impressive candidate, an ideal kind of guy to be president."

But Dukakis seemed not to realize that he had to be a good candidate before he could be a good president, he said. "The only way George Bush was made to look good was to run against a guy like Michael Dukakis," Buchanan said.

Darden said Dukakis could have been right on all the issues and still lost the election, because "it was the non-issues that Dukakis was on the wrong side of."

Aside from these post-mortems, the Greatest Political Show on Earth is over. Yet, as intense as all the sound and fury was at times, it always seemed to die so quickly. During the primary season, the candidates had all headed to the next state before the votes were counted in the last.

Convention demonstrations subsided as soon as the music stopped, and the networks cut away to a commercial. And even when Bush finally triumphed, within 15 minutes of the end of his victory speech, the balloons were all popped and the celebrants had all gone home.

In the beginning, Campaign '88 promised to be a political watershed year, at least. Now it all seems like a Phantom of the Operatives.

Bill's notes: I was in a bad mood when I wrote this story. I had spent the previous morning driving from Sioux Falls to Des Moines through the "ground blizzard" I described in the article. In the afternoon, upholding the sadomasochistic tradition of the reporter roving through Iowa in the winter, I boarded a plane to catch a can't-miss Paul Simon (the Senator) event in Waterloo. I didn't realize I was flying back into the storm I had just driven out of. The small plane made an approach to the Waterloo airport, but it suddenly shot back up. The pilot pulled back the cloth drape of his cockpit and muttered to Simon's campaign manager, "I can't see the runway." What had I done in boarding this plane? On the second pass, though, the dark clouds parted slightly and we landed safely. That was nearly three decades before the 2019-2020 campaign, and the point of the article is still valid, maybe even more now than back then. In 1988, there were seven Democratic presidential candidates, and most people thought that was way too many. Now there are a couple dozen of them, and people are still making the same complaints — and still placing far too much value on the numbers from the Iowa caucuses.

D ES MOINES, IOWA —The caucus campaign here is a Spring Break for sadomasochists.

Like the college kids who mindlessly trek to Florida every April seeking sex and sun, the politicians and journalists come to Iowa every fourth January in search of the misery of each other's company.

They inflict upon each other painfully long campaign schedules in some of the worst weather imaginable. They endure the Chinese water torture of endlessly repeated rhetoric and whipping by the rawest of winter winds.

Along the way, they practice a sort of mutual butchery, the press slicing off the also-ran candidates with strokes of their pens and the politicians skewering the press any chance they get. And this year, the excesses are even more pronounced.

"Quite frankly, I've never seen anything like it," said Hugh Winebrenner, a political scientist at Drake University in Des Moines.

All the television networks had their resident Iowa teams in place a month before the Feb. 8 caucuses, and most of the nation's major newspapers have groups of reporters living in the state, he said.

The campaigns of the 13 candidates in both parties have stepped up their efforts correspondingly, and all this is a significant increase over the intensity levels of the caucuses. About 300 news organizations were in Des Moines on Friday night to cover a debate among the Democratic candidates.

"It all just continues to grow geometrically," Winebrenner said. "It's almost as if it were the weekend before the national election already."

Winebrenner's recently published book, "The Iowa Caucuses, The Making of a Media Myth," contends that the over-hyped caucus coverage gives Iowa a disproportionately large influence on the selection of the next president. "Nevertheless, he added, the situation only continues to get further out of hand. Perception is ever more the reality, but the reality is still irrelevant," Winebrenner said.

All that the candidates receive after many long months of campaigning here is a fraction of a small group of delegates to the national nominating conventions, plus whatever small share of the general public's attention they can capture.

The only payoff for the press is someone to call a front-runner for a while. At least the college kids return from Florida with some comparative benefits, such as sunburns and hangovers.

Still they march on, the Light Brigade that produces mostly sound and fury. A few impressions of life on the campaign trail of the '88 Iowa Caucuses:

* Even the candidates seem to know in their hearts that something is seriously out of whack. Former Arizona Gov. Bruce Babbitt, widely regarded as the most candid of the candidates, spoke during a debate last week about being burned out on Iowa. "I get up in some strange motel, wondering where I am, what town I'm in; then I get up, give five or six speeches in the day; then at night, I'm lonely and homesick and I call home to check on the kids," he said. Babbitt said that since there must be someplace where the process starts, Iowa must suffice; but, he added, he'd prefer Arizona.

* U.S. Rep. Richard Gephardt of Missouri, who has been here the longest and probably devoted the most of his campaign resources to Iowa, is showing some of the strains of his non-stop campaigning. At the same debate in Sioux City, Gephardt stumbled on one of his stock catchphrases. Intending to decry the plight of the nation's poor, Gephardt instead deplored the

circumstances that make some elderly people choose "between heating and eating their homes."

* Covering the renascent Gary Hart campaign is something like covering a guerrilla war. "Rumored presence of the candidate at the Ottumwa Kmart," the rumor flashes through the Iowa press corps. Hart is trying to make a plus out of having hardly any campaign organization to support his comeback. So, as if they were trying to find the guerrilla action, the reporters scramble to their rental cars and head for the hinterlands to trail after the candidate.

As much a cause as a campaign, Hart's party travels with its own built-in martyr, Hart's wife, Lee and its own built-in enemy, the press. Hart deferentially introduces his wife at all his stops as "The First Lady of Kitteridge, Colo." She silently serves as a shield to anyone who would dare to fire questions about adultery or character at him. And as the long-suffering faithful wife, she attracts much sympathy, some of which may transfer to her husband.

At the same time, Hart is masterfully using the press attention to fuel his comeback, he brands the journalists as the bad guys. He can honestly say that he didn't invite the pack of news people who follow him around, so he can skewer them at will.

For example, while he was answering questions from the public after a speech in a restaurant in Iowa Falls last week, a man in the audience questioned Hart about his judgment in frequenting a South Florida resort that was also allegedly a hot spot for drug dealers. Hart curtly turned the question aside and got a favorable response from the crowd. But several reporters went to the questioner to obtain the man's name.

That small cluster was in the rear of the restaurant. Their conversation was inaudible to people just a few feet away from them. But Hart saw an opening for an attack. He interrupted his answer of another question and angrily demanded, "If you people want to interview that gentleman, would you please step outside, so the rest of us could talk?" The crowd applauded the candidate's stick-it-to-'em attitude.

It is a challenge just to survive an Iowa January, much less try to cover a frantic political campaign.

Besides the expected snow and cold, Iowans periodically suffer a meteorological miracle they call a "ground blizzard." This is when blizzard conditions develop without any appreciable new snow. Cold is a constant during winter on the Great Plains.

So, most of whatever snow has fallen so far in the season is still out there in the open fields. When, as happened last week, the winds hit gale force, the leftover snow makes for a fine blizzard, even if no new stuff is falling.

Driving through one of these ground blizzards is like ice-skating blindfolded. You're never exactly sure where on the road you are; and if you're in danger of a crash, you'd never know it until it was too late. You can be following a semitrailer thinking it's safer, only to have the truck swallowed by the whiteout in an instant.

Then what do you do? Keep going until you bump the truck that you know is somewhere in front of you?

Curves in the road can't be detected by looking ahead; the best way is to try to follow any bends in the lane-marking lines. Thankfully, there are few curves on the Iowa highways.

These storms don't happen every day, but when they do, the candidates try their best to slog through some of the nation's worst winter weather. The schedule must be adhered to; besides, retelling the stories of campaigning through a blizzard makes for great war stories, when the campaign staffs and the press meet for drinks at the end of a 16-hour day.

Why this ever-growing hunger for an event that has about as much real, numerical impact on the presidential election as the first spring training game has on the World Series? It's because at this stage, any hard numbers of actual votes, no matter how irrelevant, come like fresh spring water to wanderers lost in a desert of speculation.

The candidates and the press have been here so long — some for more than a year already — that the caucus results will have an explosive force megatons beyond the few actual delegates that are at stake.

And this year, everyone stands to get bit by the blast. The polls show the Democratic candidates so closely bunched that the best bet is that there will be no breakaway winner.

That means they all are really battling hardest for perceived wins. Illinois Sen. Paul Simon's staff is busy trying to dismiss polls that put him above 30 percent so that a 25 percent showing will be perceived as a big win. Gephardt's forces are trying to depict their recent 13 percent showing, after a year-and-a-half in the state, as a big surge. Hart's people, who have no campaign, concede they'll go nowhere in the actual delegate race, although they'll be happy with anything above 5 percent of the initial preferences stated by the caucus-goers.

"Wouldn't it be pathetic," Winebrenner said, "if these candidates spent 900 or so days here and millions of dollars, and the results turn out indecisive?"

Well, maybe not. For the revelers in this tortuous spring break, pathos can be a plus. A healthy dose can humanize a candidate's image. And it certainly makes for better news copy.

So, while the inveterate caucus junkies may curse the process with one breath, most of them are booking motel rooms in Muscatine with the next.

Bill's notes: I had so much fun at the Democratic convention of 1984 that I got assigned to do the same to the Republicans. You can't be in Dallas in August without being stunned by the heat, and you can't be in Dallas anytime without encountering stunning displays of conspicuous consumption. The two themes melted together in this story. At the polo event, I recall spending as much time as possible under the food tent, hovering near the station where they were serving scallops the size of silver dollars.

D ALLAS — BY day the beautiful people exude plain old sweat, and they buy perfume by night.

At least that's the way it was for a polo-and-Neiman-Marcus doubleheader on the last day of preliminaries to the Republican National Convention. A large contingent of conventioneers was among the sun-fricasseed spectators at a world-class polo match staged in mansion country north of Dallas, and in the evening an even bigger group of party stalwarts had a world-class — world-class is a cheap adjective in Texas — department store all to themselves for cocktails, canapes, and a little cash-register jingling.

The polo match was held in 106-degree conditions, when even the mad dogs and Englishmen knew enough to stay in the shade.

There was a truckload of foxhounds on the grounds of the polo club, but after a brief exhibition, they were kept in a slack-tongued stupor in their van.

A group, including some Englishmen, did venture out onto the polo field for an exhibition game of cricket, but they repaired to the bar in short order.

Posey Parker, one of the organizers of the event, estimated that about half the crowd of about 3,000 were somehow related to the convention. She spotted some high-powered Republicans among them.

"There's Ambassador Armstrong," she said, referring to Anne Armstrong, former Ambassador to Great Britain, and former co-chairman of the Republican National Committee. "She's wearing a babushka, because she wants to be incognito."

As another plainly dressed woman passed by, Parker remarked, "Her daddy owns the King Ranch." The King Ranch, in southern Texas, is somewhat larger than Rhode Island.

The scene was as sophisticated as possible for a picnic in hell. Some of the polo fans enjoyed a tent-covered brunch of pate, omelets, fruit and meats, all eaten to the accompaniment of a harpist.

The property tracts around the polo club have become sites of some new, ultra-toney residences. A nearby open house showed some nine-bedroom offerings in the mid-$3 million-range, and a developer on the fringes of this area calls his $250,000-and-up homes a "rare find."

When it came time to move to the grandstands, seats in the shade were going for $50 apiece, so most of the crowd sat out in the sun, scorching their pates and soaking their sun clothes with perspiration.

The game was, of course, hotly contested, but still an exciting display of horsemanship and athletic skill. The players pushed their ponies up and down a 10-acre field (about the size of three football fields) at speeds up to 35 mph.

They change mounts after each of the six 7-minute chukkers, or periods. The idea is to drive a hard plastic ball through a set of goal posts. Often the scoring shots are made at a gallop from 60 to 90 yards away from the goal.

The two teams were billed as featuring some of the best players in the world, and they competed for a $50,000 purse and a silver trophy valued at $40,000.

Things were only slightly less frantic at Neiman-Marcus. The department store, one of the world capitals of conspicuous consumption, was used as the setting for a party to honor three of the most visible women in town for the convention — U.N. Ambassador Jeane Kirkpatrick, Transportation Secretary Elizabeth Dole and Secretary of Health and Human Services Margaret Heckler.

All the honorees appeared except Mrs. Dole, who has not yet been able to travel to Dallas because of an illness. She was represented by her husband, Sen. Robert Dole, R-Kan.

Presidential adviser Edwin Meese also was among the partygoers. The exclusive stock of Neiman-Marcus provided suitably high-ticket set decorations for the party, but there was more.

All the guests got to pet a live baby elephant. Also, they got to eat such hors d'oeuvres as chevre cheesecakes, cucumber stuffed with ceviche, Belgian endive with sour cream and strawberries served with creme fraiche, brown sugar and mascarpone.

A quiet trio started the evening's mood music, but they were raucously supplanted by a Brazilian-style percussion and dance group called Pei de Boi. After pounding their way through the first floor, the group set up in an open space in front of the second-floor designer salon and started some spirited rug-cutting.

The group's two mocha-skinned women dancers, whose costumes showed an awful lot of mocha, pulled dance partners for themselves from the crowd.

Harold Coker, a county commissioner from Tennessee, enjoyed his turn on the floor. He got his partner to do a Charleston with him.

While this was mostly a night for mingling, there was some business being transacted. Just a few registers were open, but the hottest souvenir items were an $18.50 convention special T-shirt and an $8.50 snow globe, which showers an elephant with convention-style confetti.

Some of the more esoteric convention items were red elephant tuxedo suspenders ($55), a flag-decorated walking stick (no price available) and a $1,500 elephant carved from green malachite. The gem salesmen had a steady flow of apparently serious customers. But this was Neiman-Marcus and the visibly well-to-do crowd was taking it all in stride.

Bill's notes: The assignment that got me an all-expenses-paid trip to San Francisco was to find colorful people to write about. Going to the hotel where Phyllis Schlafly was on the inside and Sister Boom-Boom and friends were on the outside seemed like a good place to start. Talk about your low-hanging fruit! Near the end of the Democratic National Convention, I was snapped back to reality, when I was diverted to cover a mass murder at a McDonald's in San Ysidro, CA.

S AN FRANCISCO, CA — Toto, I have a feeling we're not in
Kansas anymore.

Dorothy's capsule comment upon entering Oz would serve as fair warning for Democratic conventioneers arriving for their national meeting here next week.

Everybody who is against anything is already here, and there was a volatile preview Thursday of what promises to be a sidewalk convention of the Who's Who of the Discontented.

An appearance by two of the nation's leading fundamentalists — the Rev. Jerry Falwell and Phyllis Schlafly — provoked a counter demonstration by an instant coalition of pacifists, homeless skinheads, disabled feminists, assorted gay groups, not to mention the Revolutionary Communist Youth Brigade.

"People are getting angry again," said Michael Donnelly, one of the demonstrators. "A lot of people are expecting it to be like Chicago in '68. They can unite when they're all threatened by the same people."

Inside the hotel, Falwell was telling his Family Forum conference that the past three decades have been the "dark ages of the 20th century," adding that San Francisco was a center of that darkness, due to its relative tolerance of homosexuality and abortion.

Mrs. Schlafly described prospective Democratic vice-presidential nominee Geraldine Ferraro as an "advocate of the radical feminist movement." Outside, the 200 or so protesters were the incarnation of Falwell's and Mrs. Schlafly's demons, a bazaar of the bizarre.

The San Francisco Skinheads were a group of young men wearing shredded leather jackets. One had a bullet wound painted on his bald head; another had his few patches of hair arranged in a mange-like cut. Their hand gestures directed toward the Falwell hotel were not peace signs.

One woman wore a brassiere as a headband. A mustachioed transvestite stacked his bra with two soft-drink bottles.

They chanted against the Moral Majority and carried signs that said, "Polyester to hide your jackboots" and "Now playing La Cage Aux Falwell."

Still, their crusades were being conducted California style, as suggested by the woman wearing a T-shirt that said. "Out of the hot tubs and into the streets!"

Mounted, motorized and battle-ready units of the San Francisco police almost equaled the demonstrators in number, and they somehow added to the otherworldly tone of the protests.

One group of police made a show of force by riding past the jeering demonstrators in a formation of dirt bikes. A mounted officer was engaging in a back-and-forth game of trying to get some of the protesters away from the police barricades until his steed settled the issue. The horse relieved himself mightily, and a half block-length of demonstrators jumped back onto the sidewalk.

Mostly, the confrontations were a noisy game of street chess, but some protesters threw rocks, bottles and firecrackers. At least eight people were arrested, and medics reported treating eight people for minor injuries.

James Rowley, a member of the Skinheads, said his group was particularly displeased with what he claimed was unjustified police harassment of the city's street people. "We've got no place to go, so we squat in abandoned buildings, and they throw us out," he said.

The crowd swelled to more than 1,000 for an evening demonstration in downtown Union Square. Harry Britt, a homosexual San Francisco city supervisor, used a biblical reference to underline his opposition to the fundamentalists. "They think they came to Sodom and Gomorrah to save us," Britt said. "But these people are the Sodomites; they're in the Promised Land, and they don't know it."

He compared the fundamentalists to the Sodomites in the sense that he feels the fundamentalists have failed to listen to the true Christian message of compassion.

Jack Fertig, who has become a local celebrity by appearing as a transvestite nun called Sister Boom-Boom, had a message for the fundamentalists: "Filth is in the mind of the beholder." Fertig made his speech dressed in a black leather jacket, black skirt slit up the side and a nun's wimple.

Now I know we're not in Kansas, Toto.

Bill's notes: The thing I remember most about the short-lived Pat Robertson campaign is the snarling animosity that the Evangelical crusaders held for George H. W. Bush. They believed, with good reason, that Bush was really a Yankee moderate, mouthing conservative bromides he didn't really believe in. Bush won, but four years later, revenge-minded conservatives took him out, for reneging on his No-new-taxes pledge. Later, the hard-shell right wingers gobbled up the Republican Party, to the extent that a George H.W. Bush Republican is extremely hard to find anymore.

DALLAS — BROTHER Pat's Traveling Salvation Show is on the Glory Road to the White House.

Brothers and sisters, who's got the most visible signs of a lead in the race for the Republican nomination for president? Pat Robertson. Let me hear you say "Amen!" Amen.

More than 11 million times amen for each campaign dollar raised, and about 3.5 million times amen for each signer in the Robertson-for-president petition drive.

Who's winning the early straw polls and storming the caucus processes with the armies of Christian-soldier politics? Pat Robertson. Let me hear you say "Amen, amen!" Amen from the Iowa straw poll; amen from the Florida straw poll; amen from the Michigan caucuses.

Who's drawing crowds so big and so enthusiastic that any other candidate would like to have the same in a general-election campaign? You guessed it, brothers and sisters. Say amen and hallelujah!

Amid cascades of balloons, trumpet fanfares, and mock-convention hoopla staged by about 3,000 true believers in what he calls "The Second American Revolution," Robertson finished a five-state announcement tour Saturday night in Dallas.

The Dallas finale followed a Des Moines, Iowa, rally of about 1,700 supporters that was the largest campaign event put on so far by any candidate in the campaign-saturated state of Iowa. Before that there was a similarly impressive rally in Manchester, N.H.

Yet the tour also highlighted Robertson's problems and his willingness to confront them. The initial rally of the tour, staged in the Brooklyn, N.Y., neighborhood where he briefly ministered early in his career, was met with hostility by gay-rights protesters and with responses ranging from bewilderment to indignation from many black residents.

But on Robertson's swing through the early primary and caucus states and then into Vice President George Bush's Texas stronghold, the growing power of the Robertson groundswell was obvious.

Twelve times in Dallas, nine in Des Moines, and five in Manchester, the crowds roared to their feet during Robertson's speech. And each night was a celebration of patriotism and morality. There were prayers, hymns and sermon-like warm-up speeches on the agenda; and occasional amens and hallelujahs were shouted from the audience.

Robertson, who is best known as a television evangelist, brought all his showman touches to the tour —celebrity announcers and singers, entrances and exits to the theme from "Rocky,' a giant overhead projection screen in Dallas.

Yet, for all the effort the Robertson campaign places on stressing the candidate's broad background in international business, law and athletics, his crowds respond to the moral theme of his message.

"He's got the Lord behind him," said Barbara Carolan, a member of the Manchester rally audience.

"May the praise go to God if he gets it," said Jim Poyzer, a rally attendee in Des Moines. His wife, Renee, added that Robertson shares her family's "Biblical vision."

At Dallas, a bed sheet was tacked on the auditorium wall as a place where prayer groups could sign up to seek heavenly support for Robertson's campaign. And at all the rallies, earthly support was sought in the form of donation envelopes, just like at church.

Robertson certainly does not discourage the moral tone. His basic calls are for "a return to the faith of our fathers, basic honesty in government, traditional standards of family life, and moral leadership." And when Robertson really gets on a roll, it's camp-meeting time on the campaign trail.

Some of his best crowd-pleasers:

BILL OSINSKI

Education reform: Abolish the U.S. Department of Education and combat the "leftist leaning" National Education Association. "And couldn't we begin," he suggests, "by allowing God back into our schools?"

Tax reform: Increase the standard dependent deduction from $3,000 to $5,000. "If we can give tax deductions to working mothers, can't we give tax deductions to women who want to stay home and take care of their children?"

Anti-terrorism: No negotiations with terrorists, and this warning, "You lay one finger on any American citizen any place in the world, and there will be no place on earth for you to hide." That line usually got the crowd to their feet chanting "Go, Pat, Go!"

Robertson told his Manchester audience, mostly evangelical Protestants, that he wants to reach out in this campaign. "My vision includes all Americans. We're going to encompass them all in a great crusade."

So far, though, party professionals and the national media have not given much credence to Robertson's claim to be a serious candidate. Though the size of Robertson's rally crowds may have been front page news had any other candidate drawn them, all but a few of the 50 or so members of the national press who'd signed up to cover the tour had dropped off after the first day.

"I don't really care," Robertson said when asked about the lack of party recognition. "The parties exist basically to hold a convention every four years. The candidates have to do it on their own. Besides, Richard Nixon once told me, 'Ignore the party leaders.'"

Naysayers point to Robertson's low standing in the public opinion polls and to the generally high percentage of "negatives," people who tell a pollster that they definitely would not vote for Robertson. Presidential candidate Pat Robertson has "the Lord behind him," said one admirer.

Nevertheless, the politicos who do show up at a Robertson event can't help but notice that something significant is happening.

"I'm very, very impressed," said David Oman, state chairman of the Iowa Republican Party, who'd just attended the Des Moines rally. The

Robertson rally was the largest political event staged by any candidate so far, Oman said. "These people are committed, and they're workers."

Oman pointed out that Bush won the 1980 Iowa caucuses with about 30,000 votes. Robertson already has 40,000 people in Iowa who've signed his campaign petitions, he said.

Scott Match, Robertson campaign spokesman, compared the Robertson movement to the one that brought Corazon Aquino to power in the Philippines. "That's the way it is with a grass-roots movement. You don't see it, you don't see it, and then, boom, it's there."

Let me hear you repent and say, Amen!

Bill's notes: It was just another Bush campaign rally, and it held little or no interest for most of the candidate's traveling press corps. But I wanted to see how the locals respond to having the national political circus come to town, so I hung out at Luther North High School in Chicago for a couple of days. Overall, they were gracious and welcoming hosts.

CHICAGO — THE big game had just been cruelly lost, yet the pep rally was only starting.

No matter that the Luther North High School football Wildcats had their season finale scuttled by the margin of a fourth-quarter extra-point kick that thudded against the goal post and then bounced through.

However, about an hour later, the players, the band, the cheerleaders, students, fans and a few thousand guests had turned the school gym into a rally with color and sound riotous enough to approach critical mass for a nuclear pompon explosion.

What could have reversed the Wildcat spirits? George Bush, the gloom-and doom-busting Republican presidential candidate, came to Luther North.

The Bush rally in this ethnic, working-class neighborhood on Chicago's Northwest side was an artful example of the type of campaign event that has helped keep Bush in the lead for the race to the White House.

And for a campaign that relies heavily on visual imagery, Saturday's Luther North rally was a Technicolor touchdown.

Here's how a high school gym became transformed into a sound stage for a national presidential campaign:

VP DAY MINUS 3, Wednesday. Luther North Principal Roger Schmohe agrees to a request from the Bush campaign that his school be the site for a Bush rally the next Saturday evening. "Just for the kids to see the political process close-up is a big thing," Schmohe said. "They become better citizens and better-informed voters for future elections."

Having the Bush campaign come to Luther North got the student body politically charged up, he said. "The kids are talking about the political process. They're actually listening to speeches," Schmohe said. The school did not endorse Bush by allowing its facility to be used, but the Republicans know that they score political points by demonstrating their strength in Chicago neighborhoods that were Democratic bastions not so long ago.

And Luther North, a parochial, educationally distinguished school, where many of whose students' parents are working people such as firefighters and police officers, has had this purpose before. Ronald Reagan filmed a political commercial about his views on education here in 1980.

VP DAY MINUS 2, Thursday. Don Mains, the lead Bush advance man for the event, arrives at North to meet with school officials, U.S. Secret Service agents, and the small group of local Bush volunteers who will help him stage the event. Mains is the former general manager of the Hall of Fame Bowl, in St. Petersburg. But he hasn't been home since the Republican Convention ended in August.

The announcement of the rally was only a day ago, and the students already excited. "The kids are nuts," said guidance counselor Barb Braun.

Spanish teacher Carol Bach said she can see why the Bush people to come to Luther North. "If you want a backdrop, this is good place," she said. The swarm of Secret Service are "checking places that haven't been checked in years," she said.

Some of the agents weren't too happy, though, when they discovered a maze of damp, cramped piping tunnels beneath the school, all which had to be inspected.

VP DAY MINUS 1, Friday. School goes on pretty much as normal. But afterward, the Bush volunteers start the platform construction.

Rachel Haber, a senior at Luther North, passes up the Friday parties to work with the volunteers. "I support Bush totally," Haber said. "I made three posters myself. I thought it was more important to be here. This is the best!"

VP DAY, Saturday, 10 a.m. Mains' biggest problem is his missing shoelace. He also was the lead advance man for a morning rally of Bush campaign workers held on a farm in rural Illinois. At the "Alpha Phase" of the morning rally, or about two minutes before Bush was to speak, Mains noticed that the lectern was a little wobbly because it was placed atop a platform made of hay bales.

So, Mains whipped off one of his shoelaces and tied the lectern to a strand of baling wire. On the way back from the farm to Luther North, Mains talked about his perceptions of the role of the advance man.

"It's not a national advance team coming in and taking over from the locals," he said. "It's people coming in and forming a partnership with the locals, being family for 72 hours."

Mains said he always tries to keep in mind how important these events are to the local people involved in them. "It's just another stop on the national campaign trail, but to these people, it's part of their history," he said.

For example, in the little town of Gilberts near the farm rally, a small park was renamed George Bush Park, in honor of the vice president's visit, he said. But Mains also knows that it's his job to produce a smooth-running, visually captivating campaign event.

"You can't control what the vice president is going to say; what you can do is orchestrate everything around him," Mains said.

Having worked with network television crews for the Hall of Fame Bowl, Mains knows that color is the key to attractive videotape footage. He has made stages piled high with fruit for a California event, with pumpkins and hay bales and corn stalks for an Ohio event; but for the Luther North rally, it will be basic red, white and blue. The main stage and the photographers' stand already are wrapped in sheets of patriotic-colored plastic.

11:15 a.m. Upon arriving at Luther North, the worst logistical problem Mains discovers is that the vice president's lower platform, where he will go to shake hands with some of the crowd after his speech, is too big and too low.

The two-foot drop from the stage level to the platform is too steep, so Mains dispatches some workers to find concrete blocks and plywood to build up the platform. Mains reminds the lighting technicians to make sure that there is extra light on the first six rows of the crowd.

1:15 p.m. The school band comes into the gym, to leave their instruments. They wore blue jeans for the performance before the school's football game, but they will wear concert uniforms for the rally. Generally, the band members are enthusiastic about appearing on stage with the vice president, though some are disgruntled with the "dorky tunes" they're supposed to play.

One band member, Melanie Pettway, has put her Dukakis button on the underside of her overcoat lapel. She'd heard a rumor, an untrue one, that she wouldn't be allowed into the rally, if the button were visible. Though she favors the Democrats, she respects the vice president and will gladly play for him and her school. "I hope this gets more kids in the school; enrollment's down," she said.

Erica Wojdyla is a bit upset about the late afternoon rally because it might make her late for an Amy Grant Christian music concert. "It's a pain," she said.

3 p.m. The gym is emptied for the final security sweep by the Secret Service. The core of a good rally crowd is already at the school because of the football game. Luther North's heartbreaking loss seems to have dimmed their spirits only slightly.

Local Republicans have mailed out about 11,000 tickets to the rally, and while the gym is locked, a crowd of about 2,000 presses up against the one door that will be opened. On the edges of the crowd, some little girls sell candy. In the middle of the crush, an elderly woman takes off her fur coat and puts on a Republican jacket.

3:38 p.m. The door of the gym is opened, but the crowd must go in single file. Everyone has to be frisked by a Secret Service agent, and all hand-carried items must be inspected.

3:45 p.m. Everything is in rally readiness. The new platforms are complete and all wrapped in the plastic bunting. Mains, however, still hasn't found a replacement shoelace.

A group of Luther North students push their way up to the front of the audience ropes. They say they're here as much to support Bush politically as for the show. "Dukakis stands for too many of the wrong things, things that are against my morals," said Cora Cofield. She and others in her group say they believe Dukakis supports abortions, while Bush is more strongly against abortions.

4 p.m. A crowd of about 4,000 is in the getting revved up by the high school band on the stage and by a college band in the bleachers.

4:05 p.m. A Bush worker reminds the tambourine player to shake his pompon.

4:10 p.m. A large group of Wildcat football parents, and teachers are ushered into the space right in front of the stage. They will be the designated cheerers, who will shine most in the television lights.

4:20 p.m. The crowd is reminded to hold "BUSH-QUAYLE" signs backward, so they'll show up on television.

4:25 p.m. Bush workers pass out more pompons, and cowbells to the people up front. Too many hands reaching out, so the workers start tossing the campaign stuff.

4:30 p.m. Mains, a former cheerleader in high school, grabs a wireless microphone and gets the crowd roaring, "GIVE ME A B!"

4:35 p.m. A "BUSH-QUAYLE" sign is on the blue-draped armor in front of the podium, called The Blue Goose by campaign staffers. The podium is packed from rally to rally in a C-141 transport airplane that follows the candidate.

4:40 p.m. Crystal Gayle appears onstage to sing "America" and to introduce Bush.

4:46 p.m. Bush speaks. It's basically the same rally speech Bush has delivered throughout the nation. But here in ethnic Chicago, Bush adds the story of his meetings with Polish Solidarity leader Lech Walesa and with the mother of a Catholic priest murdered by Polish soldiers.

The crowd, which went wild long before Bush arrived, goes wilder. Bush already had spoken at five campaign events Saturday before he arrived at Luther North. But if the day had drained him, the reception at Luther North restored him.

He spent long minutes shaking hands with people in the crowd, obviously warmed by their response to him, a response so genuine it couldn't have been manufactured even by the best of advance man. After the rally, Bush proclaimed Luther North the "best site of the day."

That was reward enough for Mains, who strode out of the darkened gym, loose-shoed but happy.

The only person not overjoyed by the Luther North rally was the school janitor. He started pushing his broom across the gym and grumbled, "I'm glad they only have these elections once every four years."

Bill's notes: George H. W. Bush had spent much of the previous eight or nine years positioning himself to become President. By election day 1988, he knew he was going to win, and win big. So, he could easily afford to cut up a little bit with the press and coast on home. But he was often like that on the campaign trail, doing things like participating in the press corps' landing-time betting pool. For this last day before the election, he even signed a $20 bill and tossed it in the pot, so the winner would have extra money and a presidential souvenir. I spent the campaign switching back and forth between the Bush and Dukakis press planes. I voted for Dukakis, but Bush was more fun.

HOUSTON — GEORGE Bush ended his campaign for the presidency in time to get home for supper.

While his Democratic opponent, Michael Dukakis, was just beginning his last night of cross-county, non-stop campaigning, a tired but seemingly relaxed and confident Bush gathered his family around him and settled into his hometown of Houston.

Bush's final campaign rally attracted a noisy crowd of about 5,000 to a shopping mall on the city's perimeter.

For his finale, Bush mostly backed off his attack theme against Dukakis and spoke of what he has learned in the nearly 13 months he has spent traveling the country as a candidate for president.

"I've learned that people have big dreams for the United States, and what better place to talk about big dreams than here in Texas, the state where they dream the biggest dreams of all," Bush said. "Americans understand that it is big dreams, not big government, that made America great."

Before he headed for his home base, Bush touched all the bases that he has touched so many times in his campaign: a pledge not to raise taxes, support for voluntary prayer and the Pledge of Allegiance in public schools, opposition to federal gun control laws.

He also restated the underlying themes of his campaign: "strong family values, faith in God and belief in the United States of America."

After the rally, Bush let his television campaign take over. He purchased a half-hour on all three networks to give his final message to the nation. In his closing comments on the program, Bush restated the core of his candidacy.

"I believe that the low-tax and high-opportunity policies we've pursued through the last eight years are working," he said. "Americans are better off than they were eight years ago, and if you elect me president you will be better off four years from now than you are today."

Bush will make Election Day a family affair. He will cast his vote today in Houston, his legal residence, and then be joined by his five children and 10 grandchildren for a mostly private day.

He called his family "my strength and my pride," and he plans to assemble all of them to watch election returns tonight. In coming home to Texas, Bush is not only returning to his political base, he is coming to the place where he began some of the most important chapters of his adult life.

Right after Bush graduated from a Massachusetts prep school, he enlisted in the Navy and came to the Naval Air Station in Corpus Christi for pilot training. After World War II and his marriage, Bush returned to Texas to start an oil business.

"It's great to be back where for me it all began," Bush said.

The most recent statewide polls show that Texans are glad to have Bush back and proud to claim him as an adopted son. A poll published Sunday by the Dallas Morning News, the state's largest paper, gave Bush a 16-point lead over Dukakis.

At the outset of the campaign, the Democrats considered a Texas victory for Dukakis a strong possibility, and Dukakis strengthened that bid by naming Texas Sen. Lloyd Bentsen as his running mate.

Bentsen has campaigned vigorously for Dukakis in Texas. But as the campaign ends, Bentsen is running television commercials reminding voters he also is running for senator.

Bush introduced to the rally crowd a fellow Houstonian, campaign chairman Jim Baker, who many credit with devising a strategy that has allowed Bush to remain on the offensive, while keeping Dukakis on the defensive for most of the campaign.

Texas Sen. Phil Gramm also was present, and he talked about campaigning around Texas with Bush's son, George W. "We've made a hundred stops, and we've kicked Dukakis' a.. all around this state," Gramm said.

Bush couldn't resists taking a parting shot at Dukakis. Issuing a warning against what Dukakis might do to the national economy, Bush said, "Don't play Recession Roulette with the liberal governor of Massachusetts."

Bush's last day on the campaign trail was full. After flying to Michigan from the West Coast late Sunday night, he held a rally in an office complex in the Detroit suburbs, where he told the crowd he was charged up for a vigorous end to the campaign.

"The adrenaline's flowing, our family's coming together, and the country's coming in behind our candidacy," Bush said. "And I want to be elected to be your next president."

Then it was on to a rally before a crowd of about 5,000 at Ashland College, near Mansfield, Ohio, and a brief stop for a rally of about 1,000 supporters at the Missouri GOP state headquarters in suburban St. Louis.

But more than anything else, Bush seemed glad that the rigors of the campaign trail were ending. He was even relaxed enough to joke around a little bit with the press corps traveling with him. After he landed in Texas, he tossed a football for the cameras, joining in a game the reporters and cameramen often play while they wait for his motorcades to depart.

On the last flight, Bush sent a taped message to the press airplane. "We solved the vision thing, and they never use the W-word (wimp) around me anymore," Bush said.

And he reflected on his thoughts about the men and women who have followed his every move for so long. "There have been times when I saw you across the tarmac, standing out in the cold, waiting for me," he said, then added a punch line equal to the best reporters' repartee: "But I thought, 'Tough, too bad. Who cares? It's your problem. Get away, get a haircut, go get a real job.'"

Bill's notes: This article is one of the statewide political profiles I wrote for the Tampa Tribune, as part of the buildup to the first Super Tuesday primaries in March 1988. The clumping of a bunch of Southern states voting the same day in primaries was supposed to demonstrate the region's power in naming the national presidential nominee. It didn't turn out that way. The Democrats selected a Massachusetts liberal, Mike Dukakis, who went on to lose ignominiously. The Republicans tapped the anointed heir, George H.W. Bush. Still, it was a great assignment. I took a week to bounce around Louisiana, eating great food and talking politics, history and the sweet smell of scandal.

TAMPA TRIBUNE, NOVEMBER 15, 1987

STILL STANDS THE forest primeval; but under the shade of its branches dwells another race, with other customs and language. — "Evangeline," by Henry Wadsworth Longfellow

ST. MARTINVILLE, La. "Coooooo! Eet's wahn beeyewtiful day!" said the old man selling copies of "Evangeline" from his card table set up beneath the Evangeline Oak. His voice is strange but soothing, as if one of the pigeons had started a conversation.

"Things around here, they don't change so much," cooed the Cajun storyteller and tour guide, Max Greig. "So many people don't read; and the young people who do get an education, they just leave."

Talk of change sounds mostly like deja vu to Max Greig. When Greig was a newlywed, more than 50 years ago, a dynamic young politician named Huey P. Long swept into the governor's office, promising to lift people in places like St. Martinville out of the swamp of poverty.

Greig was double lucky. He got a new state job to go with his new wife. He was a pile-driver on a state crew building bridges on the Bayou Teche. He hadn't been on the job very long, though, when a man came up to the foreman waving a piece of paper. "They found out that my gran-daddy hadn't voted for Huey," Greig said. "I was out."

Now, another fresh-faced governor has won election promising another new day. Max Greig will withhold his hopes for now, thank you, and continue to try to get by, telling his Cajun stories and selling copies of a poem of a great love on the Bayou Teche.

Louisiana is as much a pretty parasite as the Spanish moss that decorates and drains its oak trees.

For generations, people here have turned corruption, decadence and joyful living into an art form; conveniently, the patrons of these arts lived somewhere else.

Louisiana's oil severance taxes ultimately were passed on to consumers in other states, while Louisiana officials used the windfall to bloat the state payroll and provide a wide variety of free services, with enough left over to make the reigning politicians and their friends quite comfortable.

Reformers have gotten elected periodically; but soon the electorate would become bored and bring in another clown-pirate to amuse and to rob them. *Laissez les bon temps rouler*. Let the good times roll.

But now, the good times are rolling on square wheels. Louisiana is about $500 million in the red. Its unemployment rate is stuck near 10 percent, the nation's highest.

Why, then, are the Cajun concertinas still squeezing out happy music at places like Mulate's, near Breaux Bridge on the Bayou Teche? Perhaps it's because the dancers of the *fais do-do* can see the rest of the nation getting in step. American presidential politics is now as wacky as Louisiana politics has always been.

Politicians who spice their lives with vice have been standard fare for public entertainment here long before adultery, plagiarism and drug use became the favored diversions of the current presidential campaign.

Seen in that light, Louisiana could be the best preview state for Super Tuesday. There is a message in the results of last month's tumultuous Louisiana gubernatorial campaign that could be resounded, when Louisiana and 19 other states, most in the South, vote in presidential primaries next March 8.

"We're seeing a Southern rebellion," said Raymond Strother, the Louisiana native and now Washington-based political strategist who plotted the campaign of Charles E. "Buddy" Roemer III, the 44-year-old maverick congressman who unseated three-time Gov. Edwin Edwards last month.

"The South has traditionally been an assemblage of outsiders," Strother said. "They're saying the system has failed and they want to look outside the system. And they want to send the bastards in Washington a message."

REVOLUTION

Four men challenged Edwards' bid for a fourth term; total spending reached well past $20 million. Why were they so eager to run a state so clearly circling the financial drain?

Well, no politician, even the president of the United States, is granted the impressive array of powers that the governor of Louisiana enjoys. Most of the state's revenues come directly into the state capital from outside sources, namely the oil companies. Thus, local property taxes are kept low, making the middle class tolerant of the governor's tendencies to divide the largesse mostly among the well-connected and the poor.

The governor directly appoints about 1,400 state officials to a state bureaucracy that has the eighth-highest per-capita rate of employees in the nation. He also appoints members to about 130 boards that control much of the commerce in the state, which has a population of about 4.5 million.

Also, he has a line-item veto — the authority to excise any single item from the state budget and a lethal weapon to use against the favorite project of any uncooperative legislator. President Ronald Reagan has often pined in vain for such power.

This campaign may have been the grandest of them all. Candidates conducted cross-state whistle-stop train rides and camp-out caravans. Millions of dollars became election day "get-out-the-vote" money, which basically consists of cash passed out to workers who help get people to the polls.

Spicing up the whole roux was the Tabasco sauce of Louisiana politics: corruption. During his third term, Edwards was tried twice on federal charges that he had gained from the awarding of state hospital contracts.

The first trial ended in a hung jury; the second time, he was acquitted. But he obviously was damaged by trial testimony that depicted him leaving the state with attache cases full of cash on gambling trips during which he used assumed names.

It was bad enough that Edwards was promoting casino gambling as a cure to the state's economic problems; what was worse, the incognito high-rolling governor also was a steady loser.

So, the inevitable happened, but in a revolutionary way. The man who dethroned the Cajun populist Edwards was Buddy Roemer, conservative Democratic congressman from northern Louisiana. At first glance, Roemer seems like a disinherited prince trying to overthrow the emperor.

Roemer's father, Charles Roemer, had been Edwards' director of administration, or the chief dispenser of patronage. The elder Roemer was caught in a federal bribery sting operation and he spent about two years in prison.

But Buddy Roemer ran against the old system of Edwards and his own father. He accepted no campaign loans, sought no endorsements, took no large contributions. He had the least money of any of the five candidates. And until less than a month before the elections, he was last in the polls.

Roemer had just enough spice to make him palatable to the voters. He plays poker, but he is righteous enough to report his poker winnings on his income tax return and shrewd enough to know that the people will notice that he had winnings to report.

He is anything but casual about finances and budgets. As a congressman with a master's degree in business administration from Harvard, he twice submitted his own version of the national budget in the form of proposed legislation.

His bills never got very far, but they did get more votes than the version President Reagan submitted to Congress.

Strother, Roemer's campaign strategist, is quick to admit that Edwards deserves much of the credit for the success of the Roemer Revolution. Many people had simply had too many helpings of the scandal-blackened Cajun governor.

BILL OSINSKI

"When people get hungry enough, some things become more important than gumbo and crawfish etouffe," Strother said. "Finally, the corruption wasn't cute anymore."

But there is much more than anti-corruption and anti-Edwards to read into this vote, he added, and the presidential candidates might do well to seek the full meaning. "The candidates keep on adjusting, when the people want change, fundamental change," Strother said.

And the presidential candidate who might be best able to capitalize on that mood is the candidate who can run a race like Roemer's late-breaking, risk-taking and anti-establishment in tone, he said. "Everybody's playing by Jimmy Carter rules in 1987," he said. "They don't understand that those rules don't apply anymore."

Others think they've heard something like that message. Louisiana Sen. John Breaux, one of those swept into office on the 1986 tide of discontent, said he thought the message was: "Run a short race, don't spend much money and tell 'em you're not a politician."

New Orleans Mayor Sidney Bartholemy said he saw "a lot of signs pointing to a large segment of the population who do want change, and that development is good for the Democratic Party." Bartholemy has endorsed Jesse Jackson, the winner of 1984's Democratic presidential primary in Louisiana.

A.J. Leibling once wrote that the level of political involvement in Louisiana was matched only in Beirut, Lebanon. It's true that they do talk a lot of politics at the daily coffee pot congregation in the drugstore in Walker, a crossroads town just east of Baton Rouge.

But at the Walker Pharmacy Coffee Club, the politics is as lighthearted as Beirut's is serious.

Jack Dease is the druggist, postmaster and chief political consultant to no one in particular. He also has a personalized Louisville Slugger baseball bat on the floor to help keep order, though he uses a croquet mallet as his gavel.

To become a full-fledged club member, nominees must be, among other requirements, "gainfully unemployed" and able to sit on bar stools for long periods of time drinking free coffee and solving world problems.

The club has its own theme song. One line says, 'The coffee's free, you don't pay no dues, and Gene Clark puts your comments in the Denham Springs News."

There's also a highly accurate political polling device. Dease has screwed a row of Mason jars into a board and slotted the tops of the jars, so a quick glance at the small change in the jars gives a readout of candidate support.

Any candidate who visits the club gets his name on a jar and four of the five gubernatorial candidates had their own jars. Now the goal is to get jars for the presidential candidates.

Achievement in other fields also is recognized, with the Local Yokel Award. A Walker police officer was honored for chasing a car thief through the swamp and getting his man without getting his hair messed up.

Billy Grout got his award for being the oldest man to become a Goldwinger, a motorcyclist who goes 1,000 miles in a day. Billy earned his claim to fame by getting on nearby Interstate 10, riding till he hit 500 miles somewhere in West Florida and then turning around and coming back in time for the next day's coffee club.

Discussion is not restricted to politics. "Football, politics and sex are all No. 1," Dease said. But a session near the Walker Pharmacy coffee pot does give a glimpse into the thinking in the rural South.

Gene Clark, a weekly newspaper columnist and club regular, said people in Louisiana have gotten tired of glib politicians who can't solve problems. "When people are unemployed and business is bad, those little jokes don't go over so good," he said.

James Hodges, a Republican, said he'd like to see a dark horse win his party's nomination but believes the favorites will prevail. "None of the Republicans love George Bush, but he'll be the nominee," Hodges said.

Hodges has plenty of time for the coffee club these days. His mobile home business is heading in the same direction as the Louisiana economy. "We ain't got no recession Louisiana," he said. "We're living in a depression.

EMPIRE

Louisiana has been enduring these cycles of boom and bust, conquest and defeat, since before there was a United States. "Louisiana is the northernmost part of Latin America," said Mark T. Carlton, history professor at Louisiana State University. "It's an outpost of the Franco-Spanish Empire."

Since it was first settled by the French and Spanish, Louisiana is the part of the country least touched by the values of the English-speaking cultures, he said. This may explain why Louisianans find enjoying life a natural thing to do; and it may also explain why tolerating corrupt governors seems natural.

"In the era of the empires of France and Spain, there was no middle class," Carlton said. "The king could do whatever he wanted. He was *Le Patron, L'Entendant.*"

Louisiana has long been what America has come to resemble in the Reagan years, a "constitutional monarchy," he said. "Every four years, Louisiana elects a king," he said, referring to the governor's races, in which the winner gets just about all the spoils. "The governor controls access to the trough; no money is dispensed without his approval," Carlton said.

In Louisiana, they add the touch of regal power to the generally Southern notion that expects a politician "not only to enlighten you but amuse you as well — the politician-clown," he said.

So, Louisiana governors have been talented country musicians (Jimmy Davis), firebrand orators (Huey P. Long), open womanizers and mentally unbalanced (Earl Long).

Edwin Edwards had enough of these elements; he was both a Catholic and a former Nazarene preacher, and a charmer who scoffed at middle-class morality to put together an act that ran longer than any of his predecessors.

Carlton remains skeptical that the regal style will leave the governor's mansion with Edwards, who's already said he may run again. "Reformers come and reformers go; the conventional way of doing things remain," he said. "Each time Earl Long left office, he was widely despised, and each time, they brought him back. There's always the pretender out there, waiting to be re-crowned and re-enthroned."

John Maginnis, editor of Gris Gris, a Baton Rouge political tabloid, suggested Louisiana more closely resembles a Latin American dictatorship. A gris gris is a small bag of herbs and other items of spiritual importance worn by voodoo believers to ward off evil. "It's a lot like a Banana Republic, with a large uneducated population and a strong central government," said Maginnis, who is also the author of "The Last Hayride," a study of Edwards' 1983 election campaign.

Despite the fact that about 75 percent of registered voters turn out for the major elections in Louisiana, he said, overall participation of voting-age people is no better than in the rest of the nation. About 800,000 eligible Louisianans simply haven't registered. "They feel they're powerless; they feel the politicians are in control of their lives," Maginnis said.

And for many years, the middle class in Louisiana has allowed this situation to continue, he said. "The middle class was willing to let the politicians do what they wanted, as long as the politicians didn't ask them for money," he said.

But now, he said, the old system has failed because the oil money is drying up. And Maginnis sees no other way for the revenues to be made up than by raising taxes on the middle class.

For Louisiana, the problem is not just that the state has an image of bad government. There are real, costly problems to solve, such as chemical pollution, illiteracy and a generally poorly regarded school system. "I'm not sure we're ready for the real revolution," Maginnis said.

EXILE

In Acadiana, the heart of Louisiana's Cajun Country, even the hard times seem to take on a gentler tone. This is a land where the present still romances the past. The graceful oaks and quiet bayous suggest this is where Longfellow's Evangeline searched for her beloved Gabriel.

In St. Martinville, the memory of the real Acadians is preserved at a state park. On the grounds, a plantation home is preserved to show

how the Acadians lived after they were exiled from Nova Scotia to the Louisiana swamp country.

Among the exhibits in the home are some of the shadow boxes that the Acadians would make to commemorate their dead. Inside the boxes are things like fruit designs made of beeswax or human hair plaited into patterns.

Above the kitchen table is hung a flat board, or "punka," which would be waved to keep the flies away while the family ate. In the sitting room is a "wishing rocker," where wishes will be granted, if the wish-maker doesn't tip over.

In the center of St. Martinville is the Evangeline Oak, where Evangeline was supposed to have ended her years of searching only to find Gabriel dying, and at the nearby church is a statue to the young Acadian woman who is believed to be the model for Evangeline.

The old storytellers under the oak give a slightly different version of the legend that became the epic poem. They say that when Evangeline found her Gabriel, he wasn't dying but happily married to someone else; and that discovery drove her insane.

Not far from St. Martinville is Avery Island, the preserve of the McIlhenny family, who gave the world Tabasco sauce.

Edmund McIlhenny, the company founder, was something of an exile. A successful banker before the Civil War, he was forced to find another means of income by the policies of Reconstruction, so he turned to selling the red-pepper sauce that he used to flavor his gourmet cooking.

The Tabasco recipe is still the same as the founder's: capsicum peppers crushed, mixed with salt and set to age in wooden barrels for three years; once the fermented mixture is strained, it's Tabasco sauce.

Paul McIlhenny, vice president of the McIlhenny Co., said his family has long been involved in the good-government movements in Louisiana politics, but he wonders how real this one is. "I'm worried that people rallied not out of a desire for good government, but because of the economic depression," McIlhenny said. "They were willing to try anybody to get out of the doldrums."

Some of Louisiana's reputation for piratical politics is undeserved, he said. "People are tired of the amoral perception of Louisiana," McIlhenny said. "I don't think we have any lock on political corruption. Politicians in other states have done the same things, but they just don't brag about it. In Louisiana, we're just honest about dishonesty."

Wherever Louisiana goes from here, it will remain in many ways the spellbinding wilderness that Longfellow's Evangeline encountered when she first tried to find Gabriel:

"Dreamlike, and indistinct, and strange were all things around them; And o'er their spirits there came a feeling of wonder and sadness, Strange forebodings of ill, unseen and that cannot be compassed."

BILL OSINSKI

LIFE AND DEATH IN
THE COAL MINES

Wildcat miners in southeastern Kentucky erect timbers to support the roof in a punch mine, where the seams of coal have been exposed by strip mining. In the past 25 months, 11 miners have died in accidents at wildcat mines in Kentucky.

Picture of a coal miner illegally working his unpermitted mine. Photo by Stewart Bowman, Louisville Courier Journal

Bill's notes: The Hamilton family put out the word they did not want to speak publicly about the mine explosion that killed four of their relatives. However, Ralph Dunlop, my partner in covering this and other mining disasters, knew a relative of the Hamiltons. This man lived near the only road into the Hamilton's hollow. A police cruiser was parked across the road, to help enforce the family's wishes. I asked him to call Mrs. Hamilton and tell her that people around the world were concerned for her. We received permission to go up to the Hamilton home. The interview reinforced my respect for mountain people who must live with the specter of death every day to mine coal. The disaster, coupled with another deadly mine explosion just a month earlier, compelled the paper's editors to launch an investigation, of which I was a part, into mine safety. The investigation became a series entitled "Dying For Coal." It was named a finalist for the Pulitzer Prize. Its conclusion was that coal mining is an outlaw industry – which was true in 1982, and is still true today

LOUISVILLE COURIER JOURNAL, JANUARY 22, 1982

CRAYNOR, KY. A widow is thankful when she has sons nearby, but it frightened Lillie Hamilton each time her four boys went to work under the mountain beside her back yard.

"I never did want them to go into the mines," Mrs. Hamilton said yesterday. "They'd always tell me that mining was no more dangerous than a trip to Dayton, Ohio. I didn't believe that."

On Wednesday morning, Mrs. Hamilton, 67, heard the hum of the ventilation fan being turned on at the small "punch mine" above her home on Mink Branch. That noise meant her sons had gone to work in the mine.

A few hours later she heard another noise, one that meant the worst nightmare of a coal miner's mother had become a reality.

An explosion rocked the mine, blasting parts of the ventilation fan onto a distant hillside opposite the mine opening. Killed were the seven men inside the mine: Lillie Hamilton's sons Donald, 39, Jack, 36, and Burnis, 31; her grandson Wade, 23; and three other miners who worked for the Hamiltons — Thurman Reynolds, 25, Palmer McKinney, 26, and Ronnie Hall, 25.

The Hamilton brothers ran the mine first as partners. But now only Purvis, 47, who was just outside the mine at the time of the explosion, is left.

Yesterday, friends and relatives gathered at Mrs. Hamilton's home to help her absorb the shock of her loss.

She was able to talk about her boys in an unbroken voice, pausing from time to time to muse aloud, "Lord, Lord." But she kept her own questions within her heart.

"Nobody can know how it feels," Mrs. Hamilton said.

But she was strong enough to tell her family story. She moved into a home along Mink Branch, a trickle of a stream in rural Floyd County, in 1933, the year she married Craig Hamilton.

Her husband, who died nine years ago, was always proud of having worked 50 years in the mines.

She didn't have the same kind of affection for the work, she said, and her sons did not automatically acquire it from their father.

As they grew up, she said, they tried factory work in Dayton, Ohio, but they all returned to Mink Branch.

They had all married women from around the same hollow, and either the mountains or the coal, or both, pulled them back to Kentucky.

Life in the hollow suited them, she said. They could feel comfortable with their preferences for not drinking or smoking.

Most of what they wanted was in Mink Branch, she said. They all built their own homes there, and they knew how to bring out the coal that would make a good life possible, she said.

The brothers worked at a number of mines. And then, about a year ago, they pooled their resources to lease the rights to the coal beneath the hill behind their mother's house.

"That's what they wanted, to have something for themselves," Mrs. Hamilton said. "I guess they liked mining, or they wouldn't have done it."

The Hamiltons' mine, which they called R.F.H. Coal Co., was a modest success.

"They were running good coal," she said. Inspectors who have visited her since the explosion have told her that her sons' mine was among the cleanest and best run in the area, she said.

BILL OSINSKI

"I guess it doesn't always matter how clean you keep it, you never know when something like this is going to happen," Mrs. Hamilton said. "It's just one of them things, I reckon."

In the days ahead, Mrs. Hamilton must find a way to come to terms with her sorrow. She is distressed at the possibility of having to say goodbye to her sons and grandson without seeing them one last time.

She said she doesn't want the coffins closed during services for the members of her family, who will be buried in a family plot.

"If I can see them, it won't be so bad," she said. "I want to see my children!"

Bill's notes: These miners knew they were breaking the law with every lump of coal they mined. They allowed me to accompany them, because they wanted people to know why they believed they were forced into breaking the law. Under any circumstances, mining coal is a dangerous business. For these men, the danger was compounded by the knowledge that they could be arrested at any time. In these mountains, there is hardly any other way to make a living.

HARLAN — THE junkyard-fugitive pickup is no match for the grade of the road going up the muddy scab of an abandoned strip-mine bench above the creek.

Two-thirds of the way up the steepest switchback, the truck gives up and starts sliding back down.

Its brakes are lined primarily with hope, so the driver has to turn the wheels into the hill to keep control.

Back at the bottom, the driver grinds through the gearbox in search of a ratio low enough to conquer the switchback. That accomplished, the pickup churns past the black scars and brown heaps and gray pools of a mountain turned inside out.

It's early, and the wildcat miner has arrived at his work site. The easiest part of his day is over.

He turns on the power switch that provides working light and a warning of approaching inspectors. A friend at the bottom of the hill will cut off his power if a government official nears, giving the miner time to get away by the backside of the hill.

But as long as the line stays open, he'll be loading coal by the shovel and breaking the law with every lump until long past dark.

The mine is in a small section of the southeastern Kentucky coalfields where officials estimate that about 50 wildcat mines operate. A group of the miners agreed to talk to a reporter and photographer, and to show them how they work, on the condition that their names and work location not be used.

The miners say they are a different breed of wildcatter from the outlaw miner who makes big money and endangers his workers' lives. They work small punch mines on land owned by themselves or relatives, they say, scraping perhaps 30 tons of No. 5 coal out of the mountain on a good working day.

A few of them have power-driven scoops, but most load by hand, into wheelbarrows or homemade buggies. They sell at tipples, where they can deal mostly in cash, and so they usually take whatever rate the tipple operator sets.

Bring a load in once, they say, and you may get $23 a ton; the next time, maybe $18. Take it or leave it.

The people along the creek have worked small mines in this fashion for decades, but mining laws and regulations have long ago made it illegal.

During the recent meeting, the miners said they were not outlaws by choice. "I don't mind paying my taxes, but you can't pay taxes without a license," one of the miners said.

It is the preliminary costs of licensing, permitting and engineering totaling from $10,000 to $15,000 that these miners consider the single most important contributor to their outlaw status. They say the costs are prohibitive, and they complain that they are being driven underground by regulations that favor the big mine.

"The state says you have to be wealthy to mine your own coal," one of the miners said. "But this coal is the only thing this valley's got. If we can't get it honest, we'll have to get it dishonest."

The land-reclamation bonding requirements are particularly galling to the miners, because they feel they must be willing to forfeit the minimum $5,000 bond before they can go legal.

This is because most of them work in small punch mines, where the seams of coal have been exposed by strip mining, most of which was done in the era before any of the current environmental laws were in effect.

As a result, they are making what amounts to pock marks in places that are already large wounds on the land. Hundreds of thousands of dollars wouldn't reclaim the land where they work, they believe, so they feel they must be ready to give up the bond.

Environmental officials contend that the bonding requirements of the law were enacted to prevent additional mining-related devastation. The law is being researched by officials of the Kentucky Department for Natural Resources and Environmental Protection to determine whether there is any legal flexibility in the bonding requirements.

Under the current interpretation of the law, no exceptions can be made, regardless of the conditions of the land prior to the permit application, department officials say. Their only choice, as the wildcatters see it, is to take whatever royalties the large coal companies are willing to give for their coal or to wildcat it themselves.

"The big man is rooting us out," one of the wildcatters said.

One of the men and his son, along with two to four helpers, operate a punch mine that is typical of the wildcat mines in the area.

Stepping inside is like entering a vanished era of mining. Only the chain saw used to cut timbers and the electrically powered drill tell the visitor he's not in the 1920s.

But it's not a menacing place. It's spacious and cool, with a smooth sandstone roof that gives the miners confidence. The operators work an 80-inch seam of two veins of coal that are separated by a layer of coal mixed with shale, so there is at least room enough to stand inside.

The air is always good, and the mine shallow enough so that the men can come outside when they're ready to detonate an explosion.

The favorable natural factors and the comparatively low production rate about 30 tons a day, when things are going right, make them feel they operate very safely.

The man and his son are not high-volume miners. Whatever coal they shoot, they load by shovel. They have two buggies they've fabricated from old truck beds to which they affixed a sheet-metal bucket that can hold perhaps two tons of coal.

When the buggies don't run, the wheelbarrows roll. "I can remember one day loading 30 tons out of here on wheelbarrows," the father said. "They'd load and I'd roll. Buddy, if you don't think that's earning your money!"

The owner's wildcatting practices have gotten him into trouble with the law. An earlier conviction on charges related to illegal mining makes him a parole violator every time he works the coal on his own land.

But he feels he has no alternative. "The court cases took everything I had," he said. "I went to get food stamps, and I was honest with them and said I still had an old coal truck that was worth a little. They said, "'You've got a coal truck, you can't have food stamps.'"

So, they wildcat. The man's son Ernie functions as foreman and shot firer. On a recent day, he loaded six sticks of explosives into each of four holes he had drilled — an illegal practice.

As he put each of the last charges in, he sliced the stick of explosive as if he were deboning a trout. The sliced charge served to stem the blast — an illegal practice.

Once outside, Ernie shouted, "Fire in the hole!" and set off the charge. The men stopped to eat their sandwiches, while they waited for the smoke from the explosion to clear. "It's terrible," one of the workers muttered over his bologna, "to think of putting a man in jail for working."

Bill's notes: It is extremely hard to report on people's grief, especially when it's only moments old. I was sent to Topmost to get that sort of a story, and even in the atmosphere of tragedy, the people seemed to know I had a job to do, and as long as I did it respectfully, they helped me. I wanted to tell the inescapable truth that going inside a mountain to dig out coal is a job inextricably linked to sudden death. In those days, we lugged around early computers, with metal cases and tiny screens. They required connection to landline phones to transmit. My partner Ralph Dunlop and I had no time to get back to our motel to file our stories. So, we trudged through the mud until we came to a house. We knocked on the front door, and told our needs to the homeowner, who allowed us to come in and use his phone — but we were asked to leave our boots on the porch.

LOUISVILLE COURIER JOURNAL, DECEMBER 8, 1981

T OPMOST, KY. — The levee that had held back the grief for eight hours exploded as suddenly as the mountain had.

"Oh God! Hear me, dear Lord!" a man wailed, leading the mourners who had gathered in a grade school gymnasium to await word of the fate of eight miners trapped inside a coal mine by an explosion yesterday.

When state troopers gathered the immediate relatives into the gym, closed the doors and read the litany of the dead, a chorus of screams broke out — screams of the kind that have echoed in these mountains too many times before.

About 50 relatives had been waiting at Beaver Creek Elementary School for news about the men trapped in Adkins Coal Co.'s Mine No. 18 by the 2:30 p.m. explosion.

The outburst of grief was a standard part of a mountain mining tragedy, according to the Rev. Charles M. Wilcox, a chaplain for the Appalachian Regional Hospital system. Wilcox, who has tried to help families during similar disasters at Scotia and Hyden in recent years, said, "The worst moment is when they receive the word."

Not much can be done for the families at such a time, he said, except to let them express their grief. "You simply have to hear them out, let them vent their feelings," he said.

The scene inside the gymnasium conveyed the depth of the sorrow the survivors felt. Young women who had just been told they'd lost their husbands or brothers screamed and fell to the floor in shock. An older man tried to lead the mourners in a spontaneous prayer. Most people just hung their heads and sobbed.

On the bleachers in the back of the gym, two young boys sat off by themselves, silently sharing their sorrow. Among the mourners were Susie Johnson of Brinkley, the mother-in-law of one of the dead miners, and her granddaughter, Josephine Slone, 20, whose father was one of the men killed. Ms. Slone is the eldest of seven surviving children, and her mother is due to have another child next week.

"Take it easy on account of Mommy," Mrs. Johnson said as she tried to console Ms. Slone. "That cryin' won't bring him back."

"Nothing's going to bring him back," the younger woman replied. "Daddy's never coming home again."

Mrs. Johnson said she was most concerned now about her daughter, whom she feared would have to be hospitalized. She said her son-in-law was "a good man, who worked hard for his family." Taking care of the family his death has left fatherless, she said, won't be easy "but we'll try."

Before the first list of the dead, which included five names, was read about 10:15 p.m., those who had gathered at the school were going through what Wilcox called "the denial phase" of such tragedies.

People talked in small groups, mostly whispering about community events, mining, basketball, carefully avoiding any discussion of their families, of the worker who died in a 1980 blast at the same mine, or of the men now trapped in the mine.

One group of miners leaned against a wall of the school lobby, their faces still black from their day's work, wordlessly awaiting word of their friends.

Inside the school office, a small group of red-eyed women had gathered to wait for the phone to ring.

Amid the quiet tension, a group of cheerleaders and their mothers came into the gym, after returning from an out-of-town basketball game.

They sensed the gravity of the situation and muffled their enthusiasm as they arranged for their rides. Their bright uniforms seemed incongruous under the circumstances.

BILL OSINSKI

Those who had been through such vigils before said that one never develops a tolerance for mining tragedies.

Henry Causey, a Hazard Red Cross representative, said he remembers an explosion in the late 1930s. "I helped get them out, but then I told my dad that I'd had enough," he said. "Then I went off and joined the Army. It made a career soldier out of me."

Hershel Lawson and his brother Paul, who both work in nearby mines for the same company that owned the mine where the explosion occurred, said they lost a first cousin in the accident.

Hershel Lawson said such tragedies make a man think twice about mining for a living. But in these hills, he said, there's no real alternative: "That's the only way you're going to feed here, buddy."

The men who were killed were working on a seam of coal less than three feet high, Lawson said, which is about the smallest vein that is mined underground in this region.

In response to reports that the explosion was caused by powder used to blast the coal loose, Lawson said that working with such explosives is an everyday danger for the men in the mines.

Normally, Paul Lawson said, the explosives are kept a good distance away from where the miners are working, and it is usually quite difficult to set them off accidentally.

"I've seen a pretty good-sized rock fall on that powder, and nothing happen," Lawson said. He said an explosion is the worst of the dangers of mining, because a blast "never gives you no warning. When there's an explosion there ain't nothing left."

Bill's notes: I volunteered to help the young miner make it to his grave. I rode up the mountain to the family burial plot in the funeral director's SUV. But it couldn't make it all the way. So, I helped carry the casket for the last 50 yards. I was honored. Like the preacher who couldn't preach a long sermon, I deliberately kept this story short. Grief demands to be under-written.

LOUISVILLE COURIER JOURNAL
DECEMBER 10, 1981

HUEYSVILLE, KY. THE only ship that can sail in these mountains is the Ship of Zion.

That vessel of transport to a hoped-for better place began making its stops yesterday for the eight men who died Monday in a coalmine explosion at Topmost.

The boarding call for 25-year-old Keith Crager, the first of the men to be buried, was sounded by a chorus of gospel singers. Their voices, a cappella, resounded through the mountains: "Get on board the old Ship of Zion, it will never pass this way again."

That note of final departure was too difficult to accept for one grief-stricken woman, who went to the coffin and wept during the song. And many others at the Hall Funeral Home in Martin cried with her at the loss of a young man who was born and raised in these hills.

Crager had been a miner for about five years, his friends said, and he had recently saved enough to build himself a house behind his parents' home. He had planned to move there with the young woman he intended to marry.

Five more funerals for the Topmost victims will be held today; the last two will be buried tomorrow.

Preaching Crager's service, Elder Sterling Bolen noted that the grief of Crager's family and friends was shared throughout the coalfields of

Kentucky, Tennessee and West Virginia, where 23 other miners have died in accidents during the past week.

"There's much grief throughout three states this morning," Bolen said. "I know many hearts are broken. At times, when the trouble comes in, it seems like a flood."

Bolen's brother, Bethel, also a minister and a friend of the Crager family, said he could deliver only a short sermon. "There's no use trying to preach today; I've got too much grief," Bethel Bolen said. "Of all the funerals I've been called to, this one's hit me the hardest. I don't think there could be anything sadder than the situation we're in today."

The service was simple, punctuated by hymns and Sterling Bolen's ringing sermon, delivered in a chant that vibrated with hope and torment. Afterward, about 50 of Crager's relations and friends went through another mountain ritual.

Traveling in four-wheel-drive vehicles, they churned along three miles of muddy roads, up to the Crager family cemetery. The small plot is on a ridge in a place called Salt Lick, and yesterday it had a view of snow-dusted hills in every direction.

During a short ceremony on the wind-swept hilltop, Sterling Bolen tried to comfort Crager's inconsolable fiancee. "Even as Christians, there's things we don't understand," he said. "But we realize that such a great catastrophe that has happened has brought grief to many homes."

Once the family had started back down the hill, the Appalachian way of death was completed with a final ritual. Twenty or more of Crager's male friends stayed behind on the Salt Lick Ridge, and took turns throwing clay on his coffin until the grave was full.

Bill's notes: This day was calm in the coalfields but hectic at the newspaper. In the morning, I took a brief ride in a coal company helicopter to overlook the first convoy of loaded coal trucks moved out of the mines. I took a photograph of the convoy of about 30 trucks snaking down the mountain road. There was no staff photographer with me. When I called in, the news desk was more interested in my picture than in my story. They dispatched photographer/pilot Billy Davis to fly all the way from Western Kentucky to the Eastern Kentucky mountains to pick up my single roll of film. My shot of the convoy ran at the top of the front page. However, my photograph of the gun-happy security guard interviewed for this story was not used, even though I thought it was damned good. I had asked the guard to place his guns on the hood of the truck for the photo, but the photo editors decided, correctly, that this made the picture a posed shot, which was taboo for news coverage.

LOUISVILLE COURIER JOURNAL MARCH 14, 1978

ALLEN, KY. — The guard at the bottom of the coal road sucked his cigar and displayed his 6-1 shot carbine handgun and his .44-caliber pistol.

"It's open season on 'em now," he said, referring to striking union miners who yesterday defied a federal back-to-work order.

The guard at the non-union mine in Floyd County, which has more union mines than any other county in Eastern Kentucky, blamed union pickets for the dozens of two-inch-long roofing tacks he'd found in his coal road and for such things as a coal truck windshield that had been smashed with the driver still inside. But there was nothing for the guard to shoot at yesterday.

With a Taft-Hartley injunction in effect, picketing at union mines was illegal, and the security guard said he now felt the law was on his side. "When you stick a gun in their face and pull back the hammer then they'll listen," he said.

No members of the United Mine Workers worked at any of some 500 Floyd County mines. At least five nonunion strip mines in the area did operate yesterday, as they have been throughout most of the 98-day strike. From those mines, the loaded Mack truck rigs with names like "Nitro Express," "Metro Bound" and "Black Magic" ventured onto the state highways, often tailed by Kentucky State Police cars.

One state mining official, who asked not to be identified because of the negotiations in progress, said he felt the lack of violent incidents yesterday was partly because of the miners' anticipation that a settlement might be near. He said he has been in touch with high-level officials in the coal operators' association, who have told him that a tentative agreement on a contract could come within two days.

"The miners are too close to something good to spoil things now," the state official said. He said inspectors from his district are already checking mines so the miners can return as soon as a contract is ratified.

Although there was outward calm in Floyd County yesterday, some miners were not sure how the day would turn out.

At one truckstop, a table of miners watched a loaded coal truck pass by, as their coffee refills came with an extra helping of tension. They talked of paving the lot with the truck's contents.

One of their companions was a nonunion coal truck driver who said he has parked his rig since the strike began in December. "I'd like it to be in one piece when the finance company comes to pick it up," he said.

The union men left the cafe and went to a meeting of about 50 UMW members in a nearby city park. During the meeting, several miners expressed concern that some of their members would break ranks and return to work yesterday.

They said they were worried that if the "crazy miners from West Virginia" heard about such a thing, the West Virginians would come to Floyd County to give the returning workers some lessons in union solidarity. Before noon, however, it was apparent that the UMW men in Floyd County had closed ranks.

The miners at the park meeting said they were angry at Pres. James Carter and at Gov. Julian Carroll for tactics that the miners felt might lead to violence. Some men felt that Carter's endorsement of separate settlements in the strike was an overt attempt to break the UMW. "He's trying to start murder here," one miner said.

BILL OSINSKI

MORE MISADVENTURE!

Picture of Alfonso Salinas helping to load his pickup truck with scrap metal to sell to finance his family's migration from the Rio Grande Valley to the farm fields of Ohio. Photo by Bill Osinski

Bill's notes: I wanted to experience the migration with the migrants. Baldemar Velasquez, a farm labor union organizer in Toledo, Ohio, set me up with the Salinas family in Brownsville, Texas. I spent more than a week with them, paying for my room in their home and chipping in for gas money for the interminably long drive to the tomato fields of Western Ohio. I helped the father, Alfonso, break up a car body with a sledgehammer to collect scrap metal to sell. I ate at their table with the males, while the females waited their turn. I took several of the long turns at the wheel of the truck, and when I was too tired to drive any more, I paid for a couple of cheap motel rooms. When we finally reached Ohio, and the work they had expected was not there for them, they accepted the situation with a resolute determination to find other ways to earn money on their summer "vacation." The Salinases, like most migrants, do not want their jobs taken by undocumented workers. But they do want to be treated like human beings.

*E*L VIAJE, THE journey, starts with a silent prayer in a pickup with no spare.

In the front seat, Otalia Salinas crosses herself and dabs a few tears from cheeks that have been cured to a cordovan hue by 10 summers of sun and sweat in the vegetable fields of the Midwest. She must leave the Rio Grande Valley again, trading the brick home built with harvest dollars for a succession of trailers, cabins, shacks or floors in friends' homes.

And she must leave her grandchildren.

In the back end of the camper-topped truck, Sergio Garcia cries more openly. He doesn't know what lies ahead, since this is his first summer to go to pick the crops; but he does know that a 9-year-old boy who speaks little English might as well be on another planet as soon as he leaves his barrio in Brownsville, Texas.

And he must leave his grandparents.

It's time for summer camp, migrant-worker style — four months in the sun for kids and parents alike. There are plenty of open spaces and food all around; but this is no picnic.

The eight people in the truck will make a 1,500-mile migration from Brownsville to Northwest Ohio. The group includes Alfonso and Otalia Salinas; three of their children, Mireya, 17, Glorisella, 14, and Hugo, 11; their neighbor, Adela Garcia, and her son, Sergio; and a reporter for the Beacon Journal.

They all have stashed themselves and their personal gear into the camper, along with enough frijoles (beans) and corn-meal flour for tortillas to survive a summer amidst foreign supermarkets, a towbar for the used car they hope to buy in the North, and a half dozen hoes. Their plan is to work for a couple of weeks in the Ohio sugar-beet fields before moving on to pick strawberries and cherries in Michigan.

Then it will be back to Ohio for the tomato harvest. If the crops are good and the truck holds together, the pooled profits for the Salinas family might be about $3,000 to $3,500.

That figure is about one-half to one-third of what Alfonso Salinas makes during the rest of the year, when he has steady work as a carpenter or an iron-cutter. However, work has been anything but steady in the last year, so Salinas' only other source of income has been scavenging and selling scrap metal.

Though these people are a vital human link in the nation's food chain, they could not set their own dinner table without food stamps. And they would not have a decent home to stay in unless they left it each summer for the fields of the Midwest, where there will be five breadwinners in the Salinas family instead of one.

Now they must go. A plywood slab is laid over the bags and pans in the truck bed, so the back-enders can stretch out. The truck tiptires through ravines cut into the barrio street by rain and neglect.

Not a mile has been passed on smooth roads when Salinas stops the truck, which is owned by Mrs. Garcia. He goes to the back and asks if she has a spare tire. She says she does, but it's in Mexico.

Alfonso Salinas works in the fields when he can work nowhere else, a situation in which he has found himself off and on for 40 years. He first came to pick cotton in Texas during World War II as one of the *mojaditos*, literally the "wet ones," the illegal aliens from Mexico.

Since getting his passport and status as a legal alien residing in Brownsville, he has picked tomatoes and pickles in Ohio, fruit in Michigan, worked the sugar beet fields in Idaho and picked tomatoes in Florida.

BILL OSINSKI

"Mexican tourists," as he laughingly calls his road-bound family and those like them, always take working vacations. "I work wherever I can work, wherever I can make money," Salinas said.

His decision to make migrant workers out of his family was a matter of basic arithmetic; 10 or 12 hands can pick more than two. "I was the only one working in Texas," he said. "To make a better living, I had to have the whole family working with me. I don't like to take my whole family away from home, but I have to. There's no satisfaction in this work."

But Salinas has few complaints about his treatment as a migrant. He finds his work by contacting farmers directly, so he does not have to deal with the crew chiefs who sometimes exploit the workers they recruit.

Aside from the few times he and his family have been dusted with pesticide while they picked the crops, Salinas does not have a long spiel of misery from his life as a migrant. Most farmers he has worked for have treated him decently, he said, but many have made him feel that he was of a different class of human being.

"The farmers don't think of themselves as migrants, but they are migrants, too," Salinas said. "Their ancestors all came from somewhere else, just as we do now."

Alfonso Salinas was a teen-ager when he made his first illegal crossing of the Rio Grande to work in the Texas cotton fields. Manpower was short during the war years, so no one cared how many illegals were among the pickers.

He went back and forth in this fashion for the next few years, until he got immigration papers. Then he was able to go to Houston and San Antonio, where he found work as a carpenter and in a factory mixing pesticides.

After getting married in the early '50s, he found work as a stone crusher in Brownsville. In the '60s, he worked in Houston again for several years, saving his money and coming back to Brownsville, which is about 250 miles south, every other weekend or so.

Since then, he has stayed with his family in Brownsville, except for the past nine summers, when they have headed north. In 1978, he joined a union, the Farm Labor Organizing Committee.

It happened while he was having a beer with the farmer who employed him. Union picketers came to the field where he worked as a crew chief, calling out for the workers to join *la huelga*, the strike.

The farmer wanted him to stay; this would be the farmer's last year planting tomatoes, and he needed this harvest. But Salinas made his stand while he still had work to lose, and he joined the strikers.

Salinas described his explanation to the farmer, who was of German heritage, this way: "I told him, 'If those were German people out there and they asked you to join them, what would you do?' These are my people."

The farmer never spoke to him after that, Salinas said. And even now, Salinas does not announce his union affiliation when he goes to a new farm; he needs the work.

For the Salinases, income from the stoop-labor summers means the difference between bare survival and a life with a few comforts.

Each year, Salinas has put a sizable portion of his fieldwork earnings into his home. The first year, there was just enough for a concrete-slab foundation; then came a framework. For a year, the family lived in the house when it was a shell with a roof and no windows.

Construction of the house was mostly a cooperative effort among Salinas, his relatives and friends. He'd repay them by helping on their homes. Now his house has a television, carpets in the three bedrooms, a well-appointed kitchen and a couple of fans for fighting off the heat of tropical Texas.

The walls are decorated with religious icons, pictures of Salinas' two married children and his three grandchildren. He likes to call the babies "*los primitos*," the little cousins. At 53, Salinas does not like to own up to being a grandfather.

One thing that prevents the Salinases from having the nicest-looking house on their block is that they must use parts of their yard for salvage storage. Everything from old transmission housings to rusted bedsprings can be found piled in the grass, awaiting transport to the recycling center.

Salinas, aided mainly by his wife, scours the landfills for anything that can be resold. He advertises in the weekly shoppers for old appliances that people want to discard.

Selling junk is not a full-fledged business for Salinas. His primary tools are a rusty winch, which he hangs from a wooden frame he takes apart and reassembles with a claw hammer as he moves about, and a pickup truck that is all but indistinguishable from the commodities it hauls.

This truck, now retired from the Texas-to- Ohio-to- Michigan-to- Texas run, has a pitted tailgate that resembles metallic Swiss cheese. It's supposed to have an automatic transmission, but practically every change of gears requires a protracted labor-management negotiation.

When he wants the truck to go from forward to reverse, or vice versa, Salinas must get out, open the hood and jam a shaft into the desired set of gears while his helper keeps one foot on the gas and the other on the brake.

However reluctantly, the truck still hauls, and a few days before leaving for Ohio, Salinas coaxed the pickup into making a few runs to the recycling center 25 miles away.

His first load consisted mostly of the carcass of an old sports car. To get it into the pickup bed, he patiently worked his winch-and-frame system until the car's front end was in the truck and the back end was propped up by a piece of lumber.

There wasn't enough room in the truck bed for the whole car body; Salinas solved the dilemma by getting out his sledgehammer and pounding the little car in half.

Two more loads of scrap from the yard were piled into the pickup truck, both higher than the local ordinances and the laws of gravity would seem to allow. But each trip was made without mishap, and the three loads brought Salinas $168, a little more than he'd need for gas money to Ohio.

Gas stops are the only thing that break up the first evening and night on the road. The freeway-pounded kidneys of the back-end riders need relief as often as the gas tank needs refilling, so at each stop most of the group forms a fast line at the restrooms.

A ride across Texas will quickly convince the traveler that Texans' bragadocio on the size of their state is more fact than brag. After 14 hours on the road, the truck is still in Texas.

The long night starts to make the center line wiggle, and the drivers miss a couple of highway markers where they were supposed to have turned, but there is no room in the budget for a night at a Holiday Inn.

Dawn and the rear left tire break just outside Texarkana, Arkansas. Salinas trims away the tread that was separating from the tire and decides to roll on, hoping the tire cord holds until Hope.

At Hope, Ark., the state operates a rest stop exclusively for those on the fieldworker flyway. For a $1 registration fee, the Migrant Farm Labor Center offers the migrants a clean, cool room where they can rest, and the use of the center's bathhouse and picnic grounds.

To help keep them moving toward their goals, the center gives those migrants who qualify a $20 gasoline credit. Attendance at the church mission across the road is voluntary, but those who go can get some second-hand clothes for the children and some comic books in return for listening to a little proselytizing.

The Salinas entourage makes a long stop at Hope. Everyone gets a shower and a freshly grilled meal, and Salinas gets a new tire and wheel for the truck.

It almost fits.

Migrant children almost never fit into Midwestern schools. Mireya Salinas can remember hating Septembers in Ohio, when she went to elementary school while the older members of the family picked tomatoes.

"We'd get into a lot of fights, and the kids who lived there would call us names," she said. Since she has been in high school, Mireya, now 17, has not had to deal with Ohio schoolmates. She and her older brother, Javier, leave after Labor Day on a two-day bus trip back to Brownsville.

This year, however, Javier did not make the migration, staying instead to attend summer sessions at a Brownsville college. Mireya does not want to make the bus trip by herself, so she will stay with her parents this season, and try to catch up when she gets back.

BILL OSINSKI

Mireya can remember good and bad things from her summers in the Midwest. It is the only time of the year, she said, when she gets to see some of her best friends. Migrants from different cities in the Rio Grande Valley rarely get to see each other, except when they gather in the camps.

Some of the camps were clean and some of the farmers were friendly, she recalls, but there were some camps where the housing consisted of shacks with only thin frame walls between the occupants and the chill of September nights.

There were also some nights that were spent mostly in the fields, she said.

When her family picked cucumbers for pickles, they were responsible for picking the entire block of pickles; they had to stay with it for as long as it took, because another day in the sun might mean more growth for the pickles and a lower price for the farmer.

Still, she does not complain. "The pickles are harder work, because you have to stoop over all the time. With the strawberries, you can kneel down," she said. "I don't mind working the pickles, because you can make more money, but it's hard on my mother."

For her part, Mrs. Salinas does not complain, either. "I like to go north, because it's cooler in the summer and we all have work," Mrs. Saunas said. She doesn't necessarily like leaving her home and her grandchildren, but she knows the grandchildren will be there when she returns, and she knows that the home is there only because they leave it each summer.

The extra income also enables them to keep a house on a dusty back alley for her aged father in Matamoros, Mexico, just across the river from Brownsville.

The only complaint about the migration was a wistfully silent one from Glorisella, the youngest daughter. On the night before departure, the Salinas children went to a beach near Brownsville. Glorisella wrote her name and her boyfriend's in the sand, and then watched the next wave wash them away.

By the time the truck reaches the Mississippi River, the restorative effects of the dose of Hope have long since been swept away by the hot winds of the freeway. It is nightfall again, and the truck is more tired than its occupants.

The engine has been spitting oil all day. But the group reaches its goal, another migrant rest center in Cairo, Illinois.

This place is as foreboding as the first center was congenial. A semicircle of wooden shacks is hemmed in by the marshy, bug-ridden banks of the river on two sides and by grain elevators and factories on the other two.

In the gravel driveway in front of the office, a bunch of migrant children snicker at a drunken transient claiming to be a country-western singer.

Salinas goes in to ask for a place to rest. The lady in the office tells him she is all out of shack space; then she adds that the amount of gas money she can give him has been cut in half since last year. She sees him off with a $10 gas chit and a vaya-con-Dios smile.

No one in the group, least of all the two drivers, can face the prospect of driving through the night again, so the search for a motel begins. The first place encountered looks nice enough; its pool a shimmering oasis.

The motel manager emerges from his office to confront the group. Before they can even get inside, he says, "I'm full." When it is pointed out to him that it is 10 p.m. on a Thursday night and there are only two cars in his parking lot, the manager says, "Sorry, but I've got a reunion coming in here later tonight. They've booked the whole place."

The search is then narrowed to the overnight accommodations available for those unlucky enough to be caught in downtown Cairo for the night. The truck rolls into another motel, this one with a vacancy sign and three surly-looking characters drinking beer in the parking lot.

The rooms are arranged with a manager who stays inside his locked enclosure. By the time the overnight bags are unloaded, though, the parking-lot habitues have gotten nasty. They're taking beer-palsied swings at each other, cursing and threatening to pull their knives.

The disturbance is reported to the manager, who, from the safety of his booth, declines to call the police, saying, "It's all right. They stay here a lot. They're nice boys."

Hugo, the youngest of the Salinas boys, can still keep a boy's outlook on the migrant life. "It's not really work," he said, talking about the times he picks cherries in the orchards of upstate Michigan. "I have my sack on my chest, and I put all my fingers at once on the cherries, like this, and then, 'ploop,' I put them in my sack."

Picking and nibbling are not mutually exclusive, Hugo said, but the desire to nibble usually doesn't match the available pickings. "When I'm picking the cherries, I want to run over and eat the strawberries, and when I'm picking the strawberries, I want to run over and eat some cherries," Hugo said.

To Hugo, the migrant camps in the Michigan orchards are mostly happy places. There, the fields are cleared of workers at about 4 p.m., unlike the Ohio crop harvests, which usually require 11-hour days of the workers.

After a day in the orchards, his father can take him to a swimming lake in the evening. Hugo is an operator, fluent in English and Spanish and able to maneuver well in both cultures. He knows how to make the most out of a bargain-hunting border crossing, how to pour picked strawberries into a hamper to fill it with less fruit, how to navigate his father's junk truck, and how to please the church ladies at the migrant center so they'll give you extra treats.

But Hugo is also a child of the fields. Though he spent his earlier summers in the camps' child-care centers, he can recall helping his family since he was 5, by doing things like carrying empty hampers out to the pickers. His age still disqualifies him from doing some types of field work, but he is not far from becoming a full-fledged member of the family work force.

He has saved the money his father gives him at the end of the season, $100 for each of the last five summers. It doesn't seem to bother him that his bank account currently consists of an IOU, because the money was needed to pay part of the expenses related to a serious car wreck involving his brother, Javier.

Javier is aware of the extra burden he has placed on his family. He knows that much of this summer's earnings will go to pay the bills piled up by the accident, and he knows that his staying in Brownsville will reduce the family's earning power.

But the hardships are minor compared to the goal set for Javier. "I want to become a lawyer," said the young man just starting his second year of college-level studies. "My people need lawyers."

What the people in the truck need when they finally reach their first destination, Leipsic, Ohio, is a long rest, a hot shower and a new truck. The pickup that brought them from Brownsville is still leaking oil and is now running quite hot; the clutch clangs in rebellion at each shifting of the gears; and a number of passing drivers on the Ohio roads have honked and waved, trying to tell the group in the truck that the rear tire looks ready to fall off.

But they'll get none of their needs met tonight. What they will get is a warm welcome from a household of infinite hospitality.

The eight people in the pickup have descended, uninvited and unannounced, on the home of a couple with eight children of their own still living with them. Their friends, however, act as if the arrival is the high point of the summer social season.

Tortillas are tossed onto the stove top for warming, beans are refried, and a quick run to the market produces some meat for grilling.

When the night finally overwhelms travelers and hosts alike, the furniture is pushed back so all possible floor space can be used for slumber. The overflow goes back to the truck.

As the next day begins, Salinas knows the truck should spend some time in drydock. But he kicks it into gear and heads for the road again; it is more important to find work.

First the group goes to the two farmers Salinas had called before coming to Ohio. Both had told him they expected to be able to give him work hoeing and weeding sugar beets. But at both farms, the story is the same: "Sorry, no work yet. The beets are too small. There should be some work, but I can't say just when. Check back next week."

Neither farmer gave Salinas any suggestions on how to subsist until then.

Next, Salinas begins a tour of the region he and his family have worked for the past nine summers. Everywhere they see change, and everywhere they find only disappointment.

In the towns of Findlay, Fremont and Tiffin, where there are normally many Mexican- American migrants in evidence this time of year, hardly any brown faces can be seen.

At the site of one camp where they once worked, they find only the foundations of the migrant houses. At another, they see the last of the houses being loaded on a trailer for transport to Michigan.

Fields they can remember being in pickles are now in grain, and some lie fallow. They pass by a vacant tract that used to be one of three migrant camps run by a farmer for whom they worked for several Ohio summers.

They inquire at a nearby farm and find out the farmer blew his brains out last winter. They go to the sugar plant, where the processor's field agent tells them they will hear the same story on all the farms.

The wet spring has made the plants late, some farmers have bypassed the need for hand labor for weeding by means of a potent new pesticide, and others have planted crops that do not require attention from field hands.

They go to the state employment office, but the lady there tells them local farmers are filling whatever labor needs they have with local people. Migrants from Texas are last on the priority list.

There has been a strike against the tomato growers in this region for six years now, and Salinas thinks the prolonged dispute has led to the phase-out of the hand labor. But he had counted on a couple of weeks of work here this season, reckoning that the machines and the pesticides had not taken over completely. But Ohio appears to be fading from the migrants' map.

Alfonso Salinas still has the problem of hanging on until the camps in the orchards open. He'll spend some time working on the truck and in a few days move his family to a trailer, where they can wait till it's time to go to Michigan.

Maybe the strawberries will be good this year. The strawberries may or may not be good, but they will be late, the Salinases discover.

They thought they'd have a wait of about a week until they could get work. Now it looks like three weeks, or maybe four.

The farmer who'd told them the earlier date extends his apologies. But with seven people who would all like to eat, Salinas must make new plans for the summer.

They go to the farm-workers union office in Toledo, where Salinas finds part-time work for himself and his wife and daughters.

Hugo will join union marchers on their 560-mile walk from Toledo to Camden, N. J., a protest they hope will end the five-year-old strike against Campbell Soup Co., one of the major processers of the tomatoes grown in the Northwest Ohio fields.

The rest of the family will spend the summer in a house for union volunteers. When they go back to Texas, they will be lucky if they have as much money as when they left.

Bill's notes: It was a time when countries including Brazil were making it especially tough for foreigners to adopt their unwanted babies. Mostly, the Brazilian government did not want it widely known that there were so many destitute abandoned children in their country. Two friends of ours, David and Becky Brown, wanted a child together so badly that they were willing to fight the Brazilian bureaucracy for it. They also had connections, in the form of missionaries in Brazil who were supported by their church in Akron. They allowed me to travel with them for a series of stories titled "Passport to Parenthood". David and Becky raised Elyse Ana in America, but they took her back to Brazil several times to keep her connected to her heritage. A few years after this adoption, the Browns adopted another Brazilian infant, a boy this time.

F ORTALEZA, BRAZIL – "Please give my baby my doll," said the mother who'd barely outgrown it.

The only gift the young mother could give her child, besides giving her away, was her *bonoca,* her favorite cloth doll.

The visit to the mother's home was supposed to be a courtesy call. The baby's biological mother and grandmother had asked to meet David and Becky Brown, the Akron couple who have adopted the infant.

It turned out to be a slightly awkward but genuinely loving transferal of motherhood.

The Brazilian family's apartment was located down an alley in back of a doctor's clinic in a commercial and residential district of Fortaleza. The plank-floored front room was just large enough to seat the Browns, the baby's mother, Ana, the grandmother, Maria, and George and Adele, the missionaries who have been the intermediaries for the adoption.

Maria, a woman in her late 30s, received the visitors with a kiss. She works as a department store cashier. Five of her nine children still live with her, and her husband has left the family.

Some of the children must sleep in hammocks in bedrooms with earthen floors. Maria had lived most of her life in Barbalha, a mountain village about 400 miles from Fortaleza, where George and Adele have their mission.

She contacted the mission couple when her 16-year-old daughter, Ana, became pregnant. Maria and Ana told the missionaries it would be best for the baby to be put up for adoption.

Months of paperwork had preceded Tuesday's meeting between the two families. But this meeting was strictly a human affair.

Ana was shown a picture of her child; it was the first time she had seen the baby.

She had wanted to know if the infant was pretty, both from the standpoint of a mother's pride and for a more practical reason. Ana had been worried that if the baby had a birth defect, perhaps the American couple might not want it.

But Mrs. Brown reassured Ana that they would love and raise her daughter no matter what the baby's condition. "Tell her that we know how hard it was for her to give the baby up, and it shows how much she loves the baby," Mrs. Brown told Adele, who translated.

Ana smiled one of her few smiles during the visit. For most of the time, she stood in the chipped cement archway of the front room. At the top of the arch hung one of the room's few adornments, a small picture of a mountain village like the one where the family used to live.

Ana wore a cotton shirt with the words "Hot Dog" across the front. Her baby had been born only three weeks before, but she already was able to wear form-fitting jeans again.

The Browns had brought her a gift of some costume jewelry. Ana seemed pleased. Mrs. Brown had picked the gift based on the tastes of her own daughter, who is Ana's age.

Maria said, "All that's left is for my daughter to be grateful," referring to gratitude for the baby leaving the poverty of the home in Fortaleza.

Mrs. Brown replied, "We are the ones who are grateful. You've given us so much."

Ana cried silently in the archway.

Just before the visit ended, Ana asked if the Browns would give her doll to the baby, who is named Elyse Ana. "I'd be honored to give it to her," Mrs. Brown said.

Bill's notes: This story was the next-to-last of a series of articles following a local couple, David and Becky Brown, trying to adopt a Brazilian infant. The Browns were personal friends of mine in Akron, and they graciously let me tag along for a journey that took them from the barren outback of Northern Brazil to the cosmopolitan chaos of Rio. For me, Rio was breathtaking in its natural beauty. I rented a car as soon as we landed. Big mistake. Traffic in Rio is sort of like a horse race; when the light turns green, lanes do not exist. Whichever drivers have the most guts are the ones who gain the glory of making it through the intersection. I was determined to go to a soccer match at Rio's famous Maracana stadium. I found the stadium without incident, but once I got there, I realized there was no parking lot. The crowds come mostly by bus, I later discovered. I circled around, until a security guard took pity on me and directed me to a small lot reserved for security vehicles. I enjoyed the soccer match, but I turned in my car the next day.

RIO DE JANEIRO, Brazil — The bureaucratic bloodhounds were closing hard on the heavy scent of adoption documents. It was a sure sign David and Becky Brown were getting closer to America.

"Have you filled out the long form yet?" the clerk at the U.S. Consulate here asked. And with that, she uncoiled a paper anaconda of a form that fairly dared the Browns to try to fill it out.

It certainly was the long form, nearly 3 feet in length and filled on both sides with small print. The form, for seeking a visa to enter the United States, demands to know whether the applicant has ever been arrested, treated for mental disorders, involved in prostitution, addicted to drugs, or has been or is now a member of the Communist Party.

Since the applicant in this case was the Browns' month-old Brazilian-born daughter, Elyse Ana, most of these questions were not stumpers.

"The only thing she's addicted to is milk," Brown said.

Nevertheless, his wife, Becky, was not yet ready to let herself fully relax. "I know I shouldn't be nervous because everything has gone so smoothly, but I am nervous," she said.

The U.S. Consulate has approved the adoption and given the baby the Browns' last name, but their American citizenship does not automatically transfer to the child.

The baby, like any other Brazilian who intends to come to the United States, must have an immigrant visa. There are, however, worse places in the world to be stuck in for a few days than Rio de Janeiro.

Green mountains rise up from just beyond the beaches, and the unfailing bright blue of both the Atlantic Ocean and the Brazilian sky make a marvelous backdrop for the flesh show on the sands.

Downtown Rio is also a gawker's paradise. Here, anyone who stops to look at the ultramodern skyscrapers or 16th-century cathedrals also is taking a serious risk; neither vehicular nor human traffic is kind to anyone who goes the least bit slowly.

It's all a megavolt culture shock compared to where the Browns came from to get here.

On Sunday, they said goodbye to the Valley of the Cariri, the poverty-stricken Brazilian interior region where their baby's family comes from.

Spending a night bumping through the Brazilian outback on a long-haul bus is a singular experience.

By day, the buses must contend with livestock trying to take over the highway. By night, sugar cane trucks sometimes break down and are left in the middle of the road.

After a wilted arrival in the coastal city of Fortaleza, there was a day for catching up on rest and logistical details. Then it was up before dawn again to catch the early flight to Rio.

By the time the Browns and George and Adele, the missionaries who have been the intermediaries for this adoption, arrived, they were all slightly past the ragged edge.

The baby had some head congestion and the adults' digestive tracts were under serious siege.

But at least there was an afternoon to rest before mounting the final assault on the consulate.

Mrs. Brown made the first stab at filling out the long form. After answering questions on her background, she became puzzled and went back to the official's glass window.

"Do you want to immigrate to the United States?" the official asked the Akron woman. Mrs. Brown quietly started filling out a new form.

After a few hours, which is supposedly not long at all for these matters, the process seemed to be back on track. The Brazilian papers had been inspected and approved. All that remained was to obtain a doctor's checkup for the baby and visa photographs.

A couple of taxi rides later, those errands were accomplished. The group ducked into a McDonald's for burgers and *batata fritas*, fried potatoes.

Late in the afternoon, Brown returned to the consulate thinking all he had to do was pick up the visa. But it wasn't that simple.

First, there was a minor but mandatory form that the officials had forgotten to give them in the morning. This form inquired whether the child seeking to immigrate was well-adjusted and played well with others.

So far, Brown said, Elyse Ana has shown no signs of anti-social behavior.

Then, there was the fee to pay. Brown gave the officer five cruzieros (about 35 cents) too much. The officer could not accept the overage, even though Brown told him to keep the change.

All the cashiers had left for the day, so until someone was found who could change a 10 cruzieros note with two fives, the adoption looked like it might be stalled for another day.

But just after the consulate's regular closing time, Brown left with a folder of papers nearly as precious as his child. "Everything's signed and stamped," he said. "We're done."

Then it was finally time to go find some champagne.

Bill's notes: I was vacationing with family in Florida, when I got a call from Becky Douglas, the suburban Atlanta woman I'd previously profiled for her work with people of the leprosy colonies of India. She had flown there shortly after the Christmas tsunami and was helping to raise money to help the people of the fishing villages destroyed by the tsunami. She told me to try to get over there. This was a chance to get a local angle on an international catastrophe. My boss was deeply skeptical, telling me I'd never get a visa in time. However, I enlisted a helpful aide of a U.S. Senator, who expedited the process for me. I encountered human misery on a scale I'd never imagined. Yet, the prevailing attitude of the people was calmness in the face of devastation.

ATLANTA JOURNAL CONSTITUTION, JANUARY 9, 2005

CHENNAI, INDIA —FOR generations, the fishermen of Kot-tivakkam have gone to the sea every day before dawn, launching their small boats and casting their nets.

It is a tough life, but one they love, a life with a sort of rhythm. The men catch the fish, and the women take them to market.

But that way of life was destroyed two weeks ago when the blue waters that are the source of their livelihood swelled into tsunamis, the cruelest seas ever known. Amid bodies and splintered homes, the villagers' fleet of 28 brightly painted sloops and 55 catamarans was wiped out.

Their nets were left in ruins on the beach. Emergency relief has reached this village and survivors are getting food, water and clothing. But two women —one a neighbor and the other from the Gwinnett County suburb of Peachtree Corners — are focusing on their long-term survival by getting them new boats and nets.

Becky Douglas, founder of the nonprofit Rising Star Outreach, an organization originally dedicated to aiding the children of India's leprosy victims, hurried to this fishing village of 1,800 people last week.

"I know these people," she said. "I love the Indian people. I couldn't stand to see the pictures of the suffering and just sit on my couch and feel helpless," she said.

She and her partner, Padma Venkataraman, a social activist and daughter of a former president of India, Ramaswamy Venkataraman, asked the villagers what they needed for survival.

"The boats, Madam," answered D. Vijayakumar, bidding Douglas and Venkataraman to sit and talk with him in the shade of the small temple garden in the village. Other men joined them, bringing bottles of soda for their guests.

"Once we have our boats back, we want to go back to the ocean," Vijayakumar said. "And we will go back."

Douglas and Venkataraman have already collected more than $70,000 to buy boats and nets for Kotti- vakkam and a half-dozen other villages, or "kuppams," up and down the coastline.

The tsunami, which killed at least 155,000 people in 12 Asian nations, was so staggering, said Venkataraman, that the normally self-reliant people in the fishing villages are struggling. "The fisherfolk are proud people, tough and strong," she said. "They're not used to begging, but this incident has reduced them to beggars."

SEA TOOK EVERYTHING

Throughout the disaster zone, villages of the poor living at the water's edge were hit hardest. In India alone, more than 1,000 miles of coastline — home to hundreds of fishing villages, few of them named on maps — were ravaged by the tidal waves.

Rising Star's relief concept was born as the tsunamis hit and receded. Douglas was on a Christmas night telephone call with Gopi Sundaram, director of her agency's school for children of leprosy patients — a concrete-block structure on Chennai's southern beach road, less than a quarter of a mile from the water.

"Oh Becky, I have to go. There's seawater coming up to the house!" exclaimed Sundaram, who had earlier felt the earthquake shocks.

Ten minutes later, Douglas reached Sundaram again. "There's a thousand people on the road (beside the school), screaming and crying," she said he told her.

The people were wailing that the sea had taken their families. "Pray for us," Sundaram implored in tears before the line went dead.

In the large Douglas household, filled with family members home for Christmas, Becky Douglas said she was "frantic." "We just knelt on our knees and started praying," she said.

She would learn later that Rising Star did not have any tsunami victims; all 30 of the school's children were away with relatives at inland leprosy colonies around the region. And the school was spared.

Nearby, Venkataraman witnessed the big waves from her home and joined her neighbors in helping as many as 4,000 villagers who scrambled to the safety of a vacant lot. "Now, let's do something to help them get back on their feet," she thought, after distributing water and cooking oil.

RELUCTANT VOLUNTEER

Douglas called Venkataraman, who asked for her help. Douglas, mother of nine children, hesitated. Her leper project in India already consumed her free time, she said. But Venkataraman prevailed.

The plan "just made so much sense," Douglas said. She prepared to go to India.

Venkataraman, meanwhile, sought the help of fishery experts in designing the relief program. She went to seven fishing villages to help the fishermen collect the data they'll need to qualify.

This week, she presents her plans to officials of her district disaster relief agency, hoping that other nonprofits will follow their model and raise funds for other villages.

Before the waves hit, as many as 15,000 people lived in the nearby beachfront slum of Kasi Medu, in a maze of 6-foot warrens with connected concrete walls, some with thatched roofs.

Some of the men there had earned money by casting nets for fish, but now their ruined nets are in clumps of beach litter. The survivors, wearing donated clothes, appear to be holding their own.

In one fetid doorway, a woman sadly showed visitors a photo of her month-old grandson, who survived the waves only to die of exposure after his family was forced to sleep outside.

Nevertheless, Venkataraman has faith the fisherfolk will overcome the tragedy. "They will fish again, they will earn, and they will survive," she said.

Bill's notes: My boss told me I'd never make it to India in time to cover the effects of the Indian Ocean tsunami of Christmas, 2004. But I was confident I would get some good stories; besides, Becky Douglas, the local woman I'd profiled earlier for her works with the Indian leprosy colonies, was taking a significant role in tsunami relief efforts. I was able to convince an aide for a U.S. Senator to help expedite my visa application. The paper gave me special gear to transmit stories and photos. None of it worked. I wound up dictating my stories over a phone line. Then, I had to search the large city of Chennai for an internet café, where I could have my digital photos copied onto a disc, from which they could be transmitted to Atlanta for a few rupees. Even when you're on the other side of the world, deadlines must still be met.

ATLANTA JOURNAL CONSTITUTION
JAN. 12, 2005

KILLAY, INDIA— THE people who have hardly anything have taken in the people who have nothing. This coastal town of about 10,000 was largely spared in last month's devastating tsunami by a string of tiny barrier islands two miles offshore that took the brunt of the waves.

But the killer waves obliterated four fishing villages on the islands and swept about 2,000 islanders inland, killing 37, with another 20 unaccounted for. Many of the surviving villagers were rescued by the people of Killay, who pulled them from canals, off debris and out of the mangrove swamp that lines the shore.

Elsewhere along the 1,000-mile disaster front of the South Indian coastline, many tsunami victims have been relocated to tents in refugee centers. But in Killay, the people have made room for their stricken neighbors in their thatch-roof huts and small brick houses. "We are all one people. We do not separate ourselves from the others," said V.K. Sezhiyam, the panchayat, or political leader, of Killay and the island villages.

Killay itself is far from wealthy. Its villagers could use the goods being passed out from relief agency trucks. Yet they let their needier neighbors receive the aid. More than two weeks after the unprecedented disaster, the dead in the region's coastal communities have been buried or burned, and the Indian government has paid benefits to most of their families: 100,000 rupees for individuals killed, 4,000 rupees for displaced fishermen.

Widely feared outbreaks of serious diseases have not occurred. While some people feel they have not been treated fairly, and relief efforts sometimes seem uncoordinated, patience seems to prevail in most cases.

The people in Killay have worked out a system: Families from the barrier islands have been given tokens to identify themselves as tsunami victims. When a relief truck with food and supplies stopped in the village recently, women holding their tokens sat on the street and waited their turn.

One of the women in line, named Rajakumari, was dressed in a bright blue sari. She had lived in Chinna Vaykal, one of the barrier island fishing villages. Chinna Vaykal, with the beauty and seclusion of a luxury resort, was home to about 500 people who lived in modest, thatch-roof brick dwellings only yards from the seashore.

Rajakumari said she was happy there, caring for her three sons while her husband works in Singapore at a job that pays better than fishing. Her two older sons were back in Killay; only her 3-year-old son was on the island with her when the tsunami struck.

She was inside her house, she said, when she heard the ocean roar. "I came outside, and when I saw it, I grabbed my son," she said. The fierce wave ripped him from her grasp. "I couldn't hold him," she said, in a blank, even voice.

Rajakumari — who cannot swim — body-surfed the tsunami to the Killay shore. She could see other villagers being propelled along with her. "We couldn't help each other," she said. She remembers very little about how she was rescued. Reunited with her older sons, she is certain she will never live in Chinna Vaykal again.

Though the tsunami dissipated at the edge of Killay, the villagers were deeply traumatized by seeing people washed ashore by the waves, Sezhiyam said. "When we went to rescue people, we found them floating on thatch roofs and clinging to the mangrove trees," he said.

Later, the men of Killay took their boats to search for bodies, he said. They found 37 victims and buried them in a sandy clearing outside the village. Sezhiyam said he dug some of the pits. "I was digging a pit for one body, and they brought two more," he said.

To show visitors what a tsunami can do, Sezhiyam led a tour of Chinna Vaykal. It took about 45 minutes for the slow- moving fishing boat powered by an outboard motor to cross the strait.

On the island, scattered rubble from homes — bricks and thatch roofs — was lodged against palm tree trunks, evidence that people had once lived there. Power poles lay beyond the beach, like concrete driftwood. All that remained of the fishermen's dock were a few pilings poking pitifully from the sand.

The tsunami that cleared Chinna Vaykal of human life was by far the worst disaster to ever strike this land. The villagers remember the words of a Hindu woman known as the Mother, French-born Mira Alfassa, who is revered in the region for her saintly efforts to create a world where beauty and goodness reign. "You cannot deprive death of what it is due," she wrote.

Bill's notes: I wrote a story for the now-defunct Miami News based on the seizure of a large amount of cocaine found in a banana boat from Turbo, Colombia. Because the law makes ship owners liable for such seizures, their boat was also confiscated. The operators of a cooperative of banana growers contacted me after the story. They wanted me to tell their side of the story, which was that preventing the drugs from being smuggled aboard their ships was virtually impossible. I pitched the story to my bosses, but they declined. I queried the late, great Nora Ephron, who was then an editor at Esquire Magazine. She said she'd be happy to take a look at the story. So, I took vacation time and flew to Colombia to get the story below. Ephron passed on it, but the editors of the Boston Globe liked it and ran it. The editors at The News were furious that I had made this trip despite their decision that they didn't want me to do the story. Soon after it was published, I got fired from The Miami News. I was devastated, but an old friend and colleague from Orlando, George McEvoy (George was a great guy and a throwback. Before coming to Orlando, he'd worked at New York tabloids like The Mirror, where he did their annual series on Marilyn Monroe. He never learned to drive, so his wife Ruthie had to chauffeur him to all his assignments.) got me an interview at the now-defunct Fort Lauderdale News. I had a good year there and got an offer at the Louisville Courier Journal, then a Top Ten newspaper.

T URBO, COLOMBIA – This is a one-wharf town, and the wharf is made of mud.

Bananas are the major export, but the un-manifested companion cargo, cocaine, sells on American streets at about 100 times the free market price of gold.

Turbo is located across a small gulf from the Isthmus of Panama and about 22 miles past the paved end of a bad road.

Sweet, fat, Cavendish bananas are barged up jungle canals to Turbo and then loaded onto small freighters bound mostly for Florida.

In a single week during August 1975, $30 million worth of cocaine was seized aboard three of those same ships. In June 1976, U.S. Customs agents made the largest cocaine seizure in their history aboard a Turbo banana boat docked in Tampa.

That haul of 160 pounds was given a street value of $40 million. Turbo's port and the canals that lead to it are also used for importing banana by the Boston-based United Fruit Co. None of United's ships have been found carrying cocaine, Colombian officials say, primarily because those ships' crewmen must have American seamen's papers.

For the smugglers trying to get cocaine from Turbo to Miami, the task of putting an operative aboard the other banana boats is simple. They recruit the cocaine carriers, or "mules", from the thousands of poor men here.

A mule can make enough on one cocaine run to last him several years here even if he's caught. The head of the Colombian equivalent of the FBI in Turbo has a list of about 100 mules from the Turbo area who have been caught smuggling or linked to the smugglers by US authorities, only to be processed through the American justice system, shipped home and cut loose.

Legend says that cocaine was a gift to the ancient Incas from their god, Manco Capak, who wept when he saw his people starving. Cocaine, the gift of the gods, has now become the favored stimulant of the rich of the Western world; but it is the Colombians who pay the luxury tax.

The fabulous sums connected with the cocaine traffic have tilted an already shaky economy and lured to Colombia the element of the drug culture whose power is not derived from flowers.

Many of the men who become mules have spent most of their lives working for a weekly wage of 450 pesos, about $15, in the fields of the banana plantations. They are family men, and every Sunday night they walk from their shacks with their families to hear Mass in the main streets of towns like Apartado, about 20 miles east of Turbo.

They stand in front of the priest at the altar lit by neon candles but let their gaze wander to the shiny Jeeps parked along the street. After Mass, they say goodbye to their families and head into "La Zona."

In Apartado, "La Zona" is an eight-block strip of hardpan clay with nothing but bars on either side of the street. The men drink aguardiente, a local concoction with a hint of anisette and kerosene, until their week's pay becomes a memory.

Each bar in "La Zona" is identical to the next, except their facades are painted a different pastel shade. All the bars have concrete floors, jukeboxes blaring cumbias, a few chairs and women lolling in the archways. Most of the women are spindly, some pregnant and all available.

When a man starts to look for something more than this kind of life, he usually heads for Turbo.

The newcomer goes first to a small, triangular park in the center of town and sits with the other men like himself, to wait. Two sides of the park are formed by dusty streets. On the third is the port of Turbo, an earthen embankment clogged with wooden launches.

Soon enough, the newcomer will be invited, sometimes by a woman who looks too beautiful to be in a filthy town such as this, for a drink at El Scorpion bar across from the park.

He will be told that one of the banana boats needs men who want to make good money and who can keep their mouths shut. When he accepts, he is a mule.

Getting seaman's papers for a man who has never left the banana fields is no more difficult than mentioning the right person's name at the local police headquarters.

After a few runs, the mule has earned enough for a generous divorce settlement for his wife, a contract on a new home in Turbo with a concrete floor, and a down payment on a new red Jeep.

One such man was arrested during the large cocaine seizure last August in Tampa. Two weeks later he was deported and sent home on the same banana boat he had arrived on from Turbo.

Turbo was a jungle village on the Gulf of Darien until about 10 years-ago, when the fertile black soil of the surrounding plains of the Uraba was turned to the cultivation of bananas. With the bountiful yellow harvests came electricity, a road to the interior, a population of 35,000 — and the smugglers.

At first there was a more or less friendly traffic in marijuana. Colombian Gold thrives in the plains of Uraba, and the size of a man's crop of pot was a safe topic for conversation at El Scorpion.

Tastes in America have escalated to the fashionable white snorting powder, however, and the game in Turbo is no longer bush leagues.

In April 1975, the Captain of the Port of Turbo tried to enforce a ban against dugout canoes from the jungle swarming near the banana boats. He was gunned down at midday in the center of a Turbo street. When police tried to question witnesses, no one had seen anything.

"You can disappear faster from here than with the piranhas," said the Mexican captain of one of the banana boats on the Turbo-to-Miami run. He chooses to live in Turbo' with his wife and daughters, although he is convinced the area is a major junction in the cocaine pipeline.

Carlos Ardila is a Colombian policeman partly trained in Washington, DC, who was installed as mayor of Turbo in the aftermath of the port captain's assassination, partly because his predecessor was too friendly with the smugglers.

He isn't optimistic about the prospects of fighting the smugglers. The Turbo district customs operation has 50 men scattered out over six stations, charged with watching at least 13 airstrips and 200 miles of coastline, plus the rivers and the port.

"There's too much money involved for us to stop this business. The problem is too big," Ardila said.

Bill's notes: I had more fun than the teenagers on this, my first and only time on a sailboat. I was forced, however, to conquer my fear of heights to climb up the mast to get a photograph of the "termites" climbing up after me. One evening while anchored at Fort Jefferson in the Dry Tortugas, I went with the first mate to visit one of the fishing boats also in the lagoon. We traded a bottle of liquor for a fresh-caught King Mackerel. We dug a pit in the sand, got a driftwood fire going, grilled the mackerel, and enjoyed a drink while the sun slipped into the Gulf. Best fish I ever ate!

IT HAPPENED TO be a nice day a couple of weeks ago, so the eight little hoodlums canceled their advance reservations at the state prison and went sailing instead.

Aboard the tall ship they swaggered — the car thief, the dope freak, the revolving-door runaway, the street-gang member, the hot-CB dealer, the professional truant, the breaking and entering artist and the county record holder for the highest number of junior high school expulsions.

All were card-carrying members of the Junior Chamber of Conners.

Once past the gangplank, however, they traded in the chips on their shoulders for deck mops and the smirks on their faces for salutes.

Before they left the ship, these kids who previously might have pulled a knife when ordered to clean up their bedrooms were snappily, if not happily, cleaning up other people's commodes. These eight were also the last set of "termites," or apprentice crewmen, aboard the brig Unicorn, a square-rigged sailing vessel built to the specifications of an earlier century and the needs of some modern-day misfits.

For the past six months, the Unicorn has been under loan to a unique statewide juvenile offender rehabilitation program based in Deerfield Beach. The umbrella agency for the six nautical training centers around Florida is the Associated Marine Institutes.

The Unicorn is now back in its Deerfield Beach base, and her use as an inspiration to delinquent youths has ended. Her owner died and her sale is forthcoming.

The institutes take kids in penal institutions and give them a last chance to shake the criminal label. They use the lure of the open sea and the discipline required to survive on it to give the kids a marketable skill and a measure of self-respect.

Their uniqueness among juvenile offender programs is the fact they are able to claim that they actually work. The institutes claim more than 80 per cent of their graduates stop committing crimes — a rate of success about equal to the rate of failure at state reformatories.

State taxpayers support the kids in the institutes to a tune of about $2,800 per youth for the six-month program. The cost is less than half that of the reformatories.

During this Bicentennial summer, the Unicorn has served as a reward for the insitutes' students and as a promotional vehicle for the program.

Including the Operation Sail seagoing spectacular, about 300 institute students have sailed short tours aboard her as apprentices to the permanent crew.

The vessel's owner, oil magnate William W. Smith, of Fort Lauderdale and Philadelphia, had the Unicorn transformed into replica of a Revolutionary War era brig, using the institutes' students for much of the unskilled labor.

Smith had dreamed of having the Unicorn sail among the tall ships. He died four months before his dream was realized, but the 141-foot ship was the first American flag vessel to finish in the Bermuda-to-Newport race.

Since then, the Unicorn and its crews of juvenile offenders has visited nearly every major port on the Eastern seaboard. The association between the institutes and the Unicorn will end this coming week, since Smith's estate has put the ship up for sale.

Whatever the Unicorn's future, she has provided hundreds of culturally deprived boys with adventures and experiences of which even the wealthiest can only dream. Its last set of "termites" proved to be as vulnerable to her magic as their predecessors.

The group consisted of the eight boys among the 43 students at Pinellas Marine Institute in St. Petersburg who had received the highest marks in scholarship, seamanship and behavior. As they boarded the vessel that would be their home for the next 11 days, they were not quite a motley crew.

Confronting the Unicorn's captain, Doug Hoogs, wasn't a shock for them, since Hoogs once had been a counselor at their institute. Meeting the other officers was a different story.

They soon discovered that the red-bearded Buddha chasing around telling them they should clean between their ears with a vacuum pump was the first mate, Sam Gehring.

The imposing figure with the blond beard who kept insisting that the proper form of address was "Mister," not "Huh" or "Hey," was Sailmaster Jeff Berry.

Gehring was an ocean-racing sailor and Berry an ex-Navy man and a former sailing ship captain. Neither man intended to make allowances for the kids' social problems.

The five junior members of the paid crew all had been through the apprentice stage themselves, so they knew all the games the new hands might try to play.

As the Unicorn pulled away from the dock at St. Petersburg, she encountered strong headwinds. Captain Hoogs decided to keep the sails furled and motor down to the next stop, the Dry Tortugas.

Crewmen and apprentices were divided into two watches that would rotate the duties of running the ship, and life aboard the Unicorn settled into the harmony of the waves.

Most of the apprentices' assignments consisted of the odd or dirty jobs on the ship, but each kid also got a turn at taking the helm of the Unicorn. The boys who couldn't be trusted with Dad's car keys were as steady as old salts at the wheel of a million-dollar sailing ship.

The trip to the Dry Tortugas was smooth, the only highlight being a warm summer rain. When the Unicorn tied up alongside the dock of the 130-year-old Fort Jefferson National Monument that practically covers Garden Key, the ship finally looked as if it were in its proper era.

Fort Jefferson's 42 million bricks were mortared together to ward off a British invasion, but there was never an angry shot fired from the place and most of its gun ports were only for show. For two full days the work duties were minimal, and the apprentices were given time for snorkeling, wreck diving, fishing and exploring the fort.

There was also time for them to talk about what brought them here. The kid who had probably come the farthest to reach this spot was Terry L., the only African-American boy in the group. Terry was 16 and a member of an informal street gang whose main preoccupations, by his account, were "robbin' places and messin' with women."

He was netted in a roundup after a rumble in which two people were shot. That could have earned Terry an all-expense-paid vacation at the Marianna training school, but his counselor got him into the marine institute.

When he reported, Terry could barely stay afloat in the water and he had even less success trying to read a book. It was this wiry, slow-to-talk boy, however, who led the group of apprentices in the competition to qualify for the trip.

He retained that leadership during the voyage, sometimes prodding a mate who was too quick to take a cigarette break while the others were still working.

Pride in achievement was a forceful motivator for these kids, but spite worked sometimes, too. Mike O. had already paid two extended visits to state reformatories and had been written off even by the marine institute counselors.

A tow-headed kid whose voice hasn't quite finished changing yet, Mike said the institute officials weren't very optimistic about his chances when they accepted him a second time for their program. "They didn't think I could make it when I came back," Mike said. "I just happened to prove them wrong."

When Mike was 14, he stole a car and got into a wreck that caused a fatality. A couple of slips while he was on parole at the marine institute earned him a return trip to the reformatory.

"I was planning to go back to my old friends when I got out the second time,' he said.

But he got a call from a marine institute counselor, and he decided to give it another try.

BILL OSINSKI

This time, too, he got off to a shaky start. A shoving incident cost him a huge demerit. But he wanted to make the trip, so he did enough extra work to finish in the top eight.

His work during the first leg of the trip earned him a rigging knife as the best apprentice. Mike is one of the apprentices whose behavior problems appear to be rooted in the public-school system.

"Before, I never asked questions in school," he said. "Here, they care about you. You can ask 10 questions and they take the time to make sure you know the answers," he said.

For Mike W., the answer to his problems at school was to drop out in the ninth grade. His family had moved frequently, and he kept getting older than his classmates.

"I'd hear them tell the 14-year-olds to stay away from the 17-year-olds," he said.

As the age difference grew, so did the intervals between his appearances in school. His last year, he said, he showed up about once a week.

After he dropped out, he started working at two jobs. He also started drinking. He was picked up twice for disorderly intoxication, and since he was still a minor, he was taken to a detention center.

"The next time I'll just tell 'em I'm 18, and then I'll get taken to a detox center instead of detention," said Mike, a straight-looking kid who fights a daily battle against his bitterness over being in the state's juvenile system.

Some of the apprentices found there were elements of personal struggle during the voyage.

Bob K., a shaggy-headed wise-cracker who used to do a thriving resale business in hot CB radios, dropped his eyeglasses into the Gulf on the first day out. But he insisted on squinting and straining through his turns at the helm.

When Bob F. came aboard, he carried a shoulder chip as big as the foremast. He seldom passed up a chance while in the apprentices' quarters to snap at another trainee, "You don't tell me what to do!"

But to the persons who were supposed to tell him what to do, Bob was able to rein his temper and perform as an exemplary apprentice.

Mike C., a quiet, baby-faced runaway artist who entered the institute after plowing up the lawn of his mother's ex-boyfriend, fought his tendency toward light fingers. He encountered conditions where personal integrity is required to keep personal gear in the right lockers.

If there is any outward thing that sets these kids apart from their contemporaries, it's probably the cigarette mystique. Cigarettes are much more than smokes, they are a mandatory accessory of the 16-going-on-30 lifestyle.

No job or no pose is considered complete unless it includes a cigarette-punctuated lip. Drags become so dear that the unfortunate ones who run out early in the voyage will gladly pay scalper's prices of up to $1.75 a pack.

More discipline is dished out on these trips than food, and the food is abundant.

Two of the apprentices strayed too far from their assigned partners while snorkeling and soon found themselves out of the water for the rest of the day. When some cigarettes were stolen, the kids were rounded up and all their activities were stopped until the culprit was identified and the matter resolved.

As far as incidents go, however, that was it. The behavior of these "delinquents" could have been a model for the Boy Scouts. By journey's end, their willingness to work and cooperate was drawing compliments even from red-bearded Sam.

The first night after the Unicom left the Tortugas and was headed for home, there was a chance to set a few stabilizing sails. A nearly full moon played the part of "Scotsman in the rigging," giving the teams of crewmen and apprentices free light to set the jibs and spanker.

Perhaps it was the dim light that made it hard to tell who belonged and who didn't. Their time aboard the Unicom was too short to turn any of them into real sailors, but each one made progress toward manhood.

Bill's notes: I've never been as exhausted as I was when I emerged from the cold, black heart of Mammoth Cave. I laid myself on my back on the road near the cave entrance, and the stars glowed like bonfires in the pre-dawn sky. I had no one to blame but myself; I was the one who'd come up with the idea of accompanying an expedition of cave explorers. My plan at that moment was to go to my motel and sleep the whole day. But when I called my wife to report that I had survived, she relayed an urgent summons from my boss. I showered, dressed and headed out for the next story. I gained immense respect for the spelunkers' spirit of adventure and stamina, although I also had become convinced that they were, in fact, crazy.

LOUISVILLE COURIER JOURNAL,
DECEMBER 2, 1979

I FELT AS IF I were the Creature from the Black Lagoon and I'd just been captured by someone who wanted to use me in a truss commercial. Clouded in a mist of sweat steaming away into the frigid darkness, my body was totally slathered with mud and dangling down the side of a small but steep cliff. A cloth strap wrapped around my haunches and attached to a climbing rope kept me from falling, but the inertial overload straining against the strap ruled out any more upward progress.

My arms had no more strength, and the face of the wall had no footholds. "Let me down, and pick me up on your way back," I entreated my companions. "We'd like to, but you'll be a Fudgesicle by then," they answered. I soon found a way to the top.

It took a death threat to prevent me from flunking spelunking. Such was the mild-mannered reporter's welcome to the wild side of Mammoth Cave.

It's hard to think of a wilderness served by an interstate highway. But near the midpoint of the Kentucky stretch of 1-65, just a mile or two as the mole burrows from the nearest souvenir stand, a person with a curious nature can get farther away from civilization than he'd be in the heart of the Okefenokee Swamp. The place is Mammoth Cave, but not the parts of the vast labyrinth that have been made safe for the family with an extra day to spend on their way down to Disney World.

Today's tourist trails were the terror-tinged pathways to the black heart of the netherworld for yesteryear's explorers. They pushed into the darkness with only lard-oil lamps for illumination and guts for a map. They lowered themselves in baskets into previously unplumbed depths and used flimsy ladders to bridge supposedly uncrossable crevasses. "These people faced the unknown," said Harold Meloy, a Shelbyville, Ind., attorney who has researched the history of Mammoth Cave.

After each major discovery, the entrepreneurs weren't far behind the explorers. The mummified remains of a prehistoric Indian boy were at one time hyped for the tourists as the body of a pioneer girl who took her own life rather than submit to torture. As soon as a new passage was found, the first question often was: Could a new entrance for paying customers be punched in from the topside? Yet in each new passageway of system that was lit by the wild cavers' lamps, there were always new black holes that hinted of more secrets ahead.

The process of solving one riddle and finding the clues to two new ones continues today. In October, members of The Cave Research Foundation, a group of semi-pro cavers, announced the discovery of a major underground river and a passageway that add 15 miles to the explored portion of Mammoth Cave. The discovery gives Mammoth more than 230 miles of charted passages and firms its claim as the world's longest cave.

The modern brand of caver approaches the challenge quite differently from his predecessors. Nowadays, wild cavers are anything but wild in their techniques. They sketch and survey and report on every foot of new passageway they travel, while the old-timers often treated knowledge of the cave as a commodity to be hoarded. Modern cavers explore in groups and log in their travel routes, while in past years it was often extremely important to the cave explorer that no one know where he was. Where past expeditions might have been halted by flooded passageways or supposedly bottomless pits, the caver now simply breaks out his wet suit or rappelling ropes.

That doesn't mean that things are necessarily easier now. To reach virgin cave, the explorer still must walk and crawl and squirm through the miles of previously discovered passages. Also, most of the dry, sandy caves that can be reached by walking have been found, so the primary direction of most modern expeditions is down deeper into the cold and the mud.

That is the real difference between the old-time and the modern explorer, said Lyman Cutliff, a cave-country resident who has spent all but about 20 of his 79 years probing the secrets of Mammoth Cave. "They're always seeking the deepest pit, looking for the deepest hole," Cutliff said. "I was always under the impression that was Satan's territory," he added.

If Dante is a reliable guide when he depicts Lucifer in a frozen underground chamber, then the modern cavers are getting close.

Our first stop on our foray into The Inferno makes me think we're in the wrong half of the Divine Comedy. Paradise Passageway in Mammoth Cave is just what its name implies. Mother Nature was on a rococo rampage when she designed these corridors. Almost every inch of the walls and the ceiling are part of a stone hothouse, hung with brittle orchids of gypsum. The white tapers of the gypsum flowers have been extruded through the sandstone over thousands of years. Some of them have grown up to a foot long and arched all the way back to the wall. A variety of this formation, called "cotton gypsum," is so delicate that the heat from a passing lamp can make it flutter.

After this passage was discovered in the late 1930s, plans were made to turn it into a public attraction. A surface entrance and a long stairway were built, and a tourist trail was laid. But it was later decided that there was no way to protect the stone flowers of Paradise from visitors' inclinations to snatch souvenirs. So, like uninsured jewels, the corridors that hold one of Mammoth Cave's most beautiful treasures must be kept locked up.

Authentic stories of earlier eras of cave exploration are nearly as hard to get at as the gypsum flowers of Paradise. Lyman Cutliff is one of the few men remaining who can tell them first-hand.

"I kind of grew up in the caves," said Cutliff. He started tagging after his father on cave trips when he was 8 or 9, and he was still a teenager when he started working toward becoming a guide himself. "Back then, you didn't put in no application for a tour job," he said. "You had to be a trailer, someone who brought up the rear of an expedition, for three years before you was ever let loose with a party in the cave."

Like guides before him and after him, Cutliff took care of the paying guests during his workday and satisfied his own curiosity about the unexplored passageways on his own time. "I'd get to wondering about someplace I'd passed by, and then I'd go down at night after the day's work was over," he said.

It was on such an excursion in 1938 in the Salts Cave section of the system that Cutliff and a companion, Grover Campbell, happened to meet Lost John, a somewhat less successful cave explorer from a couple of thousand years back.

Cutliff was interested in trying to prove a theory, previously expounded by his father and uncle, that Indians had explored regions of the cave that the white man didn't discover until the 20th century. He and Campbell were supervising a crew of Civilian Conservation Corps workers one day in a part of the cave where Cutliff felt evidence for his theory could be found. While one man stayed with the crew, the other would go off down a side passageway.

When Campbell came back saying he'd found a mummified bat up on a remote ledge, Cutliff knew they were on the right track. They returned to the area together, and the two men sat down for a moment after they'd finished the climb to the ledge. "Grover put his hand on something. it was a mummy's head and he said, 'What in the goddam hell is this?'" Cutliff recalled. "I told him, 'Grover, that's just what I've been looking for.'"

They'd found the remains of a prehistoric forebearer of the spirit of adventure in darkness that they were perpetuating two millennia later. The dry coolness of the cave had mummified the remains of an intrepid Indian miner, who came to be known as Lost John.

The Indian had advanced about two miles into the cave sometime about 2,300 years ago, with reed torches for his only light. He had scrambled onto the distant ledge in search of something. Meloy thinks it was gypsum to be used for ceremonial purposes; Cutliff thinks it was epsom salts that he could use for trade with other tribes. Whatever his quarry, a six-ton chunk of cave rock became his instant tombstone, crushing the lower half of his body while leaving only his head and one shoulder exposed.

In contrast to previous finders of Mammoth Cave mummies, whose initial reaction often was to convert the bones into a tourist attraction, Cutliff and Campbell were scrupulously professional in reporting their find to park authorities. This ensured that Lost John could be studied scientifically and then given a glass-encased place of honor in the cave.

The aftermath of the discovery was not particularly beneficial for Cutliff, though. Among those who flocked to the cave after the mummy find was a network radio crew that wanted to interview Cutliff. The guide's speech was apparently not backwoodsy enough to satisfy the interviewers, so they told Cutliff to add more hillbilly twang to his answer. Cutliff refused, and not too long after the park operators heard about it, he was fired.

That was hardly the end of Cutliff's caving days. He spent the next 30 years poking around below the surface of Cave Country, most of them helping the operators of a nearby resort develop tourist trails in caves. He was in his mid-60s when the physical demands of caving finally caught up with him. He was about in the middle of a 3,000-foot crawlway, when he felt a weakness in his arm and chest.

"That was the one time my spirits kinda fell," Cutliff remembers. He lay on his belly in the darkness until the heart attack subsided and some of his strength returned. Then he crawled back out again. Since then, a stroke has left Cutliff partially paralyzed, and he has passed custody of his family's caving tradition onto his son Louis, who is now the chief guide at Mammoth Cave National Park.

Cutliff was able to challenge the underworld for more than 50 years because he respected it. "I always tried to keep in mind that wherever this passage goes, I've got to come back," he said. Not all his contemporaries felt that way, and one of them, Floyd Collins, paid with his life for underestimating Mammoth Cave. "I noticed that failing in Floyd," said Cutliff, who caved with Collins on occasion. "He was too ready to take chances. You can't do that down there."

The last time Collins took a chance in Mammoth Cave, he was in a hurry to get out after he'd found a new passageway, Cutliff said. Collins, he said, was moving through a crawlway in a sandstone breakdown, a centuries-old pile of rock created by the collapse of a cave roof. It was the kind of formation, Cutliff said, in which some of the rocks were only loosely suspended in ice; the kind in which an experienced caver should know to be extremely careful with his feet. Somehow, whatever was making the breakdown solid broke down, and Collins was trapped in the cold and dark.

"You've got to think about the kind of place you're in and how you're going to get out," Cutliff said. "You can't play around and kick around." By the time Cutliff heard about Collins' predicament and arrived at the surface entrance to the cave, there was already an overabundance of rescue workers. "There was a lot of people who didn't know what they was doing," he said.

He went down as far as he could into the cave and soon saw the basic problem: The rockfall that had pinned Collins was between him and his rescuers. Cutliff got within earshot of the doomed man and heard Collins call out, "What are you doing out there?"

They were doing just about everything they could, but the situation was only deteriorating. The activity and heat generated by the rescue workers were making the breakdown even less stable. "You could hear things falling all the time," Cutliff said. Once, they got close enough to loop a harness around Collins' shoulders. The plan was to pull him out, and Collins was given another rope to pull on in case the pain got to be too great. The rescuers pulled, but so did Collins.

Then they talked of digging a separate shaft down to Collins, a move which Cutliff endorsed. By the time the plan got organized, though, Collins had died of exposure.

We began the descent from Paradise, but the trip was still mostly like a midnight hike in a rock quarry. The clay trail we followed down the broad, limestone-walled avenues was compacted and dry. Because of the detour and the attendant picture-taking, we were already running late. Just above this chamber of everlasting night, the sun was well past its zenith, so when we reached a not-too-menacing opening of a passage off the main trail, it was decided to stop for lunch.

The only picnics in Mammoth Cave National Park are held on the surface. Down below, dining is strictly a survival technique. Every surface is sloped, and every table-sized rock has been set with a natural cloth of semi-sticky muck. Hunger, however, can overcome the obstacles of eating at obtuse angles.

The fare was glorified C-rations — cans of main courses and fruits with candy-bar chasers. And the stoves — small metal tripods just big enough to hold a can over a blob of burning Sterno — would've delighted a dedicated hobo. While I slurped down a can of mandarin oranges, I noticed that the contents of my spaghetti can on my little stove was rising slowly out of its container.

My first thought was botulism, but I was informed that I just needed to stir the contents. Still, my stove kept slipping, so I had to settle for a tepid serving of a nightmare.

Cave cuisine was not always thus. The following passage is from an account in the 1844 tour book "Rambles in the Mammoth Cave" of a meal served during a cave trip made in the 1840s by Alexander Bullitt, a Louisville-based journalist: "The guide arranged the plates, knives and forks, wine glasses, etc., on a huge table of rock and announced, 'Dinner is ready!' We filled our plates with the excellent viands made at the Cave House, and seating ourselves on the rocks or nitre earth, partook of our repast with the gusto of gourmands, and quaffing, ever and anon, wines which would have done credit to the Astor or Tremont House."

That party had included a fat man who grumbled about the awkward circumstances of the meal. I identified strongly with that fellow, but I kept my own counsel, stomped on my spaghetti can so it could fit more easily into my backpack, stuffed down a candy-bar dessert, and trudged ahead into the mucky, murky passageway.

Afterwards, I was glad I'd been allowed to eat the meal under the foolish presumption that I had, up until that point, been experiencing the real thing. Had I known what lay ahead, I would've never held down my noodles.

When they're above ground, modern cavers eat just like normal people. The morning air at the Cave Research Foundation's base camp within Mammoth Cave National Park is filled with the sounds and smells of bacon spattering and coffee perking. By 8 or 9 o'clock, the expedition leader has already decided which passages will be explored that day. But the troops are just starting to stagger to the breakfast table; most of them emerged from the caves only six or seven hours ago.

Members of the foundation have done much of the significant exploration of Mammoth Cave in the past two decades. It is a private, non-profit group that also supports scientific research in speleology (the study of cave systems) and often takes stands on political and environmental issues that touch the cave. Nothing, however, is dearer to their hearts than grubbing around in the uncharted mud of Mammoth Cave.

Several times a year, usually on long holiday weekends, as many as 40 Foundation cavers come to Mammoth Cave from as far away as New Hampshire. While most people are carving turkey, the cavers will fan out in groups of four or five to spend 12 hours or more in the subterranean labyrinth. After hours of walking, crawling and sometimes floating down underground streams, they will reach a point where, after a few more hours of painstaking work in the darkness, they will have added a fraction of an inch or so to the map of Mammoth Cave.

Such expeditions operate under the auspices of the National Park Service. Destinations and expected return times for all the exploration parties are logged in with park rangers. They assemble, fittingly enough, at Floyd Collins old house to plan and launch their excursions. The green frame buildings that were once home and ticket office while the Collinses operated Crystal Cave as a tourist attraction are now the CRF base camp. The cavers are mostly young, mostly thin, mostly university-connected and all in good physical shape. Being female is no barrier to serious caving; small bodies with stamina are the ones that often do best in caves.

They start separating the persons from the impersonators at ground level. Since the explorers sometimes must squeeze their bodies through openings that wouldn't make a decent dog-trot door, they test themselves before they go down. The device, which bears more than physical resemblance to a medieval torture apparatus, is a wooden rectangle with an adjustable top edge, which can be set at desired heights from the bottom.

Those who want to go through the tighter cave passages must first get between the bars set 9, or 8, or 7 or even 6 inches apart. To make it, the candidate must lie flat on the ground, stick his or her head and arms through, and then wriggle his or her lumpier portions slowly past the bars in a sort of adult re-enactment of the birth process. Some people get no further than their thoracic cavities; others can slip through a 7-inch opening as if their torsos were plastic. For the most lithe, only the size of their heads limit how low the bars can go.

Once properly screened, the caver must be outfitted for the underworld. The most important item of standard equipment is a helmet with a lamp. Most of the CRF cavers prefer a carbide arc lamp, in which the flame is actually acetylene gas, produced by the reaction of lump carbide and water in a small chamber. Kneepads and gloves are almost always required, but the only criterion for other clothing is that it be something the caver can afford to have saturated with mud and ripped by jagged cave rocks. For trips that involve traveling underground streams, wet suits also must be carried. Small kit bags are packed with food, water, and extra carbide.

Getting in and out of the caves is only half the story of these expeditions. Every inch of passageway surveyed is documented for a permanent record. Each party leader comes back with sketches and precise measurements of the cave. A detailed trip report, describing the route taken and the problems encountered, is made part of a file for that part of the cave. The measurements are transmitted to cartographers who will add the data to a comprehensive map of the system.

"Check the map!" I shouted. "This can't be the right way!" Unfortunately for me, it was. When I was booked for this tour, something was mentioned in passing about "a little mud," but here I was on my hands and knees in muck that wouldn't let go when I wanted to move. The passageway that had looked so commodious when we started in after lunch had degenerated first into a low-roofed section that we had to sort of crabwalk through, and then into a twisting crawlspace with room for only one person at a time. And we hadn't even reached the first tough spot yet. We had received a

warning of a tight squeeze through a breakdown pile, but I wasn't prepared for things to become so tight so soon. There was no longer a passageway, just some spaces between the slime-covered rocks. After raking open my knuckles on one of those rocks, I remembered that I should be wearing my gloves. The object at this point became to slither through the spaces to the wider chamber that lay somewhere beyond. My body does not slither well, however. Only my kneepads slithered down to my shins. All of a sudden, I was pushing with my feet but not going any were. There just wasn't enough room for my shoulders and chest. I was stuck. I strained against the rocks; again, no forward progress. My sweat and my cursing steamed up the cold cave air. Then I made a startling discovery — though my own girth did not need supplementing in this kind of situation, that is exactly what I'd done by leaving my pack at my side. By pushing the pack out in front of me, I immediately became slimmer around the middle; and by relaxing and squirming rather than tensing and shoving, I found the rocks would let me pass.

I was out of that squeeze and into a passage where every now and then you could stand up. In the cave, you learn to appreciate small comforts. You also learn that the secrets of Mammoth are not easily unraveled.

It is the tradition of this labyrinth that most people who discovered its secrets were loath to share them. Secrecy was in fact the byword of the cave for more than the first century of its operation as a tourist attraction, according to historian Meloy.

Owners and trustees of the cave expressly forbade the publishing of any detailed survey of the cave until the 1930s, when steps were begun to make it into a national park. The reason for this, Meloy said, was because the owners had a vested interest in not letting it be known how extensive Mammoth Cave was. They believed that they owned the cave wherever it went, but they were pretty sure that it extended beyond their surface property lines, he said.

The owners didn't want their assumption tested in court, Meloy said, and with good reason. When a rival cave operator in the 1920s took to court his claim that he owned the part of Mammoth Cave that lay beneath his property, he was upheld.

BILL OSINSKI

Not wanting to tell about the caves did not necessarily mean not wanting to know. For the guides, who in the early days were often poor men and in the earliest days were slaves, knowing of a passageway that no one else knew sometimes meant being the favorite of the paying visitors, Meloy said.

In 1908, Meloy said, one of the cave trustees, a Washington, D.C., jurist, commissioned a secret survey of the cave. The surveyor was Max Kemper, a German military officer. He spent about four months poking around in the caves, telling the local people that he was simply a "cave buff," Meloy said.

Using his military expertise at measuring distances by pacing, and with a compass for his only tool, Kemper compiled the only comprehensive survey of the cave that existed until the establishment of the national park. It was a good thing that Kemper's work was kept secret, Meloy said, because it confirmed the cave extended beyond the operators' surface property lines.

Kemper purposely put no direction indicators and no scale legends on his cave maps, Meloy said, so that the subsurface survey could not be linked to points above ground. That relationship was not established until 1949, when Kemper's surface map was found in the trustee's estate. That map had reference points that corresponded to previously unexplained dots on Kemper's cave map. In keeping with the nature of his secret mission, Max Kemper was never seen again in Kentucky's Cave Country.

Secrecy has been a vital element in the skullduggery involved in some of the skull-digging episodes in the history of the cave. There was a 19th-century mummy-switch pulled on Bill Cutliff, the uncle of Lyman Cutliff, the mummy finder of the 20th century. Cutliff said that in 1875 his uncle was caving with two trusted friends in the Salts Cave, which was then owned by the proprietors of Mammoth Cave.

In those days, mummies were big tourist draws, and three mummies found earlier in Mammoth Cave had made the rounds of big-city museums and drawn nationwide attention to the cave.

Bill Cutliff found the mummy, then met his friends and showed them the spot, Cutliff said. The three agreed to go back the following

Wednesday and take it out, he said. But Uncle Bill's friends apparently didn't have a very reliable calendar; they came back on Tuesday. A cave operator in competition with Mammoth Cave, Cutliff said, paid them $75 for the Salts Cave mummy and then billed it as one that had been found in his cave.

According to Meloy's pamphlet on the mummies of Mammoth Cave, the Salts Cave mummy came to be known as Little Alice. Later, Little Alice became quite a celebrity, though her origins remained a bit shady. A subsequent owner of the mummy, who was also manager at Mammoth Cave and operator of the stage line into the cave, exhibited her as the original Mammoth Cave mummy. (That mummy, called Fawn Hoof, was found in 1813 and was in posthumous retirement at a Washington museum.)

Anyway, Little Alice made the rounds at the 1893 World's Fair in Chicago, escorted by a Mammoth Cave guide. After helping put Mammoth Cave on the map as a tourist attraction, Little Alice was retired to her owner's barn, according to Meloy. However, in the 1920s, a new promoter running a cave attraction in competition with Mammoth acquired Little Alice and reincarnated her as "The Lady of the Cave." The mummy was billed as "the little girl turned to stone," an Indian captive who sacrificed her life rather than endure torture.

After the national park was established, Little Alice fell onto hard times. She was shuttled from the bottom shelf of a small museum at the cave to a storage warehouse. In the late 1950s, according to Meloy's pamphlet, she was dusted off and examined scientifically. Little Alice turned out to be an Indian boy who probably lived in the first century A.D.

The circumstances surrounding the discovery of Little Alice made Bill Cutliff more secretive than before, Lyman Cutliff said. The elder Cutliff supposedly knew where two more mummies were, but never discussed the matter after his betrayal. "Uncle Bill wouldn't even tell my father where they were," Cutliff said.

But sometime after his uncle's death Cutliff was called aside by a fellow guide who'd been his uncle's best friend. The guide said he'd been present when Bill Cutliff was dying and told his wife where the mummies were. The guide gave Lyman Cutliff a sketch of Mummy's Valley, where the two other mummies might be found.

"I never could find them," Cutliff said, "but they're down there."

The climb up the minicliff had been accomplished; now the trick was not to fall back down.

No sooner had our party all managed the vertical climb described at the beginning of this story than we had to cross a pit. It was hardly bottomless, but 15 or 20 feet can seem like a long way down a cylinder of rock.

The top of the opening was about 6 feet wide; too far to jump. Again, there were no convenient footholds, so the chosen method of crossing was to hold on to some dents in the rock formations above. The theory was that by moving your hands far enough along, you could get close enough for your foot to reach something solid on the far side.

It was only a few seconds in the traverse that my feet were slipping on smooth rock, and my grip on the rocks above was all that kept me from slipping into the pit, but in that brief time, all my overdue insurance premiums flashed before my eyes. It was probably the knowledge my handhold wouldn't last much longer that made me lurch out with my floundering foot and gain the other side of the pit.

Traveling with experienced cavers was the only way I could've made this trip. However, my ego suffered every time I saw a companion waltz through a section of cave that I had regarded as a mortal challenge.

Before my quivers ended from the pit-crossing, I looked back to see Chip Welter, a student from Ohio, blithely posing for pictures at the same point where I'd just brushed with eternity. Our photographer, Stewart Bowman, needed to try a few different exposures and then to change film, and Weller straddled the pit all the while, as if there were a mattress at the bottom.

Nowadays, a person has to be inside Mammoth Cave a long time before he reaches a point where no one else has been. Earlier generations of explorers reached virgin cave a lot quicker and spent a lot longer in the unknown. Dozens of milestone discoveries have been made, but a few stand out.

The discovery that helped convert Mammoth Cave from a spent saltpeter mine into a Wonder Of The World occurred in 1838. It was then that Stephen Bishop, a slave and guide, and Hiram Stephenson, a visitor from Georgetown, Ky., crossed Impossible Pit. People had tried to make the traverse, with no luck, for about 30 years, Meloy said. Most of what now is known as Mammoth Cave lay beyond. The two men took a ladder of cedar poles with them, jammed it into the far side of the pit, and crawled across what was thought to be an unbreachable void. In the following few months, Bishop's continuing explorations approximately doubled the known size of Mammoth Cave.

A more whimsical milestone was reached in 1858, when Courtland Prentice, a son of the editor of The Louisville Daily Journal, allowed himself to be put in a basket and lowered into a pit called The Maelstrom. He, like generations of journalists that were to follow, succumbed to a temptation to rhapsodize about his excursion. An excerpt from his poem reads:

> *Swing o'er the pit of gloom*
> *Into the awful stillness*
> *And the sepulchral chill.*

Explorations for the next hundred years after Stephen Bishop's crossing of the Impossible Pit were largely extensions of the same type of high-and-dry caving. But in 1938, two guides for the Park Service, Pete Hanson and Leo Hunt, launched the deep-and-wet era.

Hanson and Hunt took an aluminum skiff and went down Roaring River, an underground stream that can only be explored under certain groundwater-flow conditions, because it tends to flood its chambers in times of high water. They used the boat to get them to side passages, and after some long crawls in the mud, found a large avenue with no prior footprint. This was called the New Discovery, the region that includes the Paradise corridors. Both Hanson and Hunt are dead now, but they left guideposts that would aid future cavers in making the next significant advance in exploring the system.

In 1972, a group of CRF cavers entered the Flint Ridge cave system, which was thought to be separate from the Mammoth Cave ridge. They were looking for a link to Mammoth Cave, and the first real indication that they were about to break through was when they found Hanson's and Hunt's initials beside an arrow marker on a mud wall. The cavers later re-entered the Flint Ridge caves, accompanied by a park ranger, and slogged through rivers and squeezed through breakdowns until they came out of a nearly flooded passage at the bottom of a steel railing on a tourist trail.

Their discovery certified Mammoth Cave's claim to be the longest cave in the world.

This had to be the end of the trail, I told myself. The passageway simply stopped at the pile of rocks ahead.

Suddenly, our party leader, Kathleen Dixon, was gone. I scoffed when a companion said she'd gone down into the rock pile. I laughed when it became clear that the plan was for the rest of us to follow.

I couldn't see an opening in the breakdown big enough to post a medium-sized manila envelope, much less insert a full-sized human. Nonetheless, I went in. The sensation was like being trapped inside a piece of modern sculpture or trying to crawl through a concertina. There was no form or direction to the passage; it went generally down, but it seemed that the bendable parts of my body were heading in different directions. When I dropped down, I realized that even though this breakdown was quite a bit tighter than the first squeeze, I'd gotten through easier.

And when we dropped through the rock pile, near our destination, I thought how incredible it was that I was comfortable. I was totally covered with sticky mud. It was cold, and I was still steaming from the exertion; yet I'd learned to live and function from within a layer of ooze. This was probably evidence of the amazing adaptability of human beings more than it was of any degree of proficiency I'd developed as a caver.

We got to the end of the last survey and got ready to plot the coordinates of the unknown. Kathleen extracted her trip leader's book to start taking down the data. Chip and his sister, Lynn, did the actual surveying, with Chip handling the long measuring tape and Lynn the compass. Chip went 40 or 50 feet into a side cavern, and Lynn took a sighting, and then they both moved up. Lynn found Chip's spot by using the little mud man he'd left as a marker.

Lynn had to take a reverse sighting back to her original point, and if her two readings disagreed by more than a single degree, she had to go back and start over again.

The channel we surveyed wasn't too impressive. The ceiling got progressively lower, until it ended back in the main chamber; just a short loop with no promising leads. It was time to go back. We'd been in the cave about nine hours, and the trip back would take another three.

Why do they do it? The answer to that question is one area where the old-time and the modern cavers can find some general agreement.

"That was our purpose, to satisfy our own curiosity," said Lyman Cutliff. "I always wanted to see what was over the next hill or around the next bend."

Kathleen Dixon said she joined CRF to do exploring, after being tantalized by the passages she passed during her days as a tour guide at the park. "I keep thinking that if I go down this crummy crawlway and through that crummy breakdown, I'll come into some big wide room," she said. "We do it for fun, for adventure, and we're a little bit crazy."

My mind marshaled whatever energy reserves I had left for the roughest spots on the return trip. That much worked; I made it through the squeezes all right.

But then, I had absolutely no strength left, and we were still miles from being out. Parts of the trail that I didn't even remember as being problems on the way in got to be practically impossible on the way out. I was fighting the rocks and losing. I could feel every extra ounce of my mud skin. My boots were so heavy, I felt like the victim of a gangland hit being readied for a visit to the fishes.

We came to a little hill that had a rope for the sissies to pull themselves up with. Everybody else scampered past the rope, but I grabbed onto it and still almost broke my neck when I slipped back down.

At that point, Kathleen, who is only slightly larger than a Kingdom of Oz munchkin, offered to carry my pack. I thanked her, handed her a muddy hunk of canvas and trudged on.

EPILOGUE – MY BEST STORY
NOBODY EVER READ

Picture of Katie Coon, regrouping during an eventful bath time for her four autistic sons. Photo by Jean Shifrin.

Bill's notes: A few years after I left newspapers, Jean Shifrin, a brilliant photographer as well as a friend and former colleague, told me she'd met an amazing family. I quickly agreed to go with her to meet them and to write a story to accompany her photos. The story turned out quite well, I thought; and Jean's photographs were incredible. I could easily envision this package as Sunday Page One material for any of the 11 newspapers where I had worked. But even though Jean and I tried for months, using all the contacts we had, we failed to find a home for it. It was the best story I ever wrote that hardly anyone read. I offer it here because it's a great story – and it illustrates how drastically newspapers have changed. The progress Katie and Brad made in raising their four sons encouraged them to expand their family again; this time, they had a healthy little girl.

THE SOLDIER CAME home from the war zone and celebrated his marriage. Nine months later, there was cause for more celebration; and ten months after that, even more.

But for Brad and Katie Coon, the battles on the home front had only begun.

The fruits of their celebrations were two sets of identical twins — all boys and all with autism to varying degrees.

According to a CDC study released in March of this year, one in 68 children — and one in 42 male children — born in the United States today has some level of autism. The number of American families touched by autism has increased by 30 per cent in just the past two years. But neither statistics nor medical science can explain how autism can strike one family four times in one year.

The Coons have no time to ponder such mysteries, when they must get four misty-minded little boys ready to go to school. Even on the most seemingly normal day, chaos is only a misplaced backpack away.

Colin, 4, demands juice to slake his sugar craving.

Devin, Colin's twin, is crying because his backpack is not in its assigned cubbyhole.

Ashton, 5, is crying because his twin, Ethan, has just done another hit-and-run, swatting him and bolting for his room.

All four boys join in a frantic choir of screeching. They are not in unison, but they all cry out in the same insistent, one-word lyric: "MOMMY!" These are the times when Katie Coon wonders how in the world she'll make it till lunchtime.

"If I had three clones of myself, I could be behind each kid," Katie said. "But I can't, and each of them has his own issues."

Other parents of children with autism frequently offer her praise, marveling at how she seems to manage so well with a houseful of special-needs boys. Even though those parents have serious problems themselves, the Coon's challenges seem to be of a higher order of magnitude. "People say I'm such a good wife and mother, blah, blah, blah. It's not that way," she said. "Sometimes, the strains are overwhelming."

The Coon family is an especially intense illustration of what appears to be an autism explosion. But how did this happen? Why does it seem to be happening more frequently? And what is going on in the minds of these little boys?

The short answer is that medical science simply does not know.

"There is a basic question of what autism is," said Dr. Gina Green, executive director of the Association of Professional Behavior Analysts, an organization specializing in developing and promoting therapeutic methods for people with autism. "More and more children are getting the diagnosis, but it's not certain what that means," she said.

Diagnosing autism is nothing like diagnosing, say, chicken pox. There are no obvious visible symptoms; in fact, the signs of delayed child development could be associated with other disorders, she said. Further, she said, "There is no accurate biological test for autism; no brain scan, no blood test." Even in the hands of a pediatric developmental specialist, the diagnosis of autism is still "quite subjective," she said. The diagnostician must rely on close observation of the child, along with accurate reporting from the parents, she said.

Despite the mysteries and the ambiguities, scientists know enough to be alarmed. "We should be very concerned, regardless of how we explain what's behind this," said Robert Ring, Chief Science Officer for Autism Speaks, a national advocacy group for Autism issues and families.

Most of the increase in autism rates can probably be attributed to increased awareness, screening and diagnostic techniques, Ring said. However, he added, there is an X-factor, a twilight zone "where the environment interacts with human biology."

There is more reason to be concerned, in that the rates reported in the CDC study may be lower than what is actually occurring, Ring said. Autism Speaks is partnering with the CDC for additional studies on autism occurrence rates.

The problem is as complicated as it is widespread, he said. "It's incredibly complex," Ring said. "There's not just one type of autism, there are hundreds of different types."

A child who might have been called shy a generation ago might now be a candidate for an autism diagnosis. And just as innocently for Brad and Katie, their exceptional family started off as a sweet little high-school romance.

It was Brad Coon's gentle way with children that first attracted Katie to him. They grew up in Worthington, Ohio, a suburban community near Columbus. Katie, a sixth-grader at the time, remembers being touched when she saw Brad pushing some younger children on a tire swing. Years later, when she was a sophomore in high school and Brad was a senior, a friend introduced them. They soon became a couple and got engaged.

Katie credits Brad with saving her life in those early years. Her home life had been a horror story. She had been adopted, and her adopted mother was imprisoned for sexually exploiting Katie. "I grew up in a home without love," Katie said. "I had never even held a baby." Her relationship with Brad was her refuge from the trauma. Brad said he wasn't any sort of therapist for Katie, just her boyfriend who gave her a safe haven. "She'd come over to my Mom's in the afternoon, and we'd watch TV together, just to get her out of her house," Brad said.

Brad enlisted in the Army, and Katie was removed from her adoptive parents' home and placed with a friend's parents, whom she now considers her true family. Katie enrolled in a local arts school, and Brad, disillusioned with Army life, resigned and came back home. He worked at a series of short-term manual labor jobs, and their relationship progressed, perhaps a bit too fast. They weren't ready for marriage, Katie said, nor for the pregnancy that came when she was not quite 20 years old.

"We were terribly headstrong, and just too young," she said.

They gave up their baby, a healthy girl, up for adoption. They were able to pick the adoptive family, and they have been able to follow their daughter's progress from afar. Shortly after the birth, Katie and Brad decided it was time to grow up. They both wanted to remain together, but as a married couple with a stable income. The first step was for Brad to re-enlist.

"After I got out the first time, I thought I'd never go back," Brad said. "But the second time around, I decided to make it work. And, as it turned out, I got treated with more respect." Not long after Brad completed his basic training, they were married. Brad was trained by the Army as an ophthalmology specialist and deployed to Iraq. It was during an 18-day R&R leave that Katie became pregnant. "I was full of the joy of new life, though we wanted only one baby to begin with," she said. The births of Ethan and Ashton in early 2009 brought the challenges that comes with having twins, but no sign of anything more serious.

"Ethan and Ashton were such good babies. They slept in the same crib. They were normal, fat and happy," Katie said. They were also a handful, for her first experience of child raising. "We only wanted one baby to start with," By the time Ethan and Ashton were three months old, Katie was pregnant again. The news was welcome; they'd planned to have a big family. Brad was reassigned to a base in Germany. Not long after the family was reunited, they all became seriously ill with a bad case of the flu.

The slightly premature birth of the younger twins didn't allow much time to assess the health of their older brothers, Katie said. "All I knew was that I was living in a third-floor walk-up flat with four babies," she said.

But when she took the boys in for a routine checkup, she reported that they showed "no progress toward any motor skills, and they had abnormally long periods of sleeping," she said. As the older boys got older but did not advance normally, she tried speech and physical therapy, but neither worked. The doctors couldn't pinpoint the problem, giving her the generic diagnoses of "severe global developmental delays" and "failure to thrive." She wasn't sure what exactly that meant, but she knew things were not good. "In my gut, I knew something was wrong with my kids," she said.

The Coons were given a "compassionate reassignment" back to the states, to Fort Jackson, in Columbia South Carolina. Still, the proper specialists were not available right away, so Katie had to spend the next 18 months not knowing what if anything she and Brad could do to help their four little boys who simply were not growing up properly. The uncertainty and near hopelessness caused some serious strains in their relationship. "We took care of the boys' basic needs, but there were times when we emotionally checked out on each other and on them," she said.

Finally, when the sets of twins were about four and three, respectively, they were examined by a visiting U.S. Marine Corps physician, who was also a pediatric development specialist. By this time, Katie had begun to strongly suspect that her older twins had some level of autism, but she held out hope that the younger boys' problems might be ones that could be treated medically. But when Colin and Devin were tested, "They failed all the questions," she said.

Being told that all four of her boys were autistic was "devastating," she said, though there was also a measure of relief that came from finally being able to put a name to the problem. "Once you get a diagnosis, then at least you can start to act," she said. Still, the diagnosis confirmed that her sons' lives would never be normal. "This is not what you want for your children," she said. Brad said the diagnosis brought him some relief after the long period of uncertainty. "We already knew they weren't normal," he said.

So, they do the best they can, focusing on the logistics of getting through the day. On a typical weekday morning, Brad reports for duty, then comes back to help Katie get the boys loaded into their van and transported to school. Then Katie drops Brad back at his work and usually has a few hours of a "sanity break" before the afternoon shuttles begin. "We're a one-car family, but at least we are lucky enough to have a car that works," she said.

They are also lucky to be stationed in an area where a special place for autistic children is available to them. The Autism Academy of South Carolina, located in downtown Columbia, was founded by a couple, Dan and Lorri Unumb, who wanted to help other families deal with the life-altering news that had been delivered to them.

When their oldest son, Ryan, was 18 months, Lorri took him in for a routine checkup and told the pediatrician that Ryan wasn't able to make any sounds that resembled words. She was referred to a specialist at Johns Hopkins University Medical Center, who told her Ryan was autistic.

"I didn't know what autism was," Lorri said. At the time, she and Dan lived in Washington, D.C. and were both attorneys for the U.S. Dept. of Justice. She was also on the faculty of George Washington University. "I read up and found this was a lifelong disability," she said. "The first thing I did was to burst into tears."

Dan took the news equally hard. "Every dream and hope you have for your child is shattered," he said.

At first, Lorri said, she was consumed by the thoughts of all that Ryan would likely be missing in his life. "Will he ever go to a prom, ever have a girlfriend, ever have any friend?" she wondered. Once the shock and denial stages had passed, the Unumbs were able to place Ryan in a special program at Johns Hopkins, though this meant a 90-minute commute each school day for two hours of treatment.

Even with their two comfortable incomes, this arrangement became financially burdensome. Their insurance did not cover the kind of therapies their doctors were prescribing, so virtually all of Lorri's salary went to Ryan's special programs. Early intervention was crucial in helping Ryan develop, but life was still overstocked with challenges.

"A trip to the grocery store usually ended in tears, Ryan's and mine," Lorri said. "We had to stop going to church as a family." Ryan also had a common tendency among autistic children called "elopement", that is, he would simply wander away at any moment. "I felt like I was in the

Secret Service, I had to maintain eye contact with him at all times, and if he got away, I'd have to plow through the crowd after him."

The Unumbs decided that more hands were needed to provide Ryan's care, so they moved back home to South Carolina, where they could count on support from their families. They downsized their house, but it was still difficult to pay for therapies Ryan needed but were not covered by their insurance. "I couldn't sleep at night, thinking 'What do families do who don't have our income?'" she said.

In 2007, Lorri started to write an article about how insurance issues add to the burdens many families with autistic children already carry. Then she started thinking about the relative merits of raising awareness versus direct action. "I decided not to write an article, but to write a bill," she said. Despite having no legislative or lobbying experience, she drafted a bill that required insurance companies in South Carolina to expand their coverage of autism-related therapy costs.

She and a small group of similarly inexperienced mothers of autistic children then marched on the statehouse. On the next-to-last day of the legislative session, the Lobby Moms succeeded in getting the Legislature to pass the bill unanimously. That night, however, the measure was vetoed by then-Governor Mark Sanford. The mothers did not give up. They protested. Even though getting a vetoed measure re-considered by the legislature within a day is an unheard-of political feat, that's exactly what they did. The Legislature overrode the Governor's veto, again unanimously, thus creating what has become known as "Ryan's Law."

Autism Speaks did more than take note of Lorri's success; they hired her to try to replicate it elsewhere around the nation. Lorri left her law practice to travel around the country lobbying state legislatures on behalf of insurance reforms. Today, 35 states have passed legislation similar to "Ryan's Law".

Ryan is one of the Unumbs' three children. The other two are not affected by autism, but they have school functions, baseball games and tennis matches for which they need a parent/chauffeur. Dan tries to meet as many of these needs as he can, while he keeps his law practice going and serves as Ryan's Dad. "'Overwhelmed' is a good word for our lives,'" Dan said. "There are no miracle life cures for autism; you're just keeping your head above water and moving forward."

In her travels, Lorri saw how autism was being treated in other parts of the country. In particular, she came across a program developed and used at Princeton University. It is called Applied Behavioral Analysis. Basically, it consists of using basic, patient, repetitive, one-on-one training to help autistic children learn to function in the real world. The Unumbs seriously considered moving to New Jersey in order to give Ryan the benefits of the Princeton program, but they decided instead to move the Princeton concepts to South Carolina. "Moving would have solved the problem for exactly one child, but what about the other children in South Carolina?" Lorri said.

Then they realized that there was no facility in South Carolina that used the ABA concept, so they decided to open one themselves. Again, they were strong on zeal but weak on practical knowledge. "We had no idea what we were doing," Lorri said. They were able to secure a partner in the Clemson University Learning Institute, they started fundraising and applying for state and federal grants, and they found a local Baptist Church that allowed them to open the Autism Academy of South Carolina using space in a church hall. However, the arrangement meant that they had to pack up the school materials and equipment before the Wednesday night and Sunday services.

Later, they found a more suitable space in a former gymnasium owned by a Lutheran church. They started operating there in late 2013. The upper floor of the building had been divided into office spaces, which were more suitable for the one-on-one training sessions. The gym space provides opportunities for programs that encourage interactions between autistic and other children. Nationwide, Lorri said, the ABA methods they use have resulted in approximately 40 per cent of young autistic children to enter elementary schools with their same-aged peers. So far, Ryan has not been included in that 40 per cent. However, she said, her son has been able to accompany her to events including national television interviews and large banquets. "The research is progressing," she said. "Years ago, we didn't know that children with autism could overcome their disabilities."

One thing Ring said he knows is that the scope of the autism issue demands "a national response." Already, the diagnosis and treatment of autism "places a huge demand on our education and health care systems, not to mention on the families affected," he said. More funding is needed for research, treatment and for changes to health insurance programs, he said.

For now, the best way to overcome many of the disabilities associated with autism is to help the child take "a million baby steps, one step at a time," Green said. After making an assessment of what the child can and cannot do, the practitioners of the ABA methods focus on one function – eating at the table, bathing, using the toilet. The function is broken down into its components, for eating, say, sitting still, using utensils, chewing and swallowing. "We teach each step, with lots of repetition and positive reinforcement," she said. The parents are then taught how to do what the therapists have done. "It gives the parents the skills to help their own children, it gives them real power."

Before her boys started at the Autism Academy, Katie had an almost desperate sense of powerlessness, when it came to toilet training. Her boys didn't just have accidents, they smeared the walls and other surfaces of their room with plaster of poop. For her, the first successes in toilet training at the academy were "a defining moment", in that it showed the worst of their behaviors could be trained away. She recalls going to a parents' meeting at the Academy and launching into a joyous report on the toilet battles, saying, "This is amazing!"

Now she has allowed herself to have the kinds of hopes and dreams for her son that all mothers have. "I want them to go to college; I want them to be contributing members of society," she said.

Brad said he knows his sons have a long way to go, before he'll be able to play baseball with them; but they are still his sons, first and foremost. "We don't think of it as, we have all these problems," Brad said. "We think of it as, this is our family."

Sometimes, Katie said, it hurts a little to see how well her boys do at school. They play well, they're even learning to read a little. It's hard to replicate all the successes at home, where it's just her and Brad and four little boys who all need individual attention nearly all the time.

She has resolved to close that gap by making herself better at working with the disabled. Somewhere in her overloaded schedule, she has been able to make time to take online courses to get her started toward a degree in special education. "My children have given me a direction in my life," she said.

For now, though, Katie and Brad will settle for an uneventful bedtime. The boys eat first, then Katie and Brad have their dinner. Next, Katie supervises, while the boys clear the clutter in their rooms and put their toys into assigned cubbyholes. Then, it's rubadubdub, four boys in a tub. After baths and brushings of teeth, Brad spends some guy time with his sons, usually roughhousing or pillow fighting. Katie comes into read a bedtime story and sing a song, then it's lights out. On a good night, the whole process comes off with only one or two "time-outs".

On one night recently, Brad and Katie went into the boys' rooms for a final check before they went to bed themselves. Katie saw that Ethan, her hardest-to-reach, most-prone-to-outbursts little boy, had climbed into his twin brother's bed and was sleeping with his arm around Ashton. It was a small but precious victory. A moment of peace, perhaps even love.